Comparative Law

This book discusses a number of important themes in comparative law: legal metaphors and methodology, the movements of legal ideas and institutions and the mixity they produce, and marriage, an area of law in which culture – or clashes of legal and public cultures – may be particularly evident. In a mix of methodological and empirical investigations divided by these themes, the work offers expanded analyses and a unique cross-section of materials that is on the cutting edge of comparative law scholarship. It presents an innovative approach to legal pluralism, the study of mixed jurisdictions, and language and the law, with the use of metaphors not as an illustration but as a core element of comparative methodology.

Seán Patrick Donlan is the Associate Dean of the Thompson Rivers University, British Columbia, Canada.

Jane Mair holds the position of Professor of Private Law at the University of Glasgow, UK.

Juris Diversitas

Rooted in comparative law, the *Juris Diversitas* series focuses on the interdisciplinary study of legal and normative mixtures and movements. Our interest is in comparison broadly conceived, extending beyond law narrowly understood to related fields. Titles might be geographical or temporal comparisons. They could focus on theory and methodology, substantive law, or legal cultures. They could investigate official or unofficial 'legalities', past and present and around the world. And, to effectively cross spatial, temporal, and normative boundaries, inter- and multi-disciplinary research is particularly welcome.

For more information about this series, please visit:
www.routledge.com/Juris-Diversitas/book-series/JURISDIV

Comparative Law

Mixes, Movements, and Metaphors

Edited by Seán Patrick Donlan and Jane Mair

Routledge
Taylor & Francis Group
LONDON AND NEW YORK

First published 2020
by Routledge
2 Park Square, Milton Park, Abingdon, Oxon OX14 4RN

and by Routledge
52 Vanderbilt Avenue, New York, NY 10017

Routledge is an imprint of the Taylor & Francis Group, an informa business

First issued in paperback 2021

British Library Cataloguing-in-Publication Data
A catalogue record for this book is available from the British Library

Library of Congress Cataloging-in-Publication Data
Names: Mair, Jane, editor. | Donlan, Seán Patrick, editor.
Title: Comparative law: mixes, movements, and metaphors/edited by Seán Patrick Donlan and Jane Mair.
Description: Abingdon, Oxon; New York, NY: Routledge, 2019. | Series: Juris diversitas | Includes bibliographical references and index.
Identifiers: LCCN 2019035200 (print) | LCCN 2019035201 (ebook) | ISBN 9781138390690 (hardback) | ISBN 9780429423246 (ebook)
Subjects: LCSH: Comparative law.
Classification: LCC K561 .C656 2019 (print) | LCC K561 (ebook) | DDC 340/.2–dc23
LC record available at https://lccn.loc.gov/2019035200
LC ebook record available at https://lccn.loc.gov/2019035201

ISBN: 978-1-138-39069-0 (hbk)
ISBN: 978-1-03-208322-3 (pbk)
ISBN: 978-0-429-42324-6 (ebk)

Typeset in Galliard
by Deanta Global Publishing Services, Chennai, India

Contents

Contributors

Emese von Bóné, *Erasmus University Rotterdam, The Netherlands*

Seán Patrick Donlan, *Associate Dean, the Thompson Rivers University Faculty of Law, Kamloops, Canada*

Sue Farran, *Professor of Laws, Newcastle University, UK*

Helen Gubby, *Senior Lecturer, Rotterdam School of Management, Erasmus University Rotterdam, The Netherlands*

Jaakko Husa, *Professor in Law and Globalisation, University of Helsinki, Finland*

Mustafa Koçak, *Professor, Okan University Faculty of Law, Turkey*

Jane Mair, *Professor of Private Law, University of Glasgow, UK*

Werner Menski, *Professor Emeritus, SOAS, University of London, UK*

Richard De Mulder, *Professor Emeritus, Erasmus University Rotterdam, the Netherlands*

Jacques du Plessis, *Distinguished Professor of Law, Stellenbosch University, South Africa*

Jan M. Smits, *Professor of European Private Law, Maastricht University, The Netherlands*

Mathilda Twomey, *Chief Justice, Seychelles*

Tammo Wallinga, *Erasmus University Rotterdam, The Netherlands/University of Antwerp, Belgium*

Laurens Winkel, *Professor Emeritus, Erasmus University Rotterdam, The Netherlands*

1 'Of mixes, movements, and metaphors'

Esin Örücü's critical comparative law

Seán Patrick Donlan and Jane Mair

The currents of comparative scholarship on law change rapidly, with a swiftness that has only accelerated over the last quarter-century. And few scholars of that period have been as important in navigating these rough waves, or indeed in parting those waters, as Esin Örücü. Now Professor Emerita with the University of Glasgow, Örücü is among the most influential contemporary comparatists or comparative lawyers. This influence is the result of the fact that her scholarship moves seamlessly from a deep and focused perspective on specific laws and legal systems, especially her native Turkey, to a wider and more jurisprudential overview of the complexity of laws and legal institutions across the globe. And neither aspect is restricted to the laws of the state. Instead, she has insisted on the importance of a wider cultural context, of norms beyond the laws. Following closely from this prescription is her emphasis on the importance of other disciplines to comparative legal studies. And Örücü has done so in a series of vivid models and arresting metaphors intended to better communicate the lessons of comparative law.

Mixes

Central to Örücü's scholarship is her experience as the product of what modern jurists refer to as a *mixed legal system*. These traditions are those in which state laws of diverse origins lie in reasonably visible and frequently discrete, identifiable sections, relatively evident to specialists and non-specialists alike. Örücü has shown how a better sense of this overt legal complexity can produce a greater sensibility towards the inherent, covert hybridity of laws and norms.[1]

Another well-known 'mixed jurist', Vernon Palmer has suggested a set of 'classical mixed jurisdictions', at both the national and sub-national levels. He produced a now-familiar list of these jurisdictions: Israel, Louisiana, Malta, Quebec, the Philippines, Puerto Rico, Scotland, and South Africa. In each, the primary focus is the mix of Western laws and institutions, especially the Anglo-American

1 See especially E. Örücü, 'Mixed and Mixing Systems: A Conceptual Search' in E. Örücü, E. Attwooll and S. Coyle (eds) *Studies in Legal Systems: Mixed and Mixing* (1996).

and continental European traditions, the well-known 'common law' and 'civil law' traditions.[2] Palmer's focus on the whole tradition allows us to avoid the traditional obsession with private law, to the neglect of public law.[3] It also invites us to better understand the role of legal culture in legal traditions.

The focus of these studies is those legal mixes which are typically created as the result of exchanging one Western sovereign for another. As a result, while the legal system is complex, there is arguably only a modest clash of that system with the underlying culture. But taking a step back, we can focus on other modern 'mixed' systems that bear more diverse traces of their construction over time. The result is a rich rainbow of mixes of legal, customary, and religious traditions. Indeed, this wider category arguably includes the majority of contemporary legal traditions.[4] And if the ingredients are often overt, frequently as a result of colonialism, they can be still more complex. This is true, for example, of Turkey itself. As Örücü has described it:

> Turkey is not a mixed jurisdiction in the classical sense. Neither does she have an overt mixed legal system. Yet, the Turkish legal system is mixed in two other and different senses. In the first sense, it is a synthetic legal system, legislatively constructed by receiving, adapting and mixing laws from various foreign western sources and melting them down in the Turkish pot, to form the overlay. In the second sense, it is a mix of these diverse laws with a people the majority of whose values reflect a different socio-culture related to one past element of the legal system, that of the Ottoman Empire – erased by the Turkish Republic – significantly different to the socio-cultures represented by the incoming laws.[5]

Consistent with a more critical movement in her thinking about all jurisdictions, Örücü has repeatedly pressed for an 'expansion' of legal research beyond European mixes to more complex and exotic hybrids.[6]

But there is also a meaningful division to be made between, as the late Joseph McKnight once put it, 'what may be termed mixed and that which has already been blended to an extent that [the] origins of rules are lost in ordinary legal

2 V. V. Palmer, *Mixed Jurisdictions Worldwide: The Third Legal Family* (2nd ed. 2012).

3 Cf. 'Public Law in Mixed Legal Systems and Public Law as a "Mixed System"' (2001) 5 (2) *Electronic Journal of Comparative Law*, https://www.ejcl.org/52/art52-2.html, accessed 27 October 2018.

4 See e.g. N. Mariani and G. Fuentes, *World Legal Systems/Les Systeme Juridiques dans le Monde* (2000) 16–17.

5 'Turkey's Synthetic Legal System and Her Indigenous Socio-Culture(s) in a "Covert" Mix' in Örücü (ed.) *Mixed Legal Systems at New Frontiers* (2010) 150.

6 See especially 'What Is a Mixed Legal System: Exclusion or Expansion?' in *Mixed Legal Systems at New Frontiers.* Earlier versions of this article can be found in (2008) 3 *Journal of Comparative Law* 34 and in (2008) 12 (1) *Electronic Journal of Comparative Law*, www.ejcl.org/121/abs121-15.html, accessed 9 November 2011.

practice'.[7] The former are easy to spot. The latter are more difficult to see, but are arguably of even greater importance for understanding law over space and time. The modern distinction between *pure* and *mixed* legal traditions is thus arbitrary in two ways. On the one hand, the conceptual distinction is largely European or Western, a result of fixing our attention on specific legal systems after the considerable changes of the nineteenth century across the West. On the other, it also reflects a very real movement from explicit legal complexity to greater levels of legal unity effectively established in the same period. Only the rise of a modern nation-state claiming, with or without justification, all legal authority – by either promulgation or ratification of legal norms – makes the modern concept of a 'mixed' legal system possible. But the value of understanding legal mixity goes much deeper.

Indeed, more than any other comparatist, Örücü has drawn out the implications of the fact that *all* modern legal traditions are both mixed and mixing. And she has done so without fear of the difficulty of the task. Instead, she seems to revel in it. Örücü's work provides the most sophisticated general analyses of legal complexity or hybridity, emphasising that '[i]nstances of mixing are complicated. They may be overt or covert, structured or unstructured, complex or simple, blended or unblended'.[8] But her research is also unflinching, an explicit and bold acceptance of the significant challenges offered by extending the gaze of comparative law across the present and past, Europe and beyond, and indeed beyond the law to other social norms.

Critical of traditional taxonomies, Örücü has noted the 'internal logic of legal systems' that cuts across national systems.[9] But she has more often underscored the unique. Her 'family trees' model consciously groups traditions according to their ingredients, 'regard[ing] all legal systems as mixed and overlapping, overtly or covertly, and groups them according to the proportionate mixture of the ingredients'.[10] That approach

> is initially deconstructive, disintegrative and critical. It rests on the assumption of fluidity. Following deconstruction, the aim is to reconstruct a more reliable map of the legal systems of the world. Distinctiveness cannot be ignored. Even when comparative law is used as an instrument of integration in Europe, one must be aware of the virtues in 'distinction' and 'diversity'. In the 'family trees' approach 'distinctiveness' matters as well as similarity, whereas in classical classifications only 'similarity' mattered. The relevant degrees of distinction and similarity decide on the place of a legal system.[11]

7 J. W. McKnight, 'Some Historical Observations on Mixed Systems of Law' (1977) 22 *Juridical Review* (ns) 177, 186.
8 'Mixed and Mixing Systems: A Conceptual Search'.
9 'An Exercise on the Internal Logic of Legal Systems' (1987) 7 *Legal Studies* 310.
10 'Family Trees for Legal Systems: Towards a Contemporary Approach' in M. van Hoecke (ed.) *Epistemology and Methodology in Comparative Law* (2004) 363.
11 'What Is a Mixed Legal System: Exclusion or Expansion?', 64.

This highlights both the singularity of different traditions while acknowledging their complex relatedness. Indeed, Örücü has also noted the importance of 'extraordinary places', those 'not ordinarily covered by conventional comparative law'.[12] These have much to teach other, apparently purer, traditions as instructive, 'out-of-the-ordinary things … happen' within them, offering comparatists an opportunity to 'best observe, analyse and understand the interaction between legal cultures and socio-cultures'.[13]

As this makes clear, Örücü's approach to comparative law places mixed and extraordinary legal systems at the centre of comparative law. In them, what is covert or hidden becomes revealed. But the law of the state is mixed with more than positive law. Örücü has repeatedly asserted that comparative law must also include 'norms of non-state law, folk law and customary law, remembering that the law is global, national and local'.[14] Over 20 years ago, she was already attentive to the degree to which mixed traditions can shade into so-called 'legal pluralism'.[15] 'All systems', she wrote, 'are … the result of an interplay of a variety of normative systems emanating from customs, nation state law, religion, corporations, institutions, organisations, neighbourhoods and families'.[16] Here we go beyond legal hybridity (narrowly understood) towards a comparative investigation of normative hybridity more generally. And this mixing or interplay of laws and norms over both space and time necessarily leads comparatists to other disciplines – e.g. anthropology, sociology, and history – from which we may learn.

Movements and metaphors

If Örücü is largely focused on the complexity of contemporary traditions, she is keenly aware of the importance of the past to the present. Over two decades ago, she wrote that '[m]ixed and mixing systems and the migration of legal institutions are two inseparable fields of study'.[17] With other scholars, she has pushed the *movement* of laws to the centre of comparative analysis and sought to move us past the limitations of, and stale squabbles surrounding, Alan Watson's well-known 'legal transplants' thesis.[18] The sophistication and breadth of Örücü's scholarship is evident in her suggestion for '[a]n analytical approach to migration'. She wrote, for example, that 'we can examine first the political and historical paths

12 'Comparatists and Extraordinary Places' in P. Legrand and R. Munday (eds) *Comparative Legal Studies: Traditions and Transitions* (2003) 468–469.

13 Ibid., 468–469 and 489.

14 See 'Developing Comparative Law' in Örücü and D. Nelken (eds) *Comparative Law: A Handbook* (2007) 60–61.

15 See 'Mixed and Mixing Systems: A Conceptual Search' 335.

16 Ibid., 341.

17 Ibid.

18 See e.g. Örücü, 'Infusion of the Diffused Four Circles of Diffusion Infusing the Legal System of Turkey' in S. Farran, J. Gallen, J. Hendry, and C. Rautenbach (eds) *The Diffusion of Law: The Movement of Laws and Norms around the World* (2015).

along which such mobility takes place', 'we can observe the methods and specific techniques employed', 'we can assess the factual consequences', and

> we can analyse conceptual and future implications such as a re-definition of the terms law, legal concept, legal rules and legal system; clashes between culture and law (legal cultural diversity, legal cultures in affinity); top-down and bottom-up explanation of law-making; law reform; and legal systems in transition.[19]

If this is an extraordinarily tall order, it is no less necessary for the scale of the challenge.

Örücü's work, here and elsewhere, also reflects an awareness of the power of language for legal study. She has contributed a wide range of both models and metaphors for understanding law's mixes and the movements that created them. She has, for example, insisted on the constant refinement of our tools and models of understanding, the need for 'new terminology [for] … a workable grid for fitting legal phenomena into explanatory frameworks'.[20] Comparativists will be well aware, too, of her use of colourful culinary terminology to describe the ways in which laws might mix. As she writes:

> When elements from socio-culturally similar and legal-culturally different legal systems come together forming mixed systems of the already mentioned 'simple' kind – the 'mixing bowls' – the ingredients are still in the process of blending but in need of further processing if a 'purée' is to be produced. Next to 'simple' mixes come the 'complex' mixed systems, where the elements are both socio-culturally and legal-culturally different. I have called this type elsewhere the 'Italian salad bowl' where, although the salad dressing covers the salad, it is easy to detect the individual ingredients clearly through the side of the glass bowl. A good example of this is Algeria. Then, there is what I called the 'English salad plate', the ingredients sitting separately far apart on a flat plate with a blob of mayonnaise at the side into which the different ingredients can be dipped before consumption. Examples of this are the Sudan and Zimbabwe – legal pluralisms – which lie towards the far end of the spectrum. The examples become more extreme along the path, ending in 'curdling', with a dysfunctional legal system, as already mentioned.[21]

19 'A Theoretical Framework for Transfrontier Mobility of Law' in R. Jagtenberg, Örücü, and A. J. De Roo (eds) *Transfrontier Mobility of Law* (1995) 17. These occur again in *Critical Comparative Law: Considering Paradoxes for Legal Systems in Transition* (1999), republished in full as an article in (2000) 4 (1) *Electronic Journal of Comparative Law*, https://www.ejcl.org//41/abs41-1.html, accessed 27 October 2018, and 'Law as Transposition' (2002) 51 *International and Comparative Law Quarterly* 205, 205.

20 'General Introduction: Mixed Legal Systems at New Frontiers' in *Mixed Legal Systems at New Frontiers*, 7.

21 'What Is a Mixed Legal System: Exclusion or Expansion?' 70.

While there may be humour in her choices of models and metaphors, Örücü takes them very seriously as devices for comprehension rather than as mere rhetoric. 'Comparative law is about communication'.[22]

And this openness is not limited to language. Instead, Örücü has recognised the contributions that can be made to comparative law by other scholars, as well as the degree to which comparatists must embrace inter- or trans-disciplinarity. Understanding legal complexity, she has noted, requires a 'wide area of knowledge', and she has explicitly linked comparative law to legal philosophy, legal history, anthropology, and sociology, as well as cultural studies and economics.[23] 'The comparative lawyer must', she argues, in her *Enigma of Comparative Law*, published a decade ago:

> develop an interest in fields other than private law and systems other than the normative-legal, in context, in mixing systems, in systems in transition and in the making, in looking beyond Europe and into both 'ordinary' and 'extraordinary' systems, in transpositions and the role of the tuners of the law, in the 'better law' approach, in the deconstruction of classifications and building of other approaches to legal systems such as the 'family trees' approach, in 'comparative law and …' studies and in deciphering the intricacies of the 'similar' and the 'different' – all demanding tasks.[24]

In what remains of this introduction, we will introduce the contributions to this collection, pointing out how each fit into Örücü's wider contributions to comparative law.

Critical comparative law

In 'Island, intersection, or in-between? Legal hybridity and diffusion in the Seychellois legal tradition, c1715–1950', Seán Patrick Donlan and Mathilda Twomey explore an 'extraordinary place'. Both a mixed legal tradition and a micro-jurisdiction, Seychelles is also both a legal and social *métissage*. As such, the idea of legal *hybridity* must be understood

> in several senses. The first is related to the complex origins and organisation of legal and normative systems, institutions, and ideas. The second … relates to the gap between the principles and practices of legal orders. … The third is the recognition that individual and communal identities in colonial encounters and post-colonial situations are singular blends of mixed parentage.

22 *The Enigma of Comparative Law: Variations on a Theme for the Twenty-First Century* (2004) 208.
23 'Mixed and Mixing Systems: A Conceptual Search' 336.
24 *The Enigma of Comparative Law*, 213.

Adopting an inter- or trans-disciplinary approach, Donlan and Twomey note that extraordinary places like Seychelles are best seen as intersections of laws and customs, as sites of *translation*, in the senses of both movement and meaning. But what makes them exotic does not guarantee autonomy. While 'the Seychellois now have the possibility to determine their own future', meaningful independence 'also requires that outside influences – the result of economic dominance and geo-political hegemony rather than choice – are not allowed to overwhelm the will of the Seychellois people'. The mixtures and movements of laws are neither inherently positive nor easily altered. Indeed, the fluid nature of legal ideas and institutions may leave extraordinary places subject to global forces they cannot control.

In 'Legislating for customary land tenure: a comparative query', Sue Farran looks at the importance of land and customary law in South Africa and Vanuatu. While she notes meaningful differences between the two, she also suggests 'shared themes', including 'the challenges of plural legal systems; the centrality of land to law and policy debates; the tensions between introduced concepts such as human rights and equality; and traditional attitudes towards status and the exercise of power'. Colonialism brought about an inevitable clash between the various imposed norms of colonisers and those of the colonised. The former honoured the latter only selectively, but customary traditions survived into independence. In the post-colonial context, competing claims of custom and land interests occur through complex power relationships and rhetorics of tradition. Not least is the question of legislating for customary land tenure; is it possible and, if so, what are the consequences? In this respect, South Africa and Vanuatu face unique challenges. And custom is central to each. Referring to Örücü's salad metaphors, Farran concludes that '[i]t would … be a mistake for comparatists or comparative law in general to omit consideration of customary law. Indeed, it would be like omitting the lettuce leaves from a green salad'.

In his chapter, Jacques du Plessis also attempts to take seriously Örücü's challenge of a comparative law that looks beyond Western laws. As he notes, the existence of meaningful, legally recognised customary law, 'the customs and usages traditionally observed by the indigenous African communities', means that the law of the South African state is more complex than other mixed systems. More particularly,

> The purpose of this essay is to take up this challenge and explore the possible implications of adopting … a broader perspective in the context of two topics which recently have enjoyed considerable judicial and academic attention in South African law. These are the role of the customary law construct of *ubuntu*, and promoting fairness in the law of contract.

If *ubuntu* lacks a clear definition, as the result of its customary origins, it is reasonably well-understood to signify a communitarian value that seeks to balance individual and community rights and responsibilities. Critically, it is also a constitutionally protected value. Du Plessis explores how South African courts could utilise *ubuntu*, perhaps alongside good faith, in contract law and adjudication. But he underscores that for this development to be successful, judicial interpretation would have to ensure that the concept remains meaningful in the context of the modern South African state. In concluding with a note to Örücü, du Plessis writes that 'there is no inevitable conflict. Unusual and complex mixes are nothing new'.

Werner Menski's 'On kites and ships: climate changes in comparative law and judicial navigation' draws both parallels and differences between the work of Esin Örücü and his own scholarship. He highlights legal and normative complexity, the role of adjudication in balancing that complexity in specific contexts, as well as the utility of models and metaphors that contribute to understanding that plurality. In his contribution here, he pays particular attention to adjudication and family law in India. In particular, he

> compares and contrasts the methods of presenting legal navigation through the image of a ship, or a kite. Both models facilitate deep plurality-conscious analysis of law. Both methods of presenting decision-making processes bring out varied power structures and influences in this constantly moving, and always somewhat liquid, structure we conceptualise as 'law'.

Following his earlier work, Menski analyses the approach of the Indian legal system to securing rights to post-divorce maintenance for women. While the problem is complex, involving apparently divergent secular and religious principles, he suggests that non-Western legal systems may navigate such issues far better than Westerners, and many comparatists, might imagine.

In another look at family law, Jan M. Smits underscores the value of 'estrangement', of a comparative legal scholarship that embraces alternative ways of thinking and disciplinary plurality. In his chapter, he writes that

> The law must always take into account alternative modes of thinking, no matter whether these are based on experience with a foreign law or are coming from other sources. The law will always benefit from *estrangement*, meaning that the familiar is compared with existing or untried solutions in order to clarify what the law ought to be. This is why, among other fields, economics, empirics, psychology, ethics and literary and cultural studies all offer approaches to law that are just as valuable as comparative analysis. They confront us with the unfamiliar and thus allow for a better grounding, or rejection, of long-accepted rules.

More specifically, Smits questions the long-standing rule that marriage is concluded for an indeterminate period of time, and ideally until death. After discussing the origins of this Western idea of marriage as a permanent bond, Smits compares an Islamic alternative (the *mutah*), a fixed-term marriage of, for example, two or five years. The introduction of this 'wedlease' would, Smits argues, have financial and emotional savings, as well as 'the distinct advantage that (future) spouses have to better think through the consequences of their marriage and reconsider their commitment at set intervals'.

As any scholar or student of comparative law will be aware, the subject of the movement of laws is of central interest to comparative lawyers. And few have made contributions to that topic that are as significant as those of Örücü. In 'What is the role of norms and values in the reception of law?', Richard De Mulder and Helen Gubby reflect on changes in law over time and the importation – or 'transposition' – of legal principles from one legal system into another. Örücü has underscored the role of norms and values, and indeed the internalisation of those norms and values by legal actors, in this process. But the authors suggest instead that interests and utility are more important. Using the 'REMP' model of man – Resourceful, Evaluating, Maximising Person – developed in economics, they argue that

> Social and economic interests drive the behaviour of people. Using that model, a legal norm will be successful if it is useful in a certain society; it works well and becomes embedded in the norms of that society because it responds to a social need and furthers individual interests. It is the utility of an imported law that is the primary factor in determining the successful transference of that law to foreign soil.

Whether the transposition will succeed depends upon whether it fits in with the social and economic *interests* of people, i.e. is useful in fulfilling a need in that society at that particular moment in time.

Any discussion within comparative law of such movements of legal ideas and institutions over time necessarily involves legal history. As a result, 'comparative legal history' is essential to understanding what Örücü has called – among other things – the 'transfrontier mobility of law'. Three of the contributors here provide descriptive case studies of these movements in the Netherlands in the nineteenth century and in contemporary Turkey. In her contribution, Emese von Bóné looks at the importation of a French legal transplant during the period of the Batavian Republic (1795–1806). More specifically, she looks at the borrowing, both imposed and voluntary, of Charles-Louis de Secondat, Baron de La Brède et de Montesquieu's now-famous division of state or governmental powers between the *legislative*, the *executive*, and the *judicial*. She notes how the *trias politica* were introduced, suffered considerable changes through the numerous constitutional changes of the Republic, and survived the establishment of the Kingdom of Holland to remain an important component of the modern Constitution of the Netherlands.

Moving to private law, Tammo Wallinga explores the Dutch legal regime concerning *alluvion*, where land surface increases through deposits of sediment from rivers or the sea. In the Low Countries, such an issue, and the resulting question of ownership, is of obvious importance. But as Wallinga notes, Dutch law in the nineteenth century was complex, given the divergent and diverging legal regimes that existed. As a result of the promulgation of a Dutch version of the *Code Civil*, the law of alluvion in the Netherlands was essentially French. In practice, this meant that new alluvium was arguably state property rather than private property and, in the courts, a series of trials pitted the Department of the Public Domain against landowners. Only the intervention of the King made clear that the department would no longer resist private claims. As Wallinga concludes:

> If we are looking for an illustrative parallel, it is not one of Esin's favourite cooking parallels that comes to mind. This is rather like a case of a medical transplant of a body part that was eventually rejected and amputated again. All seemed well initially – but then it turned out that the transplant had left a nasty infection and the patient fell seriously ill.

In this instance, 'the King came to the rescue, turning the story almost into a fairy tale', and 'the moral of this story is that legal transplants are to be considered very carefully before making them. You just might get more effects than you were hoping for'.

In his contribution here, Mustafa Koçak brings us closer to the present and to the transposition of the rule of law in Örücü's native Turkey. As he notes, the concept 'is the sine qua non of a liberal, pluralist modern democracy. It requires state authority to be bound, limited and balanced by law'. Koçak tracks a nascent rule of law from the nineteenth-century Ottoman Empire to its gradual penetration into the forms and substance of law and politics in the Turkish Republic. But his focus is largely on the events of the last decade. Explaining the chapter's title, he notes that this 'movement … can be compared to the march of an Ottoman Military Band, i.e. "two steps forward, one step back"'. While steps forward in the last decade included numerous constitutional amendments in 2010, each was – and continues to be – blunted by illiberal counterforces. Without capitulating to pessimism about the future, Koçak concludes by noting that 'the success of democracy and the rule of law are closely related to the social structure, democratic and legal culture of the country in which they are recognized'.

In 'The method of comparative law reconsidered in light of legal epistemology and the reception of Roman Law', Laurens Winkel also engages with comparative legal history. But he does so at a more abstract and prescriptive level than other contributors here, emphasising the philosophical and epistemological foundations of modern comparative law. He briefly considers how we know the law, customs and customary law, and foreign legal rules. But he also notes the importance, for much of Western law and for comparative law, of the receptions – varying in *form* and *extension* – of Roman law. With this in mind, both comparative law and European legal history are, Winkel argues,

> similar on the level of method and approach, but … also share common features on the level of epistemology. For diachronic and synchronic comparison, Roman law in whatever form is the *tertium comparationis*, not only in concrete cases, … but also where legal systems as a whole are considered. … For more general comparative remarks – at least in the field of private

> law – the institutional system is nearly always present, where it concerns contemporary law or when history of private law is involved.

Among other things, the author's focus on Roman law allows us to step back from narrow modern studies of laws crossing the borders of the nominally closed legal orders and common laws of contemporary nations and states. The result is a reminder of the deeper circulation of ideas and institutions across porous intellectual and jurisdictional boundaries.

In our final chapter, Finnish comparatist Jaakko Husa seeks to 'illustrate particular epistemic benefits of using metaphors in comparative legal literature. Accordingly, it will be argued that metaphors have a special place, especially in comparative law literature'. This importance is not merely rhetorical, but is essential to thinking comparatively. Where they succeed,

> the function of metaphors is not really to explain the differences and similarities found in scholarship. Instead, it is to offer holistic projections that help comparatists to understand their subject matter and to make it easier for readers to grasp the essential message (in the form of mental images) which the comparatist seeks to convey.

But they may not, Husa warns, always succeed.

> Simply, not everyone visualises in the form of mental imagery and understands in the form of picture-like representations. Moreover, metaphors may also confuse readers because they are necessarily imperfect as to their nature, i.e. they are able to cover certain aspects but certainly not all. … And, it goes without saying that failed metaphors end up obscuring things and prevent understanding as cognitive obstacles.

Where over-utilised, metaphors can turn 'into scholarly coquetting which nobody really benefits from'.

Conclusion

Esin is a '*critical*' comparatist, in at least two different senses. First, she is *critical or important*, indeed simply unavoidable, for those who want to engage with law in its widest sense. If she hints at the *longue durée*, the sweep of systems mixing, she provides a *grand panorama*, a broad overview of the make-up of mixed systems. But she is also *critical* in a second sense. It is her great strength that she casts a critical eye on our contemporary consensus. She sees through the fictions of discrete families and neat nomenclatures. In doing so, she embraces law's complexities and contexts.

2 Island, intersection, or in-between? Legal hybridity and diffusion in the Seychellois legal tradition, c. 1715–1950

Seán Patrick Donlan and Mathilda Twomey

Introduction

All contemporary normative and legal traditions are hybrid creations, an ongoing mix of nominally native elements and borrowed features.[1] In this sense, none are islands, all are intersections in-between rippling waves of influence that may be mastered but cannot merely be manufactured. In the West, this may be masked by nineteenth-century developments that led to the unity, or apparent unity, of legal orders and the creation of a modern legal system. After the French Revolution, European laws and legal institutions underwent profound change. The long nineteenth century witnessed a move from the *poly-juralism* common to pre-modern Europe to the organised, centralised, and exclusive systems of *common national laws*. Indeed, it was a period in which many nations and modern states – along with mature legal nationalism and legal positivism – were created. And Europe's colonial encounters were central to these developments. Here, the newly unitary and apparently holistic laws of the West were first overlaid on native traditions and subsequently replaced them, at least formally. Many native legal or normative traditions, whether meaningfully pure or transformed by colonial experience, continued to operate in practice.

Legal hybridity is obvious in Seychelles.[2] The laws and legal institutions of the Seychellois *micro-jurisdiction* very clearly reflect the *diffusion* of Europe's most influential imperial legal traditions. Located in the vast Indian Ocean and virtually uninhabited before the late eighteenth century, the archipelago would be subject alternatively to French and British rule and French and Anglo-British laws. The result was a legal *métissage* that parallels the blend of races, cultures,

1 Seán Patrick Donlan, 'Things Being Various: Normativity, Legality, State Legality' in Maurice Adams and Dirk Heirbaut (eds) *The Method and Culture of Comparative Law: Essays in Honour of Mark Van Hoecke* (2014) and 'To Hybridity and Beyond: Reflections on Legal and Normative Complexity' in Vernon V. Palmer, Mohamed Mattar, and Anna Koppel (eds) *Mixed Legal Systems, East and West* (2014).

2 Mathilda Twomey, *Legal Métissage in a Micro-Jurisdiction: The Mixing of Common Law and Civil Law in Seychelles* (2017). See also Twomey, 'The Parts That Make a Whole? The Mixity of the Laws of Seychelles' in Palmer, Mattar and Koppel, *Mixed Legal Systems, East and West* (2015).

and languages in Seychelles. And unlike other colonial encounters, the absence of an indigenous people on the islands meant that there were no systematic autochthonous normativities to complement – or resist – the laws of the imperial powers. There was, however, a jumbled and often-suppressed mix of norms that Europeans indentured from Asia or enslaved from Africa. Freed blacks and 'coloureds' – defined here as the *métis*, the offspring of white landowners and female slaves – lived in a legal in-between, where sometimes the laws of citizens applied and other times the laws for slaves applied.

Seychelles' laws were buffeted, too, by the legal and political tsunamis of the Revolution in France and the Anglo-French wars that followed. The two decades between c. 1794 and 1814 saw repeated, ephemeral capitulations to the British before its rule was clearly established over a Francophone population that was some 90% black or 'coloured'. For a time, French laws applied largely unchanged, but the English language and British laws were gradually imposed. Still, more slowly, the integration of the races began. By the early twentieth century, both laws and peoples were deeply mixed through a process of *creolisation*. And in addition to the gap between principle and practice, alternative normativities inevitably arose alongside the law: some *intra legem* (within the state legal regime), some *praeter legem* (tolerated by state law), some *contra legem* (against the law).

This chapter explores the complex history and changing legal and normative hybridity of Seychelles. Seychelles is the sort of 'extraordinary place' that Esin Örücü has suggested allows comparatists to 'best observe, analyse and understand the interaction between legal cultures and socio-cultures'.[3] By necessity, its legal complexity will be discussed most thoroughly; its normative hybridity, a far more complex topic, gets only superficial treatment, though we hope that additional research might follow.

Hybridity is used here in several senses. The first is related to the complex origins and organisation of legal and normative systems, institutions, and ideas. The second, less explored here, relates to the gap between the principles and practices of legal orders, not least in colonial regimes. The third is the recognition that individual and communal identities in colonial encounters and post-colonial situations are singular blends of mixed parentage. While other perspectives would be useful, this chapter takes a trans-disciplinary approach that draws on research on *mixed legal systems*, *legal pluralisms*, and *post-colonial theories*. We note, too, that it is too easy to portray islands like Seychelles as isolated peripheries away from the imperial centre. They are better seen as places of *translation*, in the sense of both movement and meaning. They are intersections of laws and customs that

3 Esin Örücü, 'Comparatists and Extraordinary Places' in Pierre Legrand and Roderick Munday (eds) *Comparative Legal Studies: Traditions and Transitions* (2003) 489. Note, however, that 'it is in such "extraordinary places" that the comparatist of today is least equipped to work'. Ibid.

generated complex *legalities* in-between their mother traditions. And they would, as a result, change their parents, too, as all children do.[4]

Laws and norms

Properly contextualising the legal and normative hybridity of Seychelles requires, as a preliminary matter, a discussion of the concepts used to analyse its dynamic legal tradition and present legal system. While the focus of most legal analysis is limited to state law, a wider perspective that encompasses other non-legal or non-state normativities would be more appropriate and generate more useful information about social regulation. In fact, state law is a relatively novel and recent normative form even in the West, though one particularly successful at colonising and dominating its rivals. Laws and legal institutions, identified as such, preceded the state. A unified system of national state common laws is the historical exception rather than the rule. Before the rise of the state, laws existed and competed both with rival legal regimes and with other forms of normativity. And when it finally arises, the law of the state was parasitic on an already-established, conventional concept of law as well as, more importantly in practice, pre-existing legal institutions.

As a result, any meaningful understanding of 'law' requires comparative-historical analysis broadened to capture social norms (i.e. *norms*) that don't qualify as legal norms, either as conventionally understood (i.e. *laws*) or by the standard of the state (i.e. *state laws*). 'Norms', in the sense of normative valuing, are standards of oughtness or appropriateness, of right claims and conduct. But we express normativity in radically diverse ways. Law and its cognate forms across the West have no essence or fixed meaning. Their significance comes from convention, from collective experiences and common opinion. For centuries, law has stood for a sub-set of more general normativity, an institutional normative order attended to or overseen by individuals trained in the conceptual vagaries and vocabulary of an established, meaningfully substantive normative order.

While it is rarely used in any systematic manner in legal scholarship – it is metaphorical rather than meaningful – the idea of 'hybridity' is of great utility in the study of legal and normative complexity.[5] In post-colonial studies, the concept of hybridity, as identified in the work of Homi Bhabha, serves as part of a critique

4 Seán Patrick Donlan, David Marrani, Mathilda Twomey, and David E. Zammit, 'Inside-Out/Outside-In: Education, Training, and the Legal Profession in Three Mixed/Micro Jurisdictions' in Petra Butler and Christine Morris (eds) *Small States in a Legal World* (Springer 2017).

5 But see Martha-Marie Kleinhans, 'Hybridizing Civil Law through Transatlantic Migration' (2008) 5 (1) *Atlantic Studies: Global Currents* 119. This predates Donlan's work, but he has only recently become aware of it. Compare the more metaphorical use of *hybridity* in Jaakko Husa, *A New Introduction to Comparative Law* (2015).

of binary, reified thinking about cultures and their members.[6] It emphasises the deep, dynamic complexity of *individual* identities in colonial and post-colonial contexts. As will be clear, Seychellois culture can also be explored in this manner.[7] Such language better expresses the fluid process by which Seychelles does not merely replicate other cultures but creates a new blend and new significance of the old in new contexts. But hybridity can also be used as a constructive term-of-art in a holistic, relational analysis of legal-normative complexity across both time and space.[8] This is also related to, or can easily be linked to, the scholarship of so-called 'legal pluralism'. But with the intention of attending to the totality of normative orders and influences, pluralists frequently adopt an overbroad, unconventional concept of law that excludes almost nothing. This approach is more appropriately called 'normative pluralism'. In practice, pluralists typically attend to non-state norms rather than laws, often in the shadow of a failed and imported state and a hint of cultural essentialism. But this normative pluralism, or normative hybridity, is thriving.

Outside of a core cadre of 'mixed jurists', the study of 'state legal hybridity' is less well-known. The subject is meaningfully legal, rather than normative, pluralism. Unlike normative hybridity, the focus in this scholarship tends to be limited to explicit mixes of different legal traditions that are themselves seen (incorrectly) to be pure individual types. Louisiana, for example, is described as a mix of French and Spanish private law, Anglo-American criminal law, and American public or constitutional law. The fact that each of these European traditions – French, Spanish, English, and American – is itself a complex legal-normative hybrid is ignored. But if all traditions are effectively mixed, there is a meaningful division to be made between 'what may be termed mixed and that which has already been blended to an extent that [the] origins of rules are lost in ordinary legal practice'.[9] These 'mixed jurisdictions' may be seen as a type of 'state' or 'weak legal pluralism', though this definition is, unlike that of either historians or social scientists, dependent on the idea of a unified legal system, whatever its diverse origins. In addition, the scholarship on mixed legal systems is a largely positivistic affair.

6 Homi Bhabha, *The Location of Culture* (Routledge 1994) 136. In this way, 'newness enters the world'.

7 Indeed, a similar analysis on the Mauritius and La Réunion takes place in Anjali Prabhu, *Hybridity: Limits, Transformations, Prospects* (2007).

8 See Mathilda Twomey, 'Legal Salmon: Comparative Law and Africa' in Salvatore Mancuso and C Charles Manga Fombad (eds) *Comparative Law in Africa: Methodologies and Concepts* (2015) and 'Things Fall Apart? The Mixing of Fate, Free Will and Imposition in the Laws of Seychelles' in Sue Farran, Esin Örücü and Seán Patrick Donlan (eds) *A Study of Mixed Legal Systems: Endangered, Entrenched or Blended* (2014).

9 Joseph W. McKnight, 'Some Historical Observations on Mixed Systems of Law' (1977) 22 *Juridical Review* (ns) 177, 186. The distinction is 'at once ... practical and ... psychological', obvious to those both within it and without'. Ibid. See Ignazio Castellucci, 'How Mixed Must a Mixed System Be?' (2008) 12 *Electronic Journal of Comparative Law*, www.ejcl.org/121/art121-4.pdf, accessed 1 July 2017.

Such work can be important. The category of explicit legal mixes is, in fact, very large. It includes the majority of legal systems across the globe, a fact occluded by the Western focus on its own laws and the common error of assuming that those laws and legal orders are unitary.[10] Complexity is projected as an unenlightened, or pre-Enlightenment, other, or to colonial encounters with less civilised peoples. These mixed systems, including some quite exotic hybrids, were often the result of Western expansionism and the *diffusion* of its political institutions and laws. Especially through colonialism, Western laws came into contact with numerous other legal and normative traditions. Some of these were already themselves complex hybrids, but the addition of Western laws – either by imposition or through borrowing under Western hegemony – further complicated the normative-legal spaces of much of the world. The result, globally, is a number of coherent and connected, though never closed, legal traditions. This includes, of course, Seychelles. But as William Twining and others have emphasised, this complex process of diffusion was not, and is not, unidirectional.[11] Nor was it limited to the institutions of state or its laws.

So all modern legal traditions are both mixed and *mixing*; this is an historical process that occurs across time, and that is still occurring in our time. As a result, as Esin Örücü has argued, '[m]ixed and mixing systems and the migration of legal institutions are two inseparable fields of study'.[12] The *hybridity* and *diffusion* of laws (and norms) are two sides of the same coin. Indeed, in suggesting 'an analytical approach to migration', Örücü wrote:

> As sub-categories of our subject we can examine first the political and historical paths along which such mobility takes place, that is, conquest, colonisation, re-settlement, occupation, expansion, [as well as] the inter-relationship of the member states of the EU, the external relations of the EU and the like....
>
> Secondly, we can observe the methods and specific techniques employed, that is, transplantation, imposition, reception (voluntary borrowing), parallel development (concerted or otherwise), imitation, admiration and inspiration and variations and combinations of these and the like....
>
> Thirdly, we can assess the factual consequences, such as systems in transition and mixing, mixed jurisdictions, inter-related legal systems, continuous States, re-designing a State, harmonisation, unification and standardisation....

10 For two decades, Esin Örücü has pressed the expansion of research to more complex hybrids. See, e.g. Örücü, 'What Is a Mixed Legal System: Exclusion or Expansion?' in Örücü (ed.) *Mixed Legal Systems at New Frontiers* (2010).

11 See generally William Twining, 'Diffusion of Law: A Global Perspective' (2004) 49 *Journal of Legal Pluralism* 1.

12 'Mixed and Mixing Systems: A Conceptual Search', 341. For a more recent view, see Esin Örücü, 'Infusion of the Diffused: Four Circles of Diffusion Infusing the Legal System of Turkey' in Sue Farran, James Gallen, Jen Hendry, and Christa Rautenbach (eds) *The Diffusion of Law: The Movement of Laws and Norms around the World* (2015).

> Fourthly, we can analyse conceptual and future implications such as a redefinition of the terms law, legal concept, legal rules and legal system; clashes between culture and law (legal cultural diversity, legal cultures in affinity); top-down and bottom-up explanation of law-making; law reform; and legal systems in transition.[13]

If Örücü is correct – and she is – this is no small task. This chapter cannot promise to apply all of these lessons, but examines one extraordinary legal tradition.

Conventions and comparisons

Comparative history is essential to the study of both the past and the present. And because the history of laws is deeply entangled with, indeed sprang from, other norms, this is necessarily more than mere legal history. While comparative legal historians are producing ever-more sophisticated understandings of the laws' many bodies, their work would be richer with a deeper appreciation of the geographical, social, and normative contexts of the law. For most of the Western past, and into its present, non-legal social norms and orders have played a crucial role in the regulation of individual and communal life. And the boundary between the legal and non-legal was not easily divined. Comparative legal historians could, or should, focus on the complex entanglements of past social and legal norms. This 'legal history in *normative* perspective' might be too much for individual jurists. It might require, that is, engagement with other disciplines: e.g. philosophy, the social sciences, and post-colonial thought.

Such legal-normative analysis and disciplinary cross-pollination already exist, both in Europe and (far more often) abroad. It is easiest to see in scholarship dedicated to the legal hybridity and jurisdictional complexity of the pre-modern era. It is obvious, too, to those who study the legal histories of non-European jurisdictions. For example, the 'colonial' and 'imperial' legal histories of what were once the peripheries of the British Empire are frequently set in a broader context of global entanglement and legal and normative plurality.[14] Given this orientation towards 'external' legal history, rather than merely 'internal' or narrowly disciplinary legal history, it is not surprising that comparative, colonial legal historians engage with other disciplines more often than their European cousins. These take a comparative global or normative perspective that enlarges our understanding of

13 Örücü, 'A Theoretical Framework for Transfrontier Mobility of Law' in Annie J. de Roo, Örücü, and Robert W. Jagtenberg (eds) *Transfrontier Mobility of Law* (1995) 17. She emphasised the 'political and historical path[s]' of law, the 'methods and specific techniques employed' in its movements, as well as 'the factual consequences' and 'future implications' of such analysis, including, e.g. our very understanding of 'law' as a concept. Ibid. See Örücü, 'Law as Transposition' (2002) 51 *International and Comparative Law Quarterly* 205.

14 Zoë Laidlow, 'Breaking Britannia's Bounds? Law, Settlers and Space in Britain's Imperial Historiography' (2012) 55 *Historical Journal* 807.

early-modern and modern empires and legal-normative hybridity and diffusion.[15] The finest contemporary European legal historians know that much more than Europe and law are important to legal history.[16]

Convention, including conceptual convention, is necessarily a product of time and place. Consequently, it is an appropriate subject for comparative legal history. An admittedly rough – and revisable – typology of normative institutionalisation in the West can be created for the period after the fall of Rome. Unlike (i) implicit and non-institutionalised normative practices and orders or ever-more institutionalised forms or (ii) normative regimes, a (iii) 'legal regime' (as defined in public practice) required a more developed specialisation in personnel, training, and language, the last of these assisted by the introduction of writing and archives that allowed an institutional memory of authorised or authentic norms to be maintained over time and space. But this type of legality, like normativity, took plural forms in the West. Normative and legal ordering was multi-centric, with disparate competing centres of power and persuasion. Legal regimes only rarely sought, and still less often expected, to govern their rivals. There were for centuries multiple contemporaneous normative and legal regimes co-existing and overlapping in the same geographical space and at the same time, though often affecting different individuals.

Even after Roman law was rediscovered through Justinian's *Digest*, it was only one such regime. For a long time, the legal regimes of Europe included multifarious folk-laws, local and particular *iura propria*, the romano-canonical 'learned laws', and other trans-territorial *iura communia* (including feudal law and perhaps the *lex mercatoria*). A complete picture of this normative landscape requires us to add numerous other normative and legal regimes, not to mention other non-institutionalised normative practices and orders. And norms and laws could be bent by the practical pressure of power: here from the king, there from the local aristocracy, there from the church. When they finally develop late in Western history, states and their laws are still more formally institutionalised. Indeed, (iv) *state legal regimes* began to make the novel claim to sovereign dominance or exclusivity. Other normative orders and regimes were seen, at least in increasingly important theories of state sovereignty, as reliant on the sufferance of the state. Gradually legality began to be equated with state legality. Finally, the modern Western (v) *state legal systems* of the nineteenth century were able to make such claims comparatively more meaningful while also threading together

15 For the pedagogical utility of this approach, see Seán Patrick Donlan, 'Everything Old Is New Again: Stateless Law, the State of the Law Schools, and Comparative Legal/Normative History' in Shauna Van Praagh and Helge Dedek (eds) *Stateless Law: Evolving Boundaries of a Discipline* (2015).

16 See Thomas Duve (ed.), *Entanglements in Legal History: Conceptual Approaches* (*Max Planck Institute for European Legal History – Global Perspectives on Legal History Series* 2014). See also Lena Foljanty, 'Legal Transfers as Processes of Cultural Translation: On the Consequences of a Metaphor' *Max Planck Institute for European Legal History Research Paper Series* No. 2015-09.

the diverse legal regimes that persisted into a single national *common law*, though earlier ideas and institutions might continue to exist within reformed structures and substantive law.[17] While the last half-century has brought many changes and the future promises more, this modern legal world persists and remains dominant, at least in legal terms.

Even while state power grew more meaningful and national common laws expanded, legal hybridity persisted both in Europe and in its colonies. In Britain's colonies, for example, various English laws, as well as colonial charters and legal codes based on the Bible were all important before full-scale reception – doctrinal, judicial, and legislative – of the English common law over the course of the seventeenth and eighteenth centuries. And while the diffusion of the laws of the Old World into the 'New World' generated new hybridities and entanglements, colonialism was also central to the rise of common laws in Europe. Colonial administration required a common law, e.g. English common law and Equity in British colonies and the *Coutume de Paris* (the Germanic *Customs of Paris*) in French colonies. This development would feed back into the creation of uniform laws in the mother countries, towards legal unity, monism, and centralism.

Traditions and colonies

It was in this complex situation of European legal and normative hybridity that what would become Seychelles is first encountered, or recorded, by Westerners. Its ancient history is, in fact, unknown. Pirates and other transient residents no doubt spent time in the archipelago, but it had no permanent population until Europeans established plantations in the eighteenth century. There were no indigenous peoples and consequently no indigenous laws or norms. The French took possession of Mauritius in 1715. Mauritius, known as the *Isle de France* until 1810, was administered by the French East India Company from 1722 to 1742. After it was ceded back to France in 1742, its Governor-General Mahé de Labourdonnais despatched a ship to explore the surrounding seas. He was concerned about English ambitions in the Indian Ocean and wanted Mauritius to remain a base from which French interests in India could flourish.[18] In November 1742, the ship sighted and landed on what was temporarily called the *Isle d'Abondance*, but would become *Mahé* the following year. The archipelago itself would be named *Séchelles*, perhaps after Vicomte Moreau des Séchelles, the French Controller-General of Finances.

During the era of rule *à travers* Mauritius, a number of legal regimes applied to Seychelles. The laws, or regulations, of the French East India Company

17 James Gordley, 'Classifying Laws and Declassifying Legal Systems' 2013 (2014) *Annuario di diritto comparato e di studi legislative* 94–126.

18 Richard B. Allen, *Slaves Freedmen and Indentured Labourers in Colonial Mauritius* (1999).

applied first (1722–1766).[19] When the archipelago returned to France, French royal decrees (1766–1790) were its law. This included the *Coutume de Paris* for private law and the *Code Louis* governing civil procedure. The *Code Noir* applied to slave-owning and slave relations.[20] But until 1770, no settlement was made in Seychelles.[21] In that year, the first plantation on Mahé comprised 15 whites, eight slaves, and five Indians.[22] White settlers came from Mauritius and the French *métropole*;[23] the enslaved were taken from across the African Continent.[24] By 1774, there were already 50 white families and some 775 slaves, including a further 200 native-born slave children.[25]

The laws and customs that have existed in Seychelles are complex, although the absence of indigenes makes their study simpler. For settlers, the laws were an extension of French metropolitan law by way of Mauritius. The laws were also imposed on the enslaved, and it is difficult to know whether any of their varied African customs were maintained or tolerated. In fact, the Seychellois colony was in many respects unique to the European colonial project. It was, that is, neither a *settler colony* (involving invading Europeans displacing or marginalising native communities) nor a *colony of occupation* (where Europeans settled temporarily in small numbers).[26] In the latter, Europeans were primarily engaged in the exploitation of resources while promoting and safeguarding the geopolitical interests of the metropolitan state. But neither concept applied to Seychelles. And the *coloured* and freed slaves (*les affranchis*) existed in a legal limbo. Rules applying to them were drawn from both white and slave regimes, despite the fact that an

19 There was little legislation apart from that relating to slavery. These in any case ceased to have effect after 1788. See Victor Glover, 'Legislative Drafting in Mauritius: A Developing Discipline' (2011) *Loopholes* 20. Cf. Philip J. Stern, '"A Bundle of Hyphens": Corporations as Communities in the Early Modern British Empire' in Benton and Ross (eds) *Legal Pluralism and Empires, 1500–1850* (2013) 21.

20 Note, too, that the *Code Delaleu*, also known as the *Code Jaune*, regulated the regime under which slaves were kept in Reunion and Mauritius (and consequently Seychelles as well). Jean B. E. Delaleu, *Code des Isles de France et de Bourbon* (1777).

21 Deryck Scarr, *Seychelles Since 1770: History of a Slave and Post-Slavery Society* (2000) 2.

22 Guy Lionnet, *The Seychelles* (1972) 70.

23 Ibid., 87.

24 Joseph E. Harris, *The African Presence in Asia: Consequences of the East African Slave Trade* (1971). See also Jean Houbert, 'The Indian Ocean Creole Islands: Geo-Politics and Decolonisation' (1992) 30 (3) *The Journal of Modern African Studies* 465.

25 John Bradley, *The History of Seychelles* (1950) 24.

26 See Anna Johnston and Alan Lawson, 'Settler Colonies' in H. Schwarz and S. Ray (eds) *A Companion to Postcolonial Studies* (2005) 360. An example of the former would be early settlement in South Africa. See Bill Ashcroft, Gareth Griffin and Helen Tiffin, *Post-Colonial Studies: The Key Concepts*, 2nd ed. (1995) 193. An example of the latter would be India. See D. K. Fieldhouse, *The Colonial Empires: A Comparative Survey from the Eighteenth Century* (1966).

edict of 1723 provided that they were to enjoy the same rights and privileges as those free-born.[27]

In Europe, the move towards legal unity, towards monism and centralism, continued across the eighteenth century. In an historical irony, given the situation of slaves in many Western jurisdictions and their colonies, this occurred alongside increasing criticism of legal inequality and restraints, of crown interference, and of religious influence and intolerance. In law, this more enlightened view meant a pan-European effort to teach national, common laws in the universities and usually in the vernacular. Throughout Europe, both on the continent and in Britain and Ireland, there was also a shift towards legislation, to clearer and more systematic law, and to reforms in criminal law. The progressive formalisation of law satisfied in some measure a more general demand for greater levels of equality before the law and for clearer laws that might promote both political stability and economic growth. On the continent, there were early codes or restatements of the maturing common laws. Growing out of natural law and institutional writings, these provided a more unitary digest of the law, though without abrogating existing laws. Of relevance to other, non-Western normativities, Europe's laws were, and are, deeply rooted in its religious traditions, though this connection has been downplayed in the development of a secular, purported neutral, law.

Revolutions and capitulations

The movement towards legal unity and centralisation quickened with the revolutions which rocked the intellectual and institutional foundations of Europe's old regimes from the late eighteenth century. The modern legal nationalism that slowly took hold during the long nineteenth century marked an important change from Europe's plural, juridical culture of the previous millennium. This saw the accelerated movement from poly-juralism to legal unity and the marginalisation of other normativities in the name of state law that was, directly or indirectly, in theory or in practice, rooted in legislative sovereignty and the general will of the public. This was a shift from competing common and local laws to national law, from persuasive to binding authorities, from open to closed legal systems, and from judges and jurists to legislators. Whatever its truth, the belief in, or the desirability of, a coherent, holistic legal system, a single dominant common law, and the rationalisation of traditional legal regimes had a meaningful impact.

The focus on legal positivism, on law-making and legal clarity, was linked to both the new powers of the state and demands for popular accountability. Throughout the West, there was a gradual shift towards legislation, to clearer and more systematic law, and reforms in criminal law. In continental law, this was expressed in legislation, often codal, and subsequently in exegetical interpretation. Many nineteenth-century codes were attempts to create a set of laws

27 Raymond d'Unienville, *L'Evolution du Droit Civil à L'Île Maurice (1721–1968)* (1994) 37–40.

that was authoritative, comprehensive, systematic, and internally harmonious. They were intended to abrogate any previous or conflicting laws and to unify the legal system into a national common law. While reflecting the laws of the *ancien régime*, both Roman and Germanic in origin, this movement was exemplified in the *Code Civil* (1804). And if the codes were, in fact, hybrids, they were now envisioned as an organic and unified whole. A centralist legal ideology, exemplified in France by the 'School of Exegesis', became dominant. The school suggested the completeness of the code and that, further, non-codal interpretation of the laws was unnecessary.

Ripples from the Revolution in France, the ensuing Napoleonic Wars, and, more slowly, the expanding empire of legal positivism, reached across the Indian Ocean to Seychelles. Formally, from 1790 to 1803, the edicts published by the Colonial Assembly of Mauritius ruled both Mauritius and Seychelles, including a *Code Pénal* adopted in 1793. But in the spirit of the Revolution, the Seychellois settlers set up their own Colonial Assembly, drafted a constitution without reference to Mauritius or France, invested the Assembly with both criminal and civil judicial powers, and declared themselves a separate entity. Early attempts to bring Seychelles to heel and back under the control of Mauritius failed.[28] Control was, however, re-established in 1793 with the arrival of Commandant Jean-Baptiste Quéau de Quinssy. The governorship of Charles Mathieu Isidore Decaen, Captain-General of the French settlements beyond the Cape of Good Hope, put an end to these local assemblies.[29]

Tensions between the French and the British also intensified in this period. Together Mauritius and Seychelles, and the two island groups to which they belonged, commanded the important trade route between India and the Cape. French corsairs were a constant menace to British East India Company ships sailing from India.[30] While De Quinssy's administration saw the colony flourish, there were also a number of short-lived and half-hearted capitulations to the British: in 1794, 1801, 1804, 1805, 1806, 1807, and 1810. The formal terms of these capitulations, which were ephemeral in any case, ensured that French laws would remain in force even after the final capitulation of 1804. And the French flag was flown as soon as the British had sailed, earning de Quinssy the nickname of the 'Talleyrand of the Indian Ocean'.

From 1803 to 1815, the so-called laws of *Decaen* applied in Seychelles. In addition, a version of the *Code Civil* was promulgated in Mauritius in 1805. Decaen also published the French *Code de Procédure Civile* in 1807, a modified *Code de Commerce* in 1809, and a new *Code Pénal* in 1810. Criminal affairs

28 Guy Lionnet, 'Les Effets de la Revolution Française aux Seychelles' in Claude Wanquet and Benôit Julien (eds) *Révolution Francaise et Océan Indien: Prémices, paroxysmes, héritages et déviances* (1996) 191.

29 Albert-Auguste Fauvel, *Unpublished Documents on the History of the Seychelles Islands Anterior to 1810* (1909) 189, 324–325.

30 Marcus F. Franda, *The Seychelles, Unquiet Islands* (1982) 13.

were judged by French laws of 1670 until they were repealed in the Revolution of 1793.[31] During Decaen's administration, litigants in Seychelles had the right of appeal to the Supreme Court in Mauritius. The population of Seychelles continued to grow, too, but Europeans remained a small percentage (approximately 10%) of the total. By 1804, there were 215 whites, 86 coloured, and 1,820 blacks in total.[32] Decaen again decreed the legal incapacity of the coloured and freed slave populations in 1804 on the basis of needing to maintain good conduct. And the *Code Noir* maintained its rigid and ruthless regime.

Significant change also occurred in Anglo-American laws. There, too, was a demand for legal uniformity and clarity. This was linked, in Britain, to its practical parliamentary supremacy and the rise of statute law. Over the course of the century, a persuasive precedent of law reports hardened into a narrower form of binding precedent. Referred to as *stare decisis*, this was a single judicial decision that was binding on the basis of the court's authority alone, rather than persuasive on the basis of equitable interpretation or with the idea that consistent judicial decisions represent a legal *communis opinio*. This required improved law reporting and a clearer appellate hierarchy of courts. In addition, the archaic writ system was relaxed in favour of general pleading, bringing a new focus on substantive, rather than procedural, law and an attempt to limit judicial subjectivity. Common law and equity were fused.[33]

Union Jacks and juries

By 1806, the British flag was firmly planted on Seychelles soil. As noted, De Quinssy flew the capitulation flag on all exiting ships, allowing them to pass without interference to the blockaded Port Louis in Mauritius. The result was continuing trade, indeed prosperity, despite hostilities.[34] Mauritius and Seychelles finally fell to the British in 1810. The terms of this capitulation formally ensured that the Seychellois could maintain their customs, including their religion and their laws.[35] And as the *Code Pénal* and the Code of Criminal Procedure had never been promulgated there, until 1831 the old French Criminal Ordinance of 1671 still governed. Similarly, the French Penal Law of 1791 remained law until 1838.

England had been prepared to swap its Indian Ocean islands for French possessions on the Indian subcontinent during the negotiations for the Treaty of

31 Bradley, *The History of Seychelles*, 122–123.

32 Ibid., 124.

33 Indeed, if we imagine law to be sausage-making, the century saw the various elements of English law ground and pressed into a single casing. See Seán Patrick Donlan, '"All This Together Make Up our *Common* Law": Legal Hybridity in England and Ireland, 1704–1804' in Örücü (ed.) *Mixed Legal Systems at New Frontiers*, 290. But it takes little to open, exposing the mix of different traditions beneath.

34 Jean-Louis Guébourg, *Les Seychelles* (2004).

35 Although the content of these laws remained contested in the courts in the twentieth century.

Paris (1814). But France refused. Instead, the nearby *Réunion* island was returned to France, while Mauritius and Seychelles remained British. The three jurisdictions shared similar creole languages, but developed still more distinctive legal regimes. The first English Governor was Sir Robert Townsend Farquhar, resident in Mauritius. Despite the appointment of a British Civil Agent in Seychelles, de Quinssy remained as *juge de paix* until 1815. French laws applied unchanged.[36] In fact, the laws enacted from 1810 to 1840 are collectively referred to as the *Code Farquhar*. Both the English language and its laws were tentatively introduced. During the first 30 years of British rule, local ordinances, the Governor's Proclamations, and other Public Acts or Notices of the Government were usually promulgated both in English and French. Both were deemed authoritative. After 1841, all laws, including those amending the French codes, had to be written in English.[37] Mauritian legislation later in the century reversed this restriction, authorising its legislature to amend codes in French where they were originally drafted in French or in English and French.[38] Farquhar's sympathy with the plight of the settlers played a role in maintaining French laws. He even travelled to London and, for two years, tried to persuade them not to impose English law on Mauritius and its dependencies.[39]

The integration, or rather creolisation, of the black and white populations was a long and difficult process. Both Faquhar and the white Seychellois equated slavery with custom. Despite the fact that the British abolished the slave trade in 1811, real change took longer. Another Order in Council (22 June 1829) ordered that freed slaves be given the same rights as the white population, but this did not achieve much.[40] A subsequent law abolishing slavery in Mauritius and Seychelles was promulgated in February 1835, but did not take place until 1838. In the interim, liberated slaves had to undergo an apprenticeship for life, also enabling former slave-owners to reorganise the labour force.[41] Emancipation turned many French settlers against the English administration. Indeed, a number of families left Seychelles, taking their slaves with them. Others blamed the British for depriving them of slave labour and instilling idleness in the liberated Africans. Abolition only slowly eroded the established, layered social order.

The British did not settle Seychelles, but Anglo-British, or rather English, legal doctrines were slowly introduced.[42] In 1831, for example, an Order in Council confirmed that the *Code Civil*, Commercial Code, and Code of Civil Procedure

36 Scarr, *Seychelles Since 1770*, 39.

37 Order in Council, 25 February 1841.

38 Order in Council, 25 January 1962.

39 Raymond M. d'Unienville, 'Capitulation Revisited: Ce que nous devons a Farquhar' (2012) *Mauritius Law Review* 17.

40 Ibid., 42.

41 Lionnet, 'Les Effets de la Revolution Française aux Seychelles', 98.

42 A letter from Bathurst dated 28 March 1820 confirms the retention of French laws and infuses in the mix the first English legal doctrines. Colonial Office Papers 168/6, National Archives Kew London. See also Charles Clark, *A Summary of Colonial Law, the Practice of*

would be preserved except where modification was necessary. It added, however, that English criminal law would be applied in the future. A jury was to be empanelled for criminal cases and civil courts would be presided over by a judge and two assistants. The Mauritian Court of Appeal would be reduced to four judges, two of whom would be English. The Court was given the powers of a Court of Equity, as well as of law. Similarly, Civil Commissioners were invested with the powers of English Justices of the Peace. Seychelles continued to be administered by Civil Agents and Commissioners under the direct orders of the Governor of Mauritius and under applicable Mauritian laws. Although a much later Order in Council in 1888 created a Seychellois Legislative Council and Supreme Court, both were subordinate Mauritian institutions.

Mixité and *métissage*

By the twentieth century, there was still only a single court in Seychelles, exercising civil and criminal jurisdiction not requiring a jury. Cases of appeal and serious criminal offences were the domain of the Supreme Court of Mauritius.[43] The reports of the Court of Appeal[44] (1870–1902) had already changed from a French to an English style. Seychelles became independent of Mauritius in 1903.[45] Existing laws were preserved except where incompatible with Seychellois legislation.[46] In practice, however, Seychelles' French-inspired laws eroded more quickly than those in Mauritius, not least because of the greater impact of the English language. English law was also in the ascendency in Seychelles. The English law of evidence prevailed in civil matters. Its Penal Code (1904) was a patchwork of the previous French Code, with borrowings from the British Indian Penal Code.[47] Codes of criminal and civil procedure were promulgated in 1919 and 1920, respectively. In the case of the latter, again because of the retention of the *Code Civil*, several provisions of the original French Code of Civil Procedure were also saved. Finally, some provisions of the Civil Code, notably in relation to

the Court of Appeals from the Plantations, and of the Laws and their Administration in all the Colonies (1834) 586.

43 M. Murat, 'Gordon's Eden or, The Seychelles Archipelago' (1900) *Foreign and Commonwealth Office Collection* 14.

44 Paget Bourke, *A Digest of the Ruling Decisions of the Supreme Court of Seychelles from 1903 to 1933 and the Reported Cases on appeal therefrom to His Majesty's Privy Council from 1870 to 1902* (1934).

45 Letters Patent, 31 August 1903.

46 Seychelles Legislature in Council 1903.

47 It remained in force until 1955 when it was replaced by a new code based on the Penal Code of East Africa which was itself derived from English law. See generally Mathilda Twomey, 'Mongrel Laws or Model Code? The Antecedents of the Penal Code of Seychelles' (2015) 2 *Journal of Comparative Law in Africa* 40.

the law on domicile[48] and the law of defamation[49] were also amended with the introduction of English law concepts.

Of course, the Seychellois regulated their lives with more than their formal *legal* hybridity. Social norms rooted in its various cultural strains were important, too. By 1900, the archipelago had a population of 20,000, including individuals of varied European, African, and Asian origin.[50] The *métissage* of race was paralleled by the *creolité* of Seychellois culture, expanding outward from a space in-between the *grands blancs* (the old landed families descended from the first French settlers) and the later *colonisateurs anglais* (the English colonisers).[51] This development was particularly evident in the language of the Seychellois. While both English and French were spoken, increasingly its *kreol* language was the standard language of daily life, if not its laws.[52] Indeed, the ascent of English, along with the increasing elevated place of *kreol*, did not bode well for the preservation of its particular legal hybridity. After 1945, French was replaced by English as the medium of education. And lacking knowledge of French, judges would become unable to turn to the civil jurisprudence of France. This was compounded by the use of non-native judges, who not only lacked the necessary linguistic abilities, but whose loyalties were to purer forms of (colonial) Anglo-American laws. Neocolonial traits persist in the practice of law today.

Unfortunately, the *normative* hybridity of Seychelles, as well as the relationship of its norms and laws, can only be suggested here. It requires further study. Religious norms, including its laws, are not legally recognised independently of state law. But some norms that have existed for a long-time *praetor legem* or even *contra legem* have, more recently, become internalised through judicial interpretation and creativity. They are brought *intra legem* and so make up weak/state legal pluralism. Examples are *en-ménage* relationships and *piti sonnyen*. The former, also referred to as *concubinage notoire* or de facto relationships, denotes long-term relationships between unmarried parties.[53] The latter is a traditional

48 Domicile Act, Cap 66, Laws of Seychelles.

49 Defamation Ordinance, 1948, repealed and replaced by Article 1383-3 of the Civil Code of Seychelles.

50 This is mapped out in Fernando Ortiz's concept of transculturation, where there is a progression from hostility (against the black), to compromise (by the slyly subversive slave), to adaptation (on the part of the imitative mulatto), to vindication (of blacks and mulattos) and finally to integration. Ortiz, *Etnia y Sociedad* (1993). See Supriya Nair, 'Creolization, Orality and Nation Language in the Carribean' in Henry Schwarz and Sangeeta Ray (eds) *A Companion to Postcolonial Studies* (2005) 238.

51 Scarr, *Seychelles Since 1770*, 178. See Ibid., 130 and Jean Houbert, 'The Indian Ocean Creole Islands: Geo-Politics and Decolonisation' (1992) 30 (3) *The Journal of Modern African Studies* 465, 468.

52 J. Stanley Gardiner, 'The Seychelles Archipelago' (1907) 29 (2) *The Geographical Journal* 148. See also Jean Bernabé, Patrick Chamoiseau, Raphael Confiant, *Éloge de la Creolité/In Praise of Creoleness* (1993) 75.

53 This can be contrasted to the approach taken with regard to the succession rights of a concubine, which the courts have steadfastly refused to grant. *Clarisse v Sophola* (2005) SLR 96.

arrangement in which a large, usually poor, family gives a child to a household without children. But many customary norms are marginalised by state laws. Some are even illegal. Along with custom *praeter legem*, these are part of the wider normative pluralism (also known as 'strong' or 'deep legal pluralism'). It is, for example, a criminal offence to beat drums or blow conches after nine at night. This was intended to stamp out the custom of *moutia* gatherings, a combination of story-telling and dispute resolution.[54] It is a criminal offence to deal in witchcraft.[55] Legislation, sometimes for environmental reasons, also limits the traditional consumption of some foods and beverages.[56] These are either heavily regulated or banned outright.[57]

Since 1950, foreign influences have arguably become more, rather than less, important. This is true despite Seychellois independence in 1976 and the growing sense of a collective creole identity, in-between its European, African, and Asian ancestors. Indeed, while English, French, and *kreol* are used by different sectors of the population, the decision to make *kreol* the official language in 1981 helped to cement a common identity. Of course, as in other colonial or postcolonial contexts, this is complicated by continuing inequalities in land distribution, wealth, and education. The empire of English laws has expanded. Civil administration, for example, continues to mirror the British system. The laws and official documents are all in English, which is also the working language of the courts.[58] More and more judges and legal practitioners are from a common law background and speak little French. In addition, while Article 5 of the *Code Civil* states that a judicial determination on an issue of law has no declaratory force in subsequent cases, a de facto type of *stare decisis* has crept into the civil jurisprudence of the courts.[59] Indeed, this has happened despite the fact that Article 5 of the revised Civil Code of Seychelles (1975) reads that 'judicial decisions shall not be absolutely binding ... but shall enjoy a high persuasive authority'.

54 See Drums Regulation GG 1/5/1935 and Section 183 of the Penal Code.

55 Section 303, Penal Code, Chapter 158, Laws of Seychelles. See *Eugenie v R* (1969) SCAR 71. This was an attempt to stop the customs of *gri-gri* (*gris-gris*, or grey magic of voodoo), *malfesan* (malfeasance or evil), and *bonhom/bonfam dibwa* (*bonhommes* or *bonne femmes du bois*, i.e. witchdoctors). See Lionnet, *The Seychelles*, 111–112 and Burton Benedict, *People of the Seychelles* (1966) 64.

56 This includes *kare/tortues marines carées* (green sea turtles) and *fouke/fouquet* (sea birds). Section 17 of the Public Order Act, the Penal Code, and the Licences Act, Cap 113 5 also relates to *toddy* (*kalou/calou*, or fermented coconut palm juice), *bacca* (fermented sugar cane juice), and *lapire* (*la purée*, or fermented fruit or vegetable juice). See Benedict, *People of the Seychelles*, 192.

57 See Wild Animals and Birds Protection Act, Cap 247, Laws of Seychelles. See also *R v Fayolle* (1971) SLR 119 and recently *R v Marengo and Others* SC CRS 11 of 2003. See also Lionnet, *The Seychelles*, 115.

58 Interpreters are used in court to translate *kreol* testimony into English. This is both for the court records and, often, for the benefits of non-native judges.

59 Such an approach already applied to the criminal law.

Of course, this revision of the civil code was also a translation from French to English. This was easily the biggest assault on Seychelles' French connection, its links to the legal ideas and institutions of France. While the new code remains faithful in form and structure (including the numbering of its articles), there are many deviations from French tradition. English influence is obvious and expanding. This is true, for example, in the rules relating to guardianship[60] and the partial introduction of the concept of trusts in cases of co-ownership of property.[61] Some argued that the adherence of the Seychellois to the French tradition would, ironically, be enhanced by the translation of the code. It would, that is, be more accessible and modern, as well as promoting legal harmony with other Commonwealth traditions.[62] It would also meet the new challenges of nationhood.[63] But, in the same period, the laws of Mauritius remained bilingual and bi-jural without any ossification of its laws or economic problems.[64]

Ironically, Seychelles' formal sovereignty makes the foreign and European origin of its laws more obvious. The three republics that Seychelles has known since independence have often sought to alter the laws of the past. Even adherence to French tradition can be seen as neo-colonial. This is disorienting, especially when combined with the influence, often uninvited, of Anglophone legal traditions, due to political and cultural hegemony. The policies of the government in the 1980s and 1990s – from a single, dominant party – led to many calls for economic and political reform. While these slowly occurred, they often came with strings attached. Economic assistance would lead some international bodies, including the World Bank and the *International Monetary Fund* (IMF), to impose changes in the laws of Seychelles. These reforms were arguably unnecessary and instead merely reflected the political familiarity and biases of those international organisations. More recently still, the use of 'offshore business' has meant that Seychelles must effectively cede its sovereignty to the necessities of the market.

Conclusion

Intellectually and institutionally, Seychelles is not an island, but an extraordinary intersection of peoples, laws, and norms. And in recent years, its independence has made it possible for the unique Seychellois nation to speak its collective mind,

60 Articles 402–422, 429–437 *Civil Code* of Seychelles.

61 Article 818 of the *Civil Code* of Seychelles.

62 See, e.g. A. G. Chloros, *Codification in a Mixed Jurisdiction: The Civil and Commercial Law of Seychelles* (1977) 7.

63 André Sauzier, 'The Influence of the French Judicial Model on the Seychelles' (trans. Nicole Tirant-Gherardi), http://www.bas.sc/law-journal-1/theinfluenceofthefrenchjudicialmodelontheseychelles, accessed 1 July 2017.

64 Louis Yeung Lam Ko, 'The Economic Development of Mauritius Since Independence' Research Working Paper No. 6, School of Economics, University of New South Wales, Australia, http://wwwdocs.fce.unsw.edu.au/economics/Research/WorkingPapers/1998_6.pdf, accessed 1 July 2017.

both through its *parliament* and the *jurisdiction* of its courts. *Parliament*, from the French, is rooted in the idea of speaking together to make laws; *jurisdiction*, from the Latin, was the idea of having the authority to speak the law. Whatever the origin of their institutions, the Seychellois now have the possibility of determining their own future. But the prospect of establishing laws that mirror the genuine spirit of the nation will require meaningful popular sovereignty. Internally, this requires a robust republic. But it also requires that outside influences – the result of economic dominance and geopolitical hegemony rather than choice – are not allowed to overwhelm the will of the Seychellois people.

Selected bibliography

Homi Bhabha, *The location of culture* (Routledge 1994).

Petra Butler and Christine Morris (eds), *Small States in a legal world* (Springer 2017).

Ignazio Castellucci, 'How mixed must a mixed system be?' (2008) 12 *Electronic Journal of Comparative Law*, ww.ejcl.org/121/art121-4.pdf, accessed 1 July 2017.

G. Chloros, *Codification in a mixed jurisdiction: the civil and commercial law of Seychelles* (North-Holland 1977).

Thomas Duve (ed.), *Entanglements in legal history: conceptual approaches* (Max Planck Institute for European Legal History 2014).

Sue Farran, Esin Örücü, and Seán Patrick Donlan, 'An introductory overview' and 'Endnote to mixed legal systems: endangered, entrenched, blended or muddled?' in Sue Farran, Esin Örücü, and Seán Patrick Donlan (eds), *A study of mixed legal systems: endangered, entrenched or blended* (Ashgate 2014).

Martha-Marie Kleinhans, 'Hybridizing civil law through transatlantic migration' (2008) 5 (1) *Atlantic Studies: Global Currents* 119.

Zoë Laidlow, 'Breaking Britannia's bounds? Law, settlers and space in Britain's imperial historiography' (2012) 55 *Historical Journal* 807.

Joseph W. McKnight, 'Some historical observations on mixed systems of law' (1977) 22 *Juridical Review* (ns) 177.

Esin Örücü, 'A theoretical framework for transfrontier mobility of law' in Annie J de Roo, Esin Örücü, and Robert W. Jagtenberg (eds), *Transfrontier mobility of law* (Kluwer 1995).

Esin Örücü, 'Mixed and mixing systems: A conceptual search' in Esin Örücü, Elspeth Attwooll, and Sean Coyle (eds), *Studies in legal systems: Mixed and mixing* (Kluwer 1996).

Esin Örücü, 'Law as transposition' (2002) 51 *International and Comparative Law Quarterly* 205.

Esin Örücü, 'Comparatists and extraordinary places' in Pierre Legrand and Roderick Munday (eds) *Comparative legal studies: traditions and transitions* (CUP 2003).

Esin Örücü, 'What is a mixed legal system: exclusion or expansion?' in Esin Örücü (ed.) *Mixed legal systems at new frontiers* (Simmonds & Hill Publishing 2010).

Esin Örücü, 'Infusion of the diffused: Four circles of diffusion infusing the legal system of Turkey' in Sue Farran, James Gallen, Jen Hendry, and Christa Rautenbach (eds) *The Diffusion of law: the movement of laws and norms around the world* (Routledge 2015).

Anjali Prabhu, *Hybridity: limits, transformations, prospects* (State University of New York Press 2007).

William Twining, 'Diffusion of law: a global perspective' (2004) 49 *Journal of Legal Pluralism* 1.

3 Legislating for customary land tenure

A comparative query

Sue Farran

Introduction

Perhaps one of the key characteristics of a comparatist is curiosity and a genuine interest to seek out similarities and differences in order to enrich our own and others' understandings. In an increasingly globalised world, boundaries are opaque, and laws and ideas travel or are diffused, received, rejected, or modified, leading to mixities, hybrids, contaminations, and/or legal contagion. At the same time, the localities of law should not be overlooked. Law does not exist in a vacuum but is closely linked with the histories of people, their social organisation, daily life, and values systems, as well as the wider economic and political context. There are at play, therefore, a number of interlinked pluralities.

This does not mean that comparisons cannot be made across time or continents. Where it is least expected we may find common themes or challenges, and different or similar ways of dealing with these. This chapter makes a perhaps unlikely link between South Africa and the Pacific islands. The common cause is land, and customary law, influenced by past histories. If one were to adopt imagery from Esin Örücü, perhaps the *salad* is most appropriate: a mix of salad leaves, a light tossing in variable dressings which often have similar ingredients but in different quantities, in some form of container which keeps the whole thing together – in this case the legal framework. In particular, what these rather different geographical regions have in common is a colonial past, traditional and neo-traditional social organisation in which customary leaders play a significant role, changing land use and land allocation and tension between the customs of the past and the demands of modernity.

In order to explore these various dilemmas, this chapter looks at the issues arising in the South Africa context of customary land tenure and then turns its attention to examples from the Pacific region, focussing in particular on the island country of Vanuatu. Before looking at the differences let us consider some of the similarities.

The colonial and post-colonial experience

Turning first to the colonial experience, in Africa and the Pacific island region this, as in most countries coming under the influence of Western powers, had considerable consequences for land rights, often leading to the introduction of completely new systems of tenure, the dispossession of indigenous people of their historic and traditional lands, and the imposition of radically different ways of relating to and using land. In particular, colonialism introduced practices such as the registration of land interests, the determination of land disputes in formal forums, institutions such as leasehold and freehold, and concepts such as absolute ownership and a shift from the sharing of communal resources to exclusiveness and individual titles. Introduced formal laws also saw the shift from oral narratives of land claims to documentary evidence and the consolidation of land rights through formal mechanisms such as court decisions and attempts to bring customary land tenure within the framework of written laws.[1]

This last appears to be an ongoing project in post-colonial states and the challenges that this presents reflect the complex association of people, land, and status in the determination of land rights in customary law. This mix becomes even more volatile where events trigger competing demands for the re-invigoration of customary governance of land but at the same time provide an opportunity for modernisation. In South Africa the dismantling of apartheid in the early 1990s was one such event, in the Pacific island country of Vanuatu, the resolutions of a National Land Summit in 2006 and the subsequent emergence of a political party focussed on strengthening customary land rights was another.[2]

What is also a feature of some post-colonial societies is the strengthening assertion of traditions and/or customs as markers of independence from colonial rule or oppressive colonial legacies and assertions of indigeneity, sovereignty, and national autonomy. Often the practices or controls claimed as traditional or customary do not go back to 'time immemorial' but are historically quite recent innovations. Sometimes colonial encounters blended seamlessly into custom – for example religions introduced under missionisation, legal language – such as the term ownership, and assertions of status – and titles conferred under colonial administration, demonstrating not only the flexible accommodation of custom but also its malleability. Post-colonial political and government structures have

1 For comment on this legal phenomenon in Africa see 'Integrating customary land tenure into Statutory Land Law' (*US Agency for International Development*, 1 January 2008), http://www.usaidlandtenure.net/sites/default/files/USAID_Land_Tenure_PRRG_Integrating_Customary_Land_Tenure_Into_Statutory_Land_Law.pdf, accessed 13 December 2016. In the Pacific see the Lands Codes of Kiribati (found in the Native Lands Ordinance in the Laws of the Gilbert Islands, revised edition 1977, under the heading 'Gilbert and Phoenix Islands Lands Code') and Tuvalu (Tuvalu Lands Code, Laws of Tuvalu, revised edition 1990) both accessible on the Pacific Islands Legal Information Institute (Paclii.org) website.

2 See Sue Farran and Jennifer Corrin, 'Developing legislation to formalise customary land management: deep legal pluralism or shallow veneer?' (2017) 10 (1) *Law and Development Review* 1–27.

also created hybrid opportunities for traditional leaders to claim new ground. Local and national government officers, for example, may combine novel roles with traditional status; political candidates may curry the support of voters by appealing to traditional loyalties in return for the dispensation of state benefits; or 'traditional' leaders may use their influence and voice to broker deals with private investors (not always ensuring that benefits are equitably distributed to their communities). Indeed, as will be demonstrated, in both South Africa and the Pacific islands, traditional social status is closely linked to the control of land interests, and there is ongoing tension between containing this sphere of influence and enlarging it.

Customary land in South Africa

Under apartheid, customary law in general was only recognised in so far as it had been codified or could be established by evidence in the courts. It had no formal place in the state legal system and Ntlama suggests that under apartheid customary law was recognised 'only in so far as it could be used to perpetuate ... discrimination'.[3] Indigenous people had been largely deprived of their traditional land rights and in many cases relocated to specified geographic areas – 'homelands' where land was often poor and barely able to support subsistence farming.[4] Post-apartheid and under the new Constitution, customary law is formally recognised and accommodated alongside the common law and legislation as a source of law. Section 211(2) reads: 'The courts must apply customary law when that law is applicable, subject to the constitution and any legislation that specifically deals with customary law'.

Immediately it is apparent that a plural legal order is recognised and that there is a hierarchy. Section 2, for example, reads: 'This Constitution is the supreme law of the Republic; law or conduct which is inconsistent with it is invalid, and the obligations imposed by it must be fulfilled'. Similarly, Section 39(3) states: 'The Bill of Rights does not deny the existence of any other rights or freedoms that are recognised or conferred by common law or customary law or legislation, to the extent that they are consistent with the Bill'.

The relationship between common law and customary law is not entirely clear. Ntlama suggests that at first sight customary law appears to be the 'poor cousin' of common law, because Section 8 of the Constitution omits specific reference

3 Nomthandazo Ntlama, 'The application of section 8(3) of the Constitution in the development of Customary Law values in South Africa's new constitutional dispensation' (2012) 15 (1) *Potchefstroom Electronic Law Journal* 24, http://www.ajol.info/index.php/pelj/article/download/75699/66227, accessed 31 December 2016.

4 For historical background see Elmien du Plessis, 'African Indigenous land rights in a private ownership paradigm' (2011) 14 (7) *Potchefstroom Electronic Law Journal* 44, http://journals.co.za/docserver/fulltext/perblad/14/7/perblad_v14_n7_a3.pdf?expires=1483294883&id=id&accname=guest&checksum=6377B13B0B4DEF3D20CCCCB8EAD3A619, accessed 31 December 2016.

to customary law in the provisions that provide that in seeking to give effect to fundamental rights, a court 'must apply or develop the common law' (s8(3)).[5] The implication is that the court need not take into account customary law when considering fundamental rights issues. As a consequence, it might be argued that in upholding fundamental rights, customary law might be 'trumped' by the common law. Although both sources of law are equally subject to the Constitution and its post-apartheid values, the relationship between common law, customary law, and fundamental rights is sometimes difficult particularly in the context of non-discrimination and gender equality, as will be seen further below.

Customary land in the Pacific

Throughout the Pacific region, custom is relevant to land tenure and in most of the countries of the region custom is recognised as a substantial body of law relating to land. Indeed, land held under customary land tenure represents a considerable proportion of all land tenure in the region. Although the customs that determine land rights are different, generally it can be asserted that interests in land are closely linked, first to social organisation, and second to the historical movement and relocation of people. Claims to land are therefore established through genealogies, inheritance, marriage, and adoption, first settlement, or subsequent permitted settlement. Even in Tonga, where all land is held by the Crown under a feudal system of land allocation, traditional hierarchies determine land entitlement, with nobles having greater estates than commoners.[6] Similarly, in Fiji, where most land is held under a trust for indigenous Fijians,[7] entitlement is determined by genealogical links and customary membership of clans (*mataqali*) and dominance by male chiefs. While many forms of customary land tenure are communal, not all are. For example, in Nauru, individual titles are recognised and in the Cook Islands a form of native freehold emerges when a court rules on a disputed title.[8] Elsewhere, despite being strongly resisted by official statements, there are indications of shifts towards individual titles or more nuclear family land rights.[9]

5 Ntlama, 'The application of section 8(3) of the Constitution in the development of Customary Law values in South Africa's new constitutional dispensation' 32.
6 Land Act Cap. 132 Tonga Consolidated Legislation 1988 edition.
7 See Native and Trust Act Cap. 134; Native Lands Act Cap. 133, Laws of Fiji, revised edition 1985, amended by the Native Land Trust (Amendment) Act 2002, the Native Lands (Amendment) Act 2002. In 2012 and 2013, by a series of decrees, reference to 'native' was replaced in all cases by the term '*Taukei*' in reference to indigenous Fijians.
8 Junior Ngatokarua, Sue Farran and Don Paterson, 'Cook Islands' in Don Paterson and Sue Farran (eds), *South Pacific Land Systems* (USP Press 2013) 147.
9 For example, in Samoa and in Vanuatu.

The recognition of custom lies either in the written Constitution or in legislation, or both.[10] In Samoa, for example, the Constitution of 1960 includes the preambular words 'Whereas the Leaders of Samoa have declared that Samoa should be an Independent State based on Christian principles and Samoan custom'; and that of Vanuatu 20 years later proclaims 'the establishment of the united and free Republic of Vanuatu founded on traditional Melanesian values, faith in God, and Christian Principles'. One of the most recent constitutions, the 2013 Constitution of Fiji, opens by stating 'WE, THE PEOPLE OF FIJI, RECOGNISING the indigenous people or the *iTaukei*, their ownership of *iTaukei* lands, their unique culture, customs, traditions and language' demonstrating the enduring significance of custom and indeed customary law. Constitutional recognition is not just given to custom or traditions – including traditional values,[11] but in some Pacific countries there is specific reference to land. This is seen above in the Fiji Constitution, confirming very clearly that only indigenous Fijians (*iTaukei*) have claims to customary land in Fiji, and also in Vanuatu where the Constitution returned allodial titles of all land to the custom owners,[12] and stated that 'The rules of custom shall form the basis of ownership and use of land in the Republic of Vanuatu'.[13] In Papua New Guinea, which has the largest landmass in the Pacific region, customary land tenure is recognised in the Constitution, the Lands Act 1996 and the Underlying Law Act 2000, although as in Vanuatu and indeed elsewhere, the specifics of custom are left unstated and unregulated.

In the formal legal systems, the recognition of customary law is variable. In the Solomon Islands, for example, the Customs Recognition Act 2000 (which has not yet been gazetted)[14] provides for the recognition and enforcement of customary law in respect of land, fisheries, and water, except where this would be inconsistent with the Constitution, statutory law, or unjust or contrary to the public interest.[15] In Nauru, the Custom and Adopted Laws Act 1971 states that 'the … customs and usages of the Nauruans … shall have full force and effect of law to regulate … title to, and interests in, land, other than any title or interest granted by lease of other instrument',[16] although it has been historically unclear if these customs and usages include the phosphate that once made the island

10 For an extensive overview see Guy Powles, 'Common law at bay? The Scope and status of customary law regimes in the South Pacific' (1997) 21 *The Journal of Pacific Studies* 61.

11 See for example, the Constitution of Tuvalu.

12 Article 73 states 'All land in the Republic of Vanuatu belongs to the indigenous custom owners and their descendants'.

13 Article 74.

14 See Jennifer Corrin Care and Jean Zorn, 'Legislating for the application of customary law in Solomon Islands' (2005) 34 (2) *Common Law World Review* 144.

15 Sections 6 and 8.

16 Section 3(1).

so wealthy, or the foreshore and reefs.[17] In contrast, in Papua New Guinea, the status of customary law in general is unclear as the Underlying Law Act indicates that it is only one of the sources of underlying law and is subject to non-adoption or non-application if it conflicts with written laws, basic rights or is contrary to the National Goals and Directive Principles set out in the Constitution.[18]

Similarly, in the context of land disputes, there is a wide variety of processes and forums with special land courts in Kiribati, Tuvalu, the Solomon Islands, and Samoa, but elsewhere, for example the Cook Islands and Niue, land issues are determined by the ordinary courts. In Fiji there are ministerially appointed commissioners, and in Vanuatu there was, until 2013, a hierarchy of specialist tribunals.[19] In some countries the more traditional forum allows an appeal to the formal court system,[20] elsewhere it does not,[21] or alternatively there may be a requirement to engage in traditional dispute resolution before the formal process can be used. For example, in Samoa, the Land and Titles Act 1981, Section 34, requires the parties to resolve matters through conciliation and outside court, and the Registrar of the Land and Titles Court 'may actively encourage the participants to reach an agreement which accords with Samoan custom and usage'. In the Solomon Islands all land disputes regarding customary land must first be referred to traditional dispute mechanisms and only if no acceptable solution can be found will the dispute go to the local lands court.[22] Consequently, in a number of Pacific countries traditional authorities have considerable authority over land disputes. This does not, however, necessarily reduce the number of disputes as avenues of appeal are frequently pursued. It also raises the issue of adjudication competence not only of judges in the formal courts who may be unfamiliar with localised customs but also of local traditional leaders who may feel unfettered by considerations such as burdens of proof, objectivity, or fairness. The influence of those who decide land disputes is therefore significant in the context of customary land. It is for this reason that the Custom Land Management Act in Vanuatu is controversial because its principal aim is to restore the right to determine ownership of customary land to traditional authorities.

17 See Gabrissa Hartman, Sue Farran and Don Paterson, 'Nauru' in Don Paterson and Sue Farran (eds), *South Pacific Land Systems* (USP Press 2013) 118.

18 See section 4 Underlying Law Act 2000. This Act is in force but presents problems in application. See Bruce Ottley, 'Reconciling modernity and traditions – PNG Underlying Law Act' (2012) 1 *The Underlying Law Journal: Developments in the Underlying Law of Papua New Guinea*, 5, http://www.paclii.org/cgi-bin/sinodisp/pg/cases/PGULJ/2012/5.html?stem=&synonyms=&query=Underlying%20law%20act, accessed 2 January 2017.

19 Customary Land Tribunals were abolished under the land reforms linked to the Custom Land Management Act 2013.

20 For example, in Nauru appeal to the Supreme Court from the Lands Committee is permitted.

21 For example, under the Customary Land Management Act 2013 in Vanuatu there is expressly no appeal to the formal courts. The only exception would be by way of judicial review. See also the Land and Titles Act 1981 s 71, in Samoa.

22 Local Courts Act Cap 19, Laws of Solomon Islands, 1996 edition.

Judicial intervention in land

In South Africa, the Constitutional Court has read the constitutional provision relating to customary law to include living (and therefore changing) customary law as well as codified customary law[23] or customary law already recognised in case law.[24] Du Plessis and Frantz, however, suggest that the courts have sometimes struggled to accommodate 'living' customary law, seeking instead to bring this within the constraints with which they are familiar in respect of official customary law, i.e. the state's interpretation of this.[25] Thus, for example, customary claims to land are tested against common law understandings of ownership, or the exercise of uninterrupted possession over a long period of time, or recognisable evidence of engagement with the land so as to render it not '*terra nullius*'.[26] Although the court has said that the validity of customary law must be 'determined not by reference to the common law, but to the Constitution'[27] which 'acknowledges the originality and distinctiveness of indigenous law as an independent source of norms within the legal system',[28] there is, so du Plessis and Frantz argue, a continuing tendency to try and 'fit' these norms within the familiar framework of common law – thereby adopting a legal positivist approach,[29] rather than accepting customary law as a living law on its own merits.[30]

One consequence of the courts being asked to adjudicate on customary matters in South Africa has been the passing of a number of statutes to regulate formerly unregulated customary matters or to bring existing legislation in line with the Constitution.[31] This reaction challenges the idea of living customary law not only by transforming it into state law but by freezing it in time. Unless the codification of customary law is framed in rather abstract terms, which allow

23 See for example, the Black Administration Act 1927 and the Natal Code of Zulu Law.

24 *Shilubana v Nwamitwa* (2009) 2 SA 66 (CC); *Gumede v President of the Republic of South Africa* (2009)3 SA 152 (CC).

25 Elmien du Plessis and Gino Frantz, 'African customary land rights in a private ownership paradigm' (2 June 2013), https://papers.ssrn.com/sol3/papers.cfm?abstract_id=2381922, accessed 11 January 2018.

26 For a critical appraisal of the colonial construction of customary law in texts prior to 1994 see Aninka Claassens, 'Recent changes in women's land rights and contested customary law in South Africa' (2012) 13 (1) *Journal of Agrarian Change* 71.

27 *Alexcor Ltd v The Richtersveld Community* (2004) 5 SA 469, para 50–51.

28 ibid.

29 See Gerrit Pienaar 'The methodology used to interpret customary land tenure' (2012) 15 (3) *PER* 39, http://www.saflii.org.za/za/journals/PER/2012/39.pdf, accessed 31 December 2016.

30 For a longitudinal perspective see Thandabantu Nhlapo, 'Customary law in post-apartheid South Africa: the vexed question of cultural diversity, women's rights, "living law", and appropriate law reform' (2014) *New York Law School Review*, http://www.nylslawreview.com/wp-content/uploads/sites/16/2014/11/Nhlapo.pdf, accessed 19 November 2016.

31 See for example the Recognition of Customary Marriages Act 1998, The Children's Act 2005, the Communal Land Rights Act 2004, the National House of Traditional Leaders Act 2009 etc. See ibid.

for creative interpretation so as to keep it 'alive', there is the danger that it will become out of touch with reality. Even if this approach is taken, there is the question of who is to interpret the written law in order to keep it relevant, and what happens during this interpretive process?

This is not a problem limited to the South African courts. Indeed Weiner, referring to customary land tenure in Australia and the wider Pacific, has drawn attention to 'a more general trend to simplify and idealise indigenous customs across the board'.[32] In the Cook Islands, it has been suggested that evidence of genealogies to support land claims are being modified so as to remove distracting collateral or bi-lateral links and present these in a linear fashion more acceptable to the court.[33] In Vanuatu, negotiators' certificates are more likely to be granted to those claiming to be the custom owners of the land who can produce a formal court adjudication in their favour, rather than those who have never formally litigated to secure their title, and more generally recourse to written documents is apparent in reported decisions. Even where attempts are being made to strengthen traditional control over customary land, and elevate its hitherto demeaned status or inferior status in the legal system, hybrid measures emerge as law reforms seek to straddle the practices of the past with the demands of the present.

Confronting the dilemma

All the countries considered here include a Bill of Rights within their written constitutions and two examples in the context of land rights illustrate some of the challenges encountered in giving effect to these rights: discrimination and security of tenure or the protection of property rights. Balancing contemporary concerns with both raise particular issues in the case of land held under customary tenure.

In South Africa, the application of customary law has to comply with the 'spirit, purport and objects of the Bill of rights'[34] when applied by a court or tribunal. Included among these are equality before the law and non-discrimination, as well as the unfettered right to own property.[35] This is all very well, but customary land rights are largely determined by social relations and inter-generational obligations in which the individual may be of considerably less significance than the larger group, although the nature and composition of any collective may

32 James Weiner, 'Foreword' (2011) 34 *Pacific Studies* 87, 89.

33 See Arno Pascht, 'Land rights in Rarotonga (Cook Islands): traditions and transformations' (2011) 34 *Pacific Studies* 195, and Alan Howard on the Rotuman Lands Act 1959 which sought to similarly recognise only mono-lineal inheritance: Alan Howard, 'Land issues on Rotuma' (2011) 34 *Pacific Studies* 157.

34 Section s39(2).

35 Section 25.

itself be disputed, fluctuating, and multiple.[36] Often these social relations are based on power, genealogy, and status.[37] So, for example, traditionally, women have few or more precarious land rights than men, and entitlement may depend on ranking at birth as well as issues of legitimacy/adoption.[38] This gives rise to two main issues. First, the link between land and customary titles can be a major factor in land disputes because the title is so closely associated with the right to manage and control the land. Second, the allocation of traditional titles and the roles of those who hold these titles may be seen as breaching fundamental rights to equality and principles against discrimination based on sex or status, particularly as most titles of any influence are held by men. In South Africa and in the Pacific, the role of traditional leaders remains important and in some respects has been strengthened. For example, in the South African Constitution it is stated that '[t]he institution, status and role of traditional leadership, according to customary law, are recognised, subject to the Constitution'.[39] In the Pacific, the Vanuatu Constitution establishes a National Council of Chiefs and confers upon this the right to be consulted 'particularly [on] any question relating to tradition and custom'[40] and the right to be consulted by Parliament in respect of national land law.[41] Similarly constitutional provisions are found in the Cook Islands (the House of Arikis) and Marshall Islands (the Council of Iroij), which enhance the role of traditional leaders, while in Samoa only traditional title holders (*Matai*) can be elected to Parliament. The formalisation of traditional leaders in constitutions and legislation potentially creates conflict between the idea of customary law as a constantly evolving and changing law reflecting contemporary values and accommodating changing needs, and customary law as traditional, timeless, and predominantly patriarchal, and there are vested interests in preserving this status quo. For example, in South Africa, there has been lobbying for the codification of traditional powers in statute as found in the Traditional Leadership and Governance Framework Act 41 of 2003, which empowers provincial authorities to make further laws. Similarly, in Vanuatu, the Custom Land Management Act 2013, seeks to restore and strengthen the authority of local chiefs to determine land ownership, and indeed on New Year's Day 2017 the Minister of Lands

36 On the problem of referring to land as 'communal' see du Plessis, 'African Indigenous land rights'. Other problematic terms in this context are 'ownership' and 'the trust'.

37 Bennet refers to these key components as right, power and interest, with the status of the interest holder being the first consideration. T.W. Bennet, *Customary Law in South Africa* (Juta 2004) 380.

38 Challenged in South Africa in *Bhe and others v Magistrate, Khayelitsha, and others,* 2004(2) SA 544(CC) which departed from *Mthembu v Letsela and another.* 2000 (3) SA 867 (SCA) on the issue of male succession and primogeniture.

39 Section 211(1).

40 Section30(1).

41 Section 76. The National Council of Chiefs was renamed the Malvatumauri Council of Chiefs in the Constitution (Sixth) Amendment Act 2013.

extolled the work of traditional authorities stating that 'Chiefs and communities have become the arbiters as regards the local Kastom'.[42]

This local custom, however, may not be compatible with human rights, particularly, the equal treatment of individuals, when it comes to land. These issues have come before the courts in South Africa in a number of cases regarding rights of inheritance, laws of succession, and challenges to the customary practice of male primogeniture. In 2004 the Constitutional Court held that this latter practice undermined gender equality,[43] upholding the right of a woman to succeed to a traditional leadership role, but Ntlama has criticised the case for its failure to consider 'the implications it would have on the identity of the particularly traditional communities and their institutions',[44] thereby relegating customary law to its pre-1994 inferior status. In the Pacific the issue of primogeniture has recently come before the courts in the Cook Islands in the case of *Hunt and Tupou & Ors v Miguel*, Cook Islands Court of Appeal, 19 February 2016.[45] Historically courts in the Cook Islands have applied the primogeniture rule to the inheritance of titles which carry customary property benefits including entitlement to lease rents. They have done this in the exercise of their power under Section 409(f) of the Cook Islands Act 1915.[46] In this case, as a consequence of applying the rule of precedent regarding primogeniture the particular title had remained vacant since 1994, as no eligible incumbent had appeared. The litigation arose from an appeal by the *Aronga Mana* (a customary institutional group of Cook Island traditional leaders[47]) challenging the court's authority to make a ruling on customary titles on the basis of amendments to the Cook Islands' Constitution

42 'Vanuatu kava export shipment returned from NZ due to contamination with impurities' (*Vanuatu Daily Digest*, 1 January 2017), https://vanuatudaily.wordpress.com/2017/01/01/vanuatu-kava-export-shipment-returned-from-nz-due-to-contamination-with-impurities/#more-5765, accessed 3 January 2017.

43 *Bhe and Others v Khayelitsha Magistrate and Others* (2004).

44 Ntlama, 'The application of section 8(3) of the Constitution in the development of Customary Law values in South Africa's new constitutional dispensation' 26.

45 Unreported on Paclii.org but cited at *Hunt v De Miguel* [2016] CKCA in subsequent case law – see note 49. See Miranda Forsyth, 'The challenges of legal pluralism in the Cook Islands and beyond: an insight from *Hunt and Tupou & Ors v Miguel*, Cook Islands Court of Appeal, 19 February 2016' (2016) 2 *Journal of South Pacific Law* 26–38, https://www.usp.ac.fj/fileadmin/random_images/home_middle_banners/emalus/JSPL/2016/The_challenges_of_legal_pluralism_in_the_Cook_Islands_and_beyond.pdf, accessed 12 January 2018.

46 Section 409(f) reads 'In addition to the jurisdiction elsewhere conferred upon [the Land Court] by this Act, that Court shall have jurisdiction – to hear and determine any question as to the right of any person to hold office as an Ariki or other Native Chief of any island'.

47 The composition of this group and its right to wield certain customary powers is itself contested and subject to different interpretations. See Rachel Reeves, 'Aronga Mana: traditional leaders of the Cook Islands', https://rmtreeves.com/2015/12/31/aronga-mana-traditional-leaders-of-the-cook-islands, accessed 20 November 2016.

in 1995.[48] Specifically the appellants claimed that the constitutional amendment removed the power of the formal courts to determine matters of customary title. The appeal court adopted an interesting compromise position holding that while it was for the customary authorities to determine what the custom was, it was for the court to apply that custom to the case before it, thereby making a distinction between the 'evidentiary basis for and identification of custom on the one hand, and judicial application of custom on the other'.[49] In this case the primogeniture rule regarding succession to this customary title was upheld.[50] The challenge was significant because if the courts were denied the right to determine matters of customary titles then considerations of constitutional human rights could be ignored. Indeed, this seems to be the potential consequence of the Custom Land Management Act 2013 in Vanuatu, which specifically excludes the jurisdiction of courts of law (s1(2)), allowing instead for disputes to be determined at the local level – as indicated above in the Minister of Lands statement.[51]

Issues of discrimination and customary law link closely with the challenge of determining 'living' customary law, and the issue of who determines the narrative of this living law. In South Africa, empirical research by Budlender and others[52] suggests that the living law in the areas researched indicates that women –

48 66A. Custom –
(1) In addition to its power to make laws pursuant to Article 39, Parliament may make laws recognising or giving effect to custom and usage,
(2) In exercising its powers pursuant to this Article, Parliament shall have particular regard to the customs, traditions, usages and values of the indigenous people of the Cook Islands.
(3) Until such time as an Act otherwise provides, custom and usage shall have effect as part of the law of the Cook Islands, provided that this sub-clause shall not apply in respect of any custom, tradition, usage or value that is, and to the extent that it is, inconsistent with a provision of this Constitution or of any enactment.
(4) For the purpose of this Constitution, the opinion and decision of the Aronga Mana of the Island or Vaka to which a custom, tradition, usage or value relates, as to matters relating to and concerning custom, tradition, usages or the existence, extent or application of custom shall be final and conclusive and shall not be questioned in any Court of Law.

49 Forsyth, 'The challenges of legal pluralism in the Cook Islands and beyond' A28. The idea that the courts merely provide interpretation of custom and do not define custom was upheld with approval in *Estate of Richard Pare Brown, In re* [2016] CKLC1 para 24. Here it was held that these 'judicial interpretations take their cue from the evidence put before the Court' para 25, per Justice W.W. Isaac.

50 Primogeniture has also been upheld in Tonga – *Aleamotu'a v Fielakepa* [2015] TOLC 13, where an indication was given that the order of ranking is legitimate sons, legitimate daughters, illegitimate sons.

51 The final court of appeal under the Custom Land Management Act is an Island (Lands) Court which would have to be specially convened by the chief justice as none exist, and to date none have been created.

52 Debbie Budlender, Sibongile Mgweba, Ketleetso Motsepe and Leilanie Williams, 'Women, land and customary law' (*Community Agency for Social Enquiry*, 2011), http://www.cls.uct.ac.za/usr/lrg/downloads/Women_and_Land.pdf, accessed 31 December 2016.

including single and widowed women – have greater access to land than documented customary law and practice suggests, especially since 1994. Although the research revealed a perpetuation of male-dominated practices, there was sufficient data to suggest that changes were occurring, and this, combined with those court cases which have successfully challenged discriminatory practices, may incrementally diminish the discriminatory practices of 'living' customary law. Similar developments have been noted by Claassens in respect of single women (including widows and divorcees) acquiring land in the former homelands through a process of local negotiation since 1994. This example of living customary law is in contradistinction to state customary law which, through recent legislation, appears to be entrenching all the inequalities of pre-apartheid customary law. As Claassens states:

> The new laws constitute a backlash against the kinds of locally negotiated and multi-vocal processes of change … And they put such processes at risk by changing the balance of power at the local level, vesting authoritarian powers in chiefs, and signalling that national government appears to have 'changed sides' and swung its might behind the chiefly lobby … These new laws also reassert and consolidate the ahistorical stereotypes of official customary law that continue to inform much of the public discourse about custom in South Africa.[53]

This suggests that there are plural versions of custom and customary law being 'lived' in South Africa, and it is probable that this is also occurring in parts of the Pacific.[54]

The influence of the 'chiefly lobby' to which Claassens refers, is a contentious issue. In South Africa, in the former 'homelands' a number of groups have formed Communal Property Associations to hold the land communally,[55] but have had to fight the claims of traditional leaders in court to retain their rights to manage the land in this way.[56] Indeed, the role and influence of traditional chiefs have

53 Aninka Claassens, 'Recent changes in women's land rights and contested customary law in South Africa' (2013) 13 (1) *Journal of Agrarian Change* 71, 72.

54 For example, in Vanuatu especially in peri-urban areas women are taking out leases to secure their own land rights. In the Cook Islands, where land can be acquired from both sides of the family, women are also securing titles to land.

55 Nick Branson, 'Land, law and traditional leadership in South Africa' (*African Research Institute*, 17 June 2016), http://www.africaresearchinstitute.org/newsite/wpcontent/uploads/2016/06/ARI_Land_BN_Printing_v4.pdf, accessed 21 October 2016.

56 Bakgatla-ba-Kgafela, As in the Pacific the role of chiefs was manipulated and shaped by colonial authorities. See for example the 1951 Bantu Authorities. Act which conferred land administration authority on chiefs. Indeed it has been argued that traditional chiefs never owned land on behalf of their people. Nombonisa Gasa, 'Asserting traditional leaders own land opens old wounds' (*Business Day Live*, 24 July 2015), http://www.bdlive.co.za/opinion/2015/07/24/asserting-tradtional-leaders-own-land-opens-old-wounds, accessed 10 November 2016.

been used as a political pawn in South Africa with the African National Congress (ANC) promising more power and securing the support of chiefs through the passing of the Traditional Leadership and Governance Framework Act 2003 and the Communal Land Rights Act 2004.[57] This latter Act was, though, found to be unconstitutional in 2010.[58] The 2014 Communal Land Policy similarly proposed conferring land administration on traditional councils and limiting individuals and groups to institutional use rights rather than any customarily determined rights. Claassens has argued that

> the new laws introduce a stand-off between the power of chiefs according to official customary law, and the Constitutional Court's interpretation of custom as embodying the changing practices and values of ordinary people as shaped by wider social, economic and political realities.[59]

In the Pacific, the 'chiefly lobby' is similarly a matter of concern. In Vanuatu, for example, the National Council of Chiefs – referred to above – has recently been given the power to work at a local level to determine, through resolutions of the council, custom land boundaries under the guise of 'kastom governance'.[60] There is little accountability of this organisation, its members are all male, and it is unclear what legal effect these resolutions have.

While wooing traditional leaders has been described as an 'anachronism of modern democracy',[61] the close tie between land and social organisation cannot be swept under the carpet in customary land tenure systems. Indeed, in these systems, a focus on the reciprocal social obligations attached to rights in respect of land might be more appropriate than any claim to individual rights to land. Okoth-Ogenda, for example, suggests that in African customary systems the focus should be on the way in which people inter-relate within the social order.[62] By itself this may not remove inequalities, but if the formal framework also provides

57 This latter provided for the transfer of land and title deeds from the state to chiefs in areas originally designated under the 1951 Act (above), and the relegation of occupiers land rights to 'use' rights to communal land. See also attempts to get The Traditional Courts Bill enacted.

58 On the grounds of the procedure regarding its passage rather than its substance.

59 Claassens, 'Recent changes in women's land rights and contested customary law in South Africa'.

60 Jonas Culwick, 'Malvatumauri starts piloting Custom Governance implementation' (*Vanuatu Daily Post*, 30 July 2016), http://dailypost.vu/news/malvatumauri-starts-piloting-custom-governance-implementation/article_06246bcb-c803-59ef-8e83-e22d58ae7ef1.html>, accessed 11 January 2018.

61 Anthea Jeffrey, 'Zuma's land grab urgings to traditional chiefs; desperate move by a declining force' (*BizNews*, 17 March 2015), https://www.biznews.com/thought-leaders/2015/03/17/zumas-land-grab-urgings-to-traditional-chiefs-a-desperate-move-by-a-declining-force/, accessed 11 January 2018.

62 H.W.O. Okoth-Ogendo, 'The nature of land rights' in Aninka Claassens and Ben Cousins (eds), *Land Power and Custom* (UCT 2008), 99.

for combatting the abuse of power, and fostering equality then customary land tenure may not cause constitutional offence.[63]

Equality or non-discrimination is predominantly an introduced concept in the countries under consideration, and its advocacy is evidence of change. Change is also key to calls for security of tenure and the protection of property rights. One of the triggers for insecurity of customary land tenure, even in systems in which such tenure is recognised, is the attempt, particularly in plural legal systems where common law property law has been introduced, to 'fit' customary land rights within the common law framework. Where this fails, what might have previously been a relatively secure right in customary law, becomes insecure, for example, because evidence of occupation entitlement is rejected, or the customary practice relied on today conflicts with a customary practice recognised by the courts in the past, and so precedent is favoured over and above the idea of 'living' customary law. The consequence may then be that those claiming customary land rights seek to secure these by formalising the right through registration or documentation, converting custom rights into common law rights or hybrids therefore, or assimilating custom law into the common law, for example by claiming that this right is 'like' the common law right of X. It is also often the case that where land can be offered as security for financial loans, customary land is unappealing to lenders, so that introduced and non-customary devices are used, such as leases, the incorporation of land groups into legal persona, or the establishment of trusts in order to demonstrate security of tenure.

In South Africa, security of tenure has particularly been a problem in the former 'homelands' where grants of land were made by the government under a permit system but the title remained with the state. The 1996 Constitution recognises this legacy of racially discriminatory laws in Section 25 and provides that Parliament is to enact legislation to address tenure insecurity. Following a White Paper in 1997 the Communal Land Rights Act was passed in 2004, but this was subsequently found to be unconstitutional.[64] The challenges in the South African context are deciding what form(s) of land tenure in these areas would best provide for non-discriminatory secure land rights taking into account factors such as the passage of change; the dominant influence of the common law on property rights; and the introduction of forms of landholding which were alien to traditional customary land tenure in homeland areas. Nick Branson writing for the Africa Research Institution states that 'land remains an emotive fault line in South Africa'.[65] He highlights the challenge of addressing past wrongs, especially the dispossession of land, the need to protect individual property rights[66] and

63 Anne Pope, 'Indigenous-law land rights: constitutional imperatives and proprietary paradoxes' (2011) *Acta Juridica* 308.

64 *Tongoane v National Minister for Agriculture and Land Affairs* (2010) 6 SA 214 (CC).

65 Branson, 'Land, law and traditional leadership in South Africa'.

66 This may be particularly at risk under legislation such as the Restitution of Land Rights Amendment Act 2014.

security of tenure, while ensuring economic growth, food security, and national reconciliation. He points out that around 60% of South Africans claim rights to property and land outside the formal systems and that an 'estimated 3.3 million South Africans live in informal settlements without any proof of land rights'.[67] A further 17 million reside on communal land, where their occupation is rather precariously protected by the Interim Protection of Informal Land Rights Act 1996, which is renewed as an interim measure on an annual basis. Similarly, in the Pacific, an increasing but undocumented number of people live precariously in settlements in expanding urban and peri-urban areas.

Du Plessis refers to Pienaar's suggestion that one possible solution might be to have a parallel system of registers in which alongside the title register there is an interests register reflecting the co-existence of a number of different interests and obligations generated by social obligations in respect of the land.[68] A partial reflection of this approach is found in the Solomon Islands in the Pacific where it has been recognised that there are primary and secondary rights holders over the same parcel of land and that although the former have the greater control, they cannot act without taking into account the consequences on secondary right holders. These two categories of right holders are not, however, registered. The danger with any dual system is the emergence of a hierarchy and the vulnerability of 'lesser' rights holders to the control and subjection by 'higher' rights holders. Claassens – referring to the current situation in South Africa – has suggested that 'current policies are entrenching [the] legacy of exclusion, by bolstering the power of a small elite at the expense of the majority of rural South Africans'.[69] Similar elites emerge in the Pacific region where small pockets of freehold land, in countries such as Samoa and Fiji, are held by a minority of indigenous people, or where custom owners can benefit from lucrative leasing of land in capital cities or popular tourist areas.

Conclusion

The constraints of a contribution of this nature necessarily results in a rather 'snapshot' view of a multi-faceted issue and clearly there are significant geopolitical differences between the island states of the Pacific and South Africa. Despite these differences, however, it is suggested that there are shared themes: the challenges of plural legal systems; the centrality of land to law and policy debates; the tensions between introduced concepts such as human rights and equality; and traditional attitudes towards status and the exercise of power. All legal systems face the challenges of change, but not all have to consider how customary law, which essentially draws on the past, can be respected and accommodated to provide for the future. This brief comparative excursus suggests that while there are

67 Branson, 'Land, law and traditional leadership in South Africa' 2.
68 Gerrit Pienaar, 'The land titling debate in South Africa' (2006) *TSAR* 435.
69 Aninka Claassens, quoted in Branson, 'Land, law and traditional leadership in South Africa' 3.

different approaches, finding answers remains an ongoing challenge, and indeed it may be this very dilemma which strengthens the hold of customary law within the legal systems in which it is found. It would therefore be a mistake for comparatists or comparative law in general to omit consideration of customary law. Indeed, it would be like omitting the lettuce leaves from a green salad.

Selected bibliography

Nick Branson, 'Land, Law and Traditional leadership in South Africa' (*African Research Institute*, 17 June 2016), http://www.africaresearchinstitute.org/newsite/wpcontent/uploads/2016/06/ARI_Land_BN_Printing_v4.pdf, accessed 21 October 2016.

Debbie Budlender, Sibongile Mgweba, Ketleetso Motsepe and Leilanie Williams, 'Women, Land and Customary Law' (*Community Agency for Social Enquiry*, 2011), http://www.cls.uct.ac.za/usr/lrg/downloads/Women_and_Land.pdf, accessed 31 December 2016.

Aninka Claassens, 'Recent changes in women's land rights and contested customary law in South Africa' (2012) 13 (1) *Journal of Agrarian Change* 71.

Sue Farran and Jennifer Corrin, 'Developing legislation to formalise customary land management: deep legal pluralism or shallow veneer?' (2017) 10 (1) *Law and Development Review* 1–27.

Thandabantu Nhlapo, 'Customary law in Post-apartheid South Africa: the vexed question of cultural diversity, women's rights, "living law", and appropriate law reform' (2014) *New York Law School Review*, http://www.nylslawreview.com/wp-content/uploads/sites/16/2014/11/Nhlapo.pdf.

Nomthandazo Ntlama, 'The application of section 8(3) of the Constitution in the Development of Customary Law values in South Africa's new constitutional dispensation' (2012) 15 (1) *Potchefstroom Electronic Law Journal* 24

HWO Okoth-Ogendo, 'The nature of land rights' in Aninka Claassens and Ben Cousins (eds), *Land Power and Custom* (UCT 2008), 99.

Don Paterson and Sue Farran (eds), *South Pacific Land Systems* (USP Press 2013).

Gerrit Pienaar, 'The land titling debate in South Africa' (2006) *TSAR* 435.

Gerrit Pienaar, 'The methodology used to interpret customary land tenure' (2012) 15 (3) *PER* 39, http://www.saflii.org.za/za/journals/PER/2012/39.pdf, accessed 31 December 2016.

Elmien du Plessis, 'African Indigenous land rights in a Private Ownership Paradigm' (2011) 14 (7) *Potchefstroom Electronic Law Journal* 44.

Elmien du Plessis and Gino Frantz, 'African customary land rights in a private ownership paradigm' (2 June 2013), https://papers.ssrn.com/sol3/papers.cfm?abstract_id=2381922, accessed 11 January 2018. Anne Pope, 'Indigenous-law land rights: constitutional imperatives and proprietary Paradoxes' (2011) *Acta Juridica* 308.

4 Fairness and diversity in the South African law of contract

Jacques du Plessis[1]

Introduction

South African law is usually described as 'mixed', in the sense that it has been strongly influenced by the civil law and common law traditions.[2] However, this perspective does not reflect that customary law, in other words the customs and usages traditionally observed by the indigenous African communities,[3] is also a constitutionally recognised source of law.[4] The South African legal system could therefore be more properly regarded as 'mixed' in the broader sense of containing 'Western' and 'indigenous' components, or it could also be called 'pluralist', to signify that these components have only interacted to a limited extent.[5]

In her scholarship, Esin Örücü has challenged comparative lawyers to transcend the boundaries that so often limit their enquiries to the dominant Western legal traditions[6] and has argued that legal systems are mixed in more complex

1 The support of the National Research Foundation is acknowledged with gratitude.

2 See e.g. Reinhard Zimmermann and Daniel Visser (eds), *Southern Cross – Civil Law and Common Law in South Africa* (Juta 1996) 1, 2–4; Jacques du Plessis, 'Comparative Law and the Study of Mixed Legal Systems' in Mathias Reimann and Reinhard Zimmermann (eds) *The Oxford Handbook of Comparative Law* (OUP 2006) 477, 478. On the possibility that some customary usages exist independently of state-recognised customary law, i.e. that the system is also characterised by 'strong' or 'deep' legal pluralism, see Chuma Himonga, 'State and Individual Perspectives of a Mixed Legal System in Southern African Contexts with Special Reference to Personal Law' (2010) 25 *Tulane European and Civil Law Forum* 23.

3 See Recognition of Customary Unions Act 120 of 1998, s 1; for further definitions see Enyinna Nwauche, 'Affiliation to a New Customary Law in Post-apartheid South Africa' *Potchefstroom Electronic Law Journal* 570, 576–577.

4 See Constitution of the Republic of South Africa, 1996, s 211(3); *Alexkor Ltd v The Richtersveld Community* 2004 (5) SA 460 (CC) [51].

5 See Du Plessis, 'Comparative Law and the Study of Mixed Legal Systems' 480–486.

6 See e.g. Esin Örücü, 'What Is a Mixed Legal System: Exclusion or Expansion?' (2008) 12 (1) *EJCL*, http://www.ejcl.org/121/art121-15.pdf, accessed 30 August 2016; Esin Örücü, *The Enigma of Comparative Law: Variations on a Theme for the Twenty-First Century* (Martinus Nijhoff Publishers 2004) 216. For assessments further see Sean Patrick Donlan, 'Remembering: Legal Hybridity and Legal History' (2011) 2(1) *Comparative Law Review* 1, 33–34.

and profound ways than are traditionally appreciated,[7] and that the processes of mixing are dynamic and their futures uncertain.[8] The purpose of this essay is to take up this challenge and explore the possible implications of adopting such a broader perspective in the context of two topics which have recently enjoyed considerable judicial and academic attention in South African law. These are the role of the customary law construct of *ubuntu*, and promoting fairness in the law of contract.[9] The essay commences with a brief exploration of the concept of *ubuntu*, then considers the current rules on contractual fairness, and finally explores what role, if any, *ubuntu* could play in their further development.

Diversity: the meaning and significance of *ubuntu*

Ubuntu as a concept in customary law

Ubuntu (a Zulu word), and *botho* (its Sesotho equivalent),[10] has been called African law's 'nucleus' and its 'indigenous philosophy of life';[11] its spirit is said to 'suffuse' the whole South African constitutional order.[12] Unfortunately for such a cornerstone of customary law, but also hardly surprising given its origins in a tradition where law is 'lived' rather than recorded, *ubuntu* does not have a generally accepted definition.[13] Sometimes it is used to describe a quality of a person;

7 Örücü (n 5) 9. It is uncertain how these mixes are to be classified (see Du Plessis, 'Comparative Law and the Study of Mixed Legal Systems' 477), but this does not detract from her central argument that the traditional conception of mixed legal systems (or mixed jurisdictions) was too limited.

8 Örücü (n 5) 11, 16–17 where in Map 1 she classifies pre-1996 South African law as a 'simple mix' (of substantive civil law and common law) and post-1996 South African law as a 'complex mix' or hybrid which includes customary law. Also see Mauro Bussani and Marta Infantino, 'Tort Law and Legal Cultures' (2015) 63 *American Journal of Comparative Law* 77, 107–108.

9 On the general need for comparative law in South Africa to take more account of the African context see Jacques du Plessis, 'Foreword' in Salvatore Mancuso and Charles Fombad (eds) *Comparative Law in Africa: Methodologies and Concepts* (Juta 2015) vii.

10 See Yvonne Mokgoro, '*Ubuntu* and the Law in South Africa' in Drucilla Cornell and Nyoko Muvangua (eds) *Ubuntu and the Law – African Ideals and Post-apartheid Jurisprudence* (Fordham University Press 2012) 317.

11 Dial Dayana Ndima, 'The Resurrection of the Indigenous Value System in Post-apartheid African Law: South Africa's Constitutional and Legislative Framework Revisited' (2014) 29 *SAPL* 294.

12 *Port Elizabeth Municipality v Various Occupiers* 2005 (1) SA 217 (CC) [37] (per Sachs J); *Wormald NO v Kambule* 2006 (3) SA 562 (SCA) [37].

13 For overviews see e.g. Mluleki Munyaka and Mokgethi Motlhabi, '*Ubuntu* and its Socio-moral Significance' in Munyaradzi Felix Murove (ed.) *African Ethics – An Anthology of Comparative and Applied Ethics* (University of Kwazulu-Natal Press 2009) 63, 64; T. W. Bennett, 'Ubuntu: An African Equity' in Frank Diedrich (ed.) *Ubuntu, Good faith and Equity* (2011) 3 (= T W Bennett, 'Ubuntu: An African Equity' (2011) 14 (4) *Potchefstroom Electronic Law Journal* 29); Drucilla Cornell, 'uBuntu, Pluralism and the Responsibility of Legal Academics to the New South Africa' (2009) 20 *Law and Critique* 43, 47; T. W. Bennett, assisted by A. R. Munro and P. J. Jacobs, *Ubuntu – An African Jurisprudence* (Juta 2018) 24–59 esp 29.

having *ubuntu* would mean behaving in a humane manner towards others; not to have *ubuntu* would amount to being 'inhuman'. The concept is also said to describe a way of life, a way in which persons interact or relate to each other, encapsulated in the phrase *umuntu ngumuntu ngabantu* ('a person is a person because of other people or through other people'). But the meaning of *ubuntu* at times rather easily moves from the descriptive to the prescriptive, from stating how people are to stating how they should behave.[14] A sense of *ubuntu*'s meaning can also be conveyed by examining some pronouncements on its origins. The following passage by Ngcobo J in *Bhe v Magistrate, Khayelitsha* (*Commission for Gender Equality as Amicus Curiae*),[15] a case which dealt with male primogeniture, is particularly insightful:

> [162] … The rules of indigenous law, in particular, the rule of primogeniture, have their origin in traditional society. This society was based on a subsistence agricultural economy. At the heart of the African traditional structure was the family unit. The family unit was the focus of social concern. Individual interests were submerged in the common weal. … The system emphasised duties and responsibilities as opposed to rights. …
>
> [163] A sense of community prevailed from which developed an elaborate system of reciprocal duties and obligations among the family members. This is manifest in the concept of *ubuntu – umuntu ngumuntu ngabantu* [footnote omitted] a dominant value in African traditional culture. This concept encapsulates communality and the inter-dependence of the members of a community. As Langa DCJ put it, it is a culture which 'regulates the exercise of rights by the emphasis it lays on sharing and co-responsibility and the mutual enjoyment of rights'. (footnote 185: *S v Makwanyane* para [224])

This statement reflects that the concept of *ubuntu* is traditionally applied in the context of close community structures, where interdependence is a given, and the failure to recognise it could threaten the survival of the community itself. Where a person has not respected societal norms setting out their reciprocal rights and duties, and thereby violated the value of *ubuntu*, a principal function of the law would be to restore social relations, or, to put it more broadly, its purpose is 'restorative' rather than 'retributive justice'.[16]

The quotation above further reflects that individual interests are secondary to community interests, but this requires qualification: it has been pointed out that *ubuntu* does not entail that individual identity has to be entirely subsumed within the group, or that *ubuntu* is simply to be equated with collectivism.[17] The

14 See Bennett, Munro, and Jacobs, *Ubuntu – An African Jurisprudence*, 31–32.
15 2005 (1) SA 580 (CC).
16 *Dikoko v Mokhatla* 2006 (6) SA 235 (CC) [68] sqq, [113] sqq.
17 See Yvonne Mokgoro, '*Ubuntu* as a Legal Principle in an Ever-Changing World' in Diedrich (ed.) *Ubuntu, Good Faith and Equity* 1, 2. Also see the critique of equating *ubuntu* with

individual is indeed entitled to dignity and respect, but this cannot be enjoyed in isolation; it must simultaneously be accorded to other members of the group.[18]

One further qualification can also be added. While *ubuntu* is an original creation of indigenous African law, the phenomenon that those living in customary communities subscribe to an ethos which requires some concern for others is of course not unique.[19] *Ubuntu* can be linked to concepts found outside the African cultural heritage. In this regard the courts have drawn parallels between *ubuntu* and counterparts in religious belief systems[20] or in other cultures, for example, the Western culture, where, as Mokgoro J stated in *S v Makwanyane*, 'all-embracing concepts of "humanity" and "menswaardigheid", are also highly priced'.[21] To this list, one can add another important example, which is especially significant in the law of contract, namely the concept of *bona fides* or good faith. To its relationship with *ubuntu* we will return later.

Ubuntu as a constitutional value

Despite its fundamental importance in a system of law which historically governed the lives of the vast majority of the South African population, *ubuntu* has traditionally been accorded almost no significance in 'mainstream' Western law. However, this position has changed with the advent of the new constitutional dispensation. Courts now expressly describe *ubuntu* as a 'constitutional value',[22] which is related to, but distinct from other constitutional values or rights, such as dignity.[23] This prompts the question of what significance *ubuntu* has when it is referred to in this way.

---

simple notions of communitarianism or social cohesion in Cornell and Muvangua, *Ubuntu and the Law – African Ideals and Post-apartheid Jurisprudence*, 5.

18 *S v Makwanyane*, 1995 (3) SA 391 (CC); further see *The Citizen 1978 (Pty) Ltd v McBride (Johnstone, Amici Curiae)* 2011 (4) SA 191 (CC) [215]. This type of thinking is reflected in references to the notion that 'we are not islands unto ourselves': while we may require respect as individuals, we can only do so while respecting others (see *SAPS v Solidarity obo Barnard (Popcru as Amicus Curiae)* 2014 (6) SA 123 (CC) [174]).

19 See Albie Sachs, 'Towards the Liberation and Revitalization of Customary Law' in Cornell and Muvangua *Ubuntu and the Law – African Ideals and Post-apartheid Jurisprudence*, 303, 310.

20 Chief Justice Mogoeng has for example linked *Ubuntu* to the biblical injunction that 'one should do unto others as he or she would have them do unto him or her' (*The Citizen 1978 (Pty) Ltd* (n 17) [216]).

21 (n 17) [308]. See Leonhard Praeg, *A Report on Ubuntu* (University of Kwazulu Natal Press 2014) 193 on problematic contrasts sometimes drawn between 'Western' individualism and African communalism.

22 See e.g. *Joseph v City of Johannesburg* 2010 (4) SA 55 (CC) [46] n 39; *Dikoko* (n 15) [112]; *Derby-Lewis v Minister of Justice and Correctional Services* 2015 (2) SACR 412 (GP) [58].

23 See e.g. *Dikoko* (n 15) [68]; *KwaZulu-Natal Joint Liaison Committee v MEC for Education, KwaZulu-Natal* 2013 (4) SA 262 (CC) [17]; *Advtech Resourcing (Pty) Ltd t/a Communicate Personnel Group v Kuhn* 2008 (2) SA 375 (C) [30].

Especially when *ubuntu* first came to the fore in the mid-1990s, when the interim and final constitutions were adopted, concern was expressed over it being used as a mere 'marketing device', 'to put an African imprimatur on a set of civil liberties and freedoms forged largely out of Western instruments'.[24] However, it is becoming increasingly apparent that this is not the way the courts view its function: thus, according to Sachs J, *ubuntu* is 'more than a phrase to be invoked from time to time to add a gracious and affirmative gloss to a legal finding already arrived at'.[25] This heightened relevance is apparent from more recent cases which deal with matters as varied as determining the appropriate response to defamation[26] or whether to impose duties of support on persons in relationships akin to that of family.[27]

Crucially, when courts refer to *ubuntu* in these modern contexts, they do not seek to establish some anthropologically 'authentic' meaning, based on its actual, past application in customary communities.[28] It would be absurd, for example, to enquire whether *ubuntu* demanded access to electricity centuries ago.[29] There is inevitably a change of meaning once *ubuntu* is invoked as a constitutional value in the broader context of a heterogeneous society, forged by powerful forces such as colonisation and globalisation, which cause many descendants of earlier communities to adopt increasingly more Western lifestyles.[30] This is also the context in which *ubuntu* has to be applied if it were to influence the modern South African law of contract, and especially if it were to assist in developing it to ensure more fair and equitable outcomes.[31]

24 Rosalind English, '*Ubuntu*: The Quest for an Indigenous Jurisprudence' (1996) *SAJHR* 641. On the notion that *ubuntu* was rendered ineffective as a constitutional value because it did not fit within the discourse of traditional legal thinking', or that it was a mere 'flavour of the month' see Irma Kroeze, 'Doing Things with Values II: The Case of Ubuntu' (2002) 13 *Stellenbosch LR* 252.

25 *Dikoko v Mokhatla* (n 15) [113] (Sachs J).

26 *Le Roux v Dey* 2011 (3) SA 274 (CC); Gardiol J van Niekerk, '*Amende Honorable* and *Ubuntu*: An Intersection of *Ars Boni et Aequi* in African and Roman-Dutch Jurisprudence?' (2013) 19 *Fundamina* 397.

27 *JT v Road Accident Fund* 2015 (1) SA 609 (GJ) [26].

28 See Thaddeus Metz, '*Ubuntu* as a Moral Theory and Human Rights in South Africa' (2011) 11 *AHRLJ* 532, 535.

29 See Cornell and Muvangua, *Ubuntu and the Law – African Ideals and Post-apartheid Jurisprudence*, 10.

30 See Munyaka and Motlhabi, '*Ubuntu* and its Socio-moral Significance' 80. See Praeg, *A Report on Ubuntu* for an extensive analysis of the distinction between the pre-colonial communal 'praxis' or way of life of *ubuntu*, and its modern, philosophical expression).

31 On the potential of *ubuntu* to assist in defining obligations in crucial areas of the law, including the law of contract, see generally Cornell and Muvangua, *Ubuntu and the Law – African Ideals and Post-apartheid Jurisprudence*, 24–25.

Fairness: debates and challenges in the South African law of contract

The fairness cases

Over the past two decades, the role of fairness in the South African law of contract has been strongly contested in academic and judicial circles. Much of the debate concerns the relevance of constitutional principles and values in promoting fairness in this field of law. Some key judgments have provided the framework within which much of the debate has been conducted. These judgments, which will be called the 'fairness cases', are generally concerned with challenges to the validity or enforceability of certain terms. These include provisions that limit or exclude a party's potential liability under the contract,[32] require variations to assume a certain form,[33] or enable a party to exercise a right to terminate the contract.[34] At times the cases do not only consider the terms, but also the way in which they were supposedly assented to, for example, when the parties were not in positions of equal bargaining power.[35]

In deciding these cases, the courts routinely emphasise the importance of *pacta servanda sunt*, the principle that (freely concluded) agreements must be enforced. The party alleging unfairness would typically seek to avoid enforcement by relying on a variety of grounds for relief, usually with limited success. A popular route is to rely on the rule that a contractual term is invalid or unenforceable if it is contrary to public policy.[36] Second, parties argue that it should not be possible to rely on a term if this would be contrary to good faith (*bona fides*), a concept which traditionally enjoys some recognition in South African law, albeit, as we shall see presently, that the extent of this recognition is highly disputed. And, finally, parties have relied on certain constitutional rights and values, including *ubuntu*, in arguing for new applications or development of the law of contract that would give rise to more fair outcomes. These three routes are all in effect aimed at ensuring that a court would not enforce a contract which *prima facie* appears to be freely concluded, and hence, worthy of recognition and enforcement under the *pacta servanda sunt* principle.

32 See *Afrox Healthcare Bpk v Strydom* 2002 (6) SA 21 (SCA); *Barkhuizen v Napier* 2007 (5) SA 323 (CC).

33 See *Brisley v Drotsky* 2002 (4) SA 1 (SCA).

34 See *Bredenkamp v Standard Bank of SA Ltd* 2010 (4) SA 468 (SCA); *Maphango v Aengus Lifestyle Properties (Pty) Ltd* 2012 (3) SA 531 (CC); *Mohamed's Leisure Holdings (Pty) Ltd v Southern Sun Hotel Interests (Pty) Ltd* 2018 (2) SA 314 (SCA).

35 See e.g. *Barkhuizen* (n 31) [59].

36 See *Magna Alloys and Research (SA) (Pty) Ltd v Ellis* 1984 (4) SA 874 (A) 891; *Barkhuizen v Napier* 2007 (5) SA 323 (CC).

The protagonists

The fairness cases have elicited extensive comment, some of which is crucial to the current enquiry. Grouping together individual views can be a precarious exercise, but it may assist in conveying the essence of the considerable body of learning that has arisen over the past few years. For present purposes, two main camps can be identified.[37]

The traditionalists

A traditionalist, at the risk of stating the obvious, is someone who adheres to the doctrines or practices of a particular tradition. In the present context, we are concerned with those who support the tradition in the South African law of contract of strongly adhering to the values of freedom of contract and *pacta servanda sunt.*[38] In supporting these values, reference is often made to certain prominent justifications in the case law,[39] but also, more recently to the Constitution.[40] Hallmarks of the traditionalist approach are the emphasis it places on the value of

37 Further see the distinction between a 'freedom-oriented approach' and a 'fairness-oriented approach' drawn in Luanda Hawthorne, '*Breedenkamp v Standard Bank of SA Ltd* 2009 (5) SA 304 GSJ' (2010) 43 *De Jure* 395, 408; Luanda Hawthorne, 'Constitution and Contract: Human Dignity, the Theory of Capabilities and *Existenzgrundlage* in South Africa' (2011) *SUBB Jurisprudentia* 27. Andre Louw refers to 'anti-transformationists', a rather more severe label than 'traditionalists' ('Yet another Call for a Greater Role for Good Faith in the South African Law of Contract: Can we Banish the Law of the Jungle, while Avoiding the Elephant in the Room?' (2013) 16 *Potchefstroom Electronic Law Journal* 44, 55).

38 The traditionalists include a number of prominent members of the judiciary who have made their views known from the bench but also in extra-judicial writings. See J. J. F. Hefer, 'Billikheid in die Kontraktereg volgens die Suid-Afrikaanse Regskommissie' (2000) *TSAR* 142; Joos Hefer, 'Billikheid in die Kontraktereg' (2004) 29 *JJS* 1; Fritz Brand, 'The Role of Good Faith, Equity and Fairness in the South African Law of Contract: The Influence of the Common Law and the Constitution' (2009) 126 *SALJ* 71; Carole Lewis, 'The Uneven Journey to Uncertainty in Contract' (2013) 76 *THRHR* 80; Malcolm Wallis, 'Commercial Certainty and Constitutionalism: Are they Compatible? (2016) 133 *SALJ* 545; Malcolm Wallis, 'The Common Law's Cool Ideas for Dealing with Ms Hubbard' (2015) 132 *SALJ* 940; Fritz Brand, 'The Role of Good Faith, Equity and Fairness in the South African Law of Contract: A Further Instalment' (2016) 27 *Stellenbosch LR* 236.

39 Especially the *dictum* of Sir George Jessel MR in *Printing and Numerical Registering Co v Sampson* 1875 LR 19 EQ 462, 465. For citations see A. J. Barnard-Naudé, '"Oh What a Tangled Web We Weave …" Hegemony, Freedom of Contract, Good Faith and Transformation – Towards a Politics of Friendship in the Politics of Contract' (2008) 1 *Constitutional Court Review* 155, 168.

40 See Hefer, 'Billikheid in die Kontraktereg' 14. Hefer does not consider countervailing constitutional values, such as dignity, but see Brand, 'The Role of Good Faith, Equity and Fairness in the South African Law of Contract: The Influence of the Common Law and the Constitution' 86.

certainty,[41] and on the danger of broad judicial discretions,[42] especially the unfettered discretion to strike down contracts on the basis of good faith as a so-called free-floating principle.

The traditionalists at times declare their concern about or at least awareness of the problem of unfairness in contract, but they typically only recognise a limited number of instruments to combat it. These include prohibitions on certain classic improper methods to obtain consent (misrepresentation, duress, and undue influence); the rules on mistake as grounds for escaping liability (which are useful when dealing with standard terms); the rule referred to above that contracts must not be contrary to public policy; the rules promoting fairness when interpreting contracts and reading terms, and specific statutory instruments.[43] The possibility of extending lists like these with specific new categories is not denied,[44] but traditionalists profess a strong preference for developing the law incrementally through specific rules,[45] rather than for resorting to open-ended discretions.

Traditionalists are not renowned for their willingness to explore new avenues in order to promote greater fairness in the law of contract. This is hardly surprising: those who attach great significance to certainty would tend to favour a *status quo* which only recognises limited grounds for challenging ostensibly valid contracts. Traditionalists further do not embrace the potential for resorting to constitutional values to justify these extensions; for example, through influencing the application of the rule that the content or enforcement of contracts may not be contrary to public policy, or through according greater prominence to good faith. Ideologically, they therefore are much more closely aligned to the common law tradition, than the civilian tradition, where some certainty can be sacrificed for fairness.[46] Nonetheless, they do recognise that good faith is a value or underlying principle in South African law, and that effect could be given to it by,

41 See e.g. Brand, 'The Role of Good Faith, Equity and Fairness in the South African Law of Contract: The Influence of the Common Law and the Constitution' 87; Lewis, 'The Uneven Journey to Uncertainty in Contract' 80; on the principle itself see Carole Lewis, 'Fairness in South African Contract Law' (2003) 120 *SALJ* 330, 344.

42 Reference is sometimes made in this context to the (constitutional) 'principle' of legality, which apparently entails that it may be destructive of the rule of law if rules of law were made discretionary or subject to value judgements (see Harms JA in *Bredenkamp* (n 33) [39]; Brand JA in *Pogieter v Potgieter* [36]; Lewis, 'The Uneven Journey to Uncertainty in Contract' 87). This 'principle' is not the same as the requirement of legality in the law of contract, which demands that contracts should not be contrary to public policy.

43 See Lewis, 'The Uneven Journey to Uncertainty in Contract' 83; Wallis (n 37) 4, 23; *Den Braven SA (Pty) Ltd v Pillay* 2008 6 SA 229 (W) [33]-[35] (Wallis AJ).

44 See e.g. Hefer, 'Billikheid in die Kontraktereg' 13–14.

45 See Brand, 'The Role of Good Faith, Equity and Fairness in the South African Law of Contract: The Influence of the Common Law and the Constitution' 72.

46 See Simon Whittaker and Reinhard Zimmermann, 'Good Faith in European Contract Law: Surveying the Legal Landscape' in: Reinhard Zimmermann and Simon Whittaker (eds) *Good Faith in European Contract Law* (Cambridge University Press 2008) 29–31.

for example, importing certain duties on parties to support each other through processes of interpretation or through incorporating implied terms.[47]

Traditionalists rarely refer to *ubuntu*, and when they do it is not with discernible enthusiasm. Supreme Court of Appeal Justice Malcolm Wallis, for one, has expressed scepticism about the value of statements to the effect that the law of contract must be 'infused' with constitutional values such as *ubuntu* and human dignity, and that contracting parties must relate in 'good faith', and has expressed concern that the proponents of such a process of 'infusion' do not clearly indicate in what way the law is deficient, and hence how instilling or inculcating constitutional values could benefit it.[48] He has especially questioned how *ubuntu*, which to him is associated with 'essentially human qualities and principles that guide human interaction', could be applied 'in the context of the contractual relationships between artificial persons such as companies created for trading purposes'; ultimately to him it could mean nothing more than that public policy embraces the concept of good faith and reasonableness.[49]

The constitutionalists

The approach of the traditionalists stands in marked contrast to that of a number of academics as well as some judges, who are critical of judgments (often by 'traditionalists') which to them privilege 'liberal' notions of freedom of contract and *pacta servanda sunt* over other values. These 'constitutionalists'[50] are

47 See *South African Forestry Co Ltd v York Timbers Ltd* 2005 (3) SA 323 SCA; Brand, 'The Role of Good Faith, Equity and Fairness in the South African Law of Contract: The Influence of the Common Law and the Constitution' 82–83.

48 Wallis (n 42) 17–18. His criticism is directed against academics who make such statements, but similar *dicta* emanate from the judiciary; see e.g. *KwaZulu-Natal Joint Liaison Committee* (n 22) [17]; *Everfresh Market Virginia (Pty) Ltd v Shoprite Checkers (Pty) Ltd* 2012 (1) SA 256 (CC) [71]; *Advtech* (n 22) [30].

49 Wallis (n 42) 18; further see Bennett, Munro and Jacobs, *Ubuntu – An African Jurisprudence*, 39.

50 See e.g. Dire Tladi, 'One Step Forward, Two Steps Back for Constitutionalising the Common Law: *Afrox Health Care v Strydom*' (2002) 17 *SAPL* 473; Luanda Hawthorne, 'Closing of the Open Norms in the Law of Contract' (2004) 67 *THRHR* 294; Deeksha Bhana and Marius Pieterse, 'Towards a Reconciliation of Contract Law and Constitutional Values: *Brisley* and *Afrox* Revisited' (2005) 122 *SALJ* 865; Deeksha Bhana, 'The Law of Contract and the Constitution: *Napier v Barkhuizen* (SCA)' (2007) 124 *SALJ* 269; Barnard-Naudé '"Oh What a Tangled Web We Weave ..."' 155; Deeksha Bhana, 'The Role of Judicial Method in the Relinquishing of Constitutional Rights through Contract' (2008) 24 *SAJHR* 300; Sandra Liebenberg, *Socio-economic Rights Adjudication under a Transformative Constitution* (Juta 2010) 358–376; Dennis Davis and Karl Klare, 'Transformative Constitutionalism and the Common and Customary Law' (2010) 26 *SAJHR* 403; Dennis Davis, 'Developing the Common Law of Contract in the Light of Poverty and Illiteracy: The Challenge of the Constitution' (2011) 22 *Stellenbosch LR* 845; Jaco Barnard-Naudé, 'Of Dorothy's Dog, "Post-structural" Fairy Tales ... and the Real: Power, Poverty and the General Principles of the South African Law of Contract' (2013) 29 *SAJHR* 467 (especially sources cited in notes 5–6); Louw, 'Yet another Call for a Greater Role for Good Faith in the South African Law of

uncomfortable with what they perceive as attempts to entrench these notions on constitutional grounds, by basing them on values or rights such as freedom, equality, and dignity; this practice is regarded as effectively entrenching the legal and socio-economic *status quo*, characterised by extreme inequality in wealth distribution and power relations.[51]

The role which the constitutionalists favour for the Constitution is the significantly more prominent one of being at the forefront of changing or transforming the law of contract;[52] such a development would then entail relying on constitutional values and rights (especially dignity) to achieve more progressive outcomes in the law of contract. These outcomes could entail greater protection of parties who negotiate from positions of inequality and weakness or extending the range of cases where exploitative or substantively unfair contracts would be regarded as contrary to public policy. Fears that these developments would result in intolerable uncertainty are regarded as exaggerated, and sacrificing some certainty for greater fairness is regarded as justified.[53]

In the present context, it is significant that some constitutionalists argue strongly for a more prominent or robust role for good faith. Their point, in essence, is that if courts were to interpret this concept more broadly and progressively, it would result in a greater emphasis on communitarian values and less adherence to the value of individualism, which in turn would promote fairness in the law of contract.[54] The way in which good faith would fulfil this function is not clearly indicated, but there appears to be support for the idea that courts should be able to apply good faith more *directly* as a standard, rather than (merely)

Contract' 44; Dennis Davis, 'Where is the Map to Guide the Common-law Development?' (2014) 25 *Stellenbosch LR* 3; Luanda Hawthorne, 'Concretising the Open Norm of Public Policy: Inequality of Bargaining Power and Exploitation' (2014) 77 *THRHR* 407; Deeksha Bhana, 'Contract Law and the Constitution: *Bredenkamp v Standard Bank of South Africa (Ltd)*' (2014) 29 *SAPL* 508; Deeksha Bhana, 'The Role of Judicial Method in Contract Revisited' (2015) 132 *SALJ* 122; Dennis Davis, 'Legal Transformation and Legal Education: Congruence or Conflict?' (2015) *Acta Juridica* 172 (where the term 'constitutionalists' is used at 187). Further see the judgments of Davis J in *Advtech* (n 22) [24]–[32] and *Mozart Ice Cream Franchises (Pty) Ltd v Davidoff* 2009 (3) SA 78 (C) 85F-G.

51 See e.g. Davis, 'Developing the Common Law of Contract in the Light of Poverty and Illiteracy' 845.

52 See e.g. Bhana, 'The Law of Contract and the Constitution: *Napier v Barkhuizen* (SCA)' 269; Davis, 'Legal Transformation and Legal Education: Congruence or Conflict?' 181 (Davis e.g. refers to the need for a constitutional audit of the common law).

53 See Bhana and Pieterse, 'Towards a Reconciliation of Contract Law and Constitutional Values' 866; Louw, 'Yet another Call for a Greater Role for Good Faith in the South African Law of Contract' 49–50, 68–69.

54 See e.g. Barnard-Naudé, '"Oh What a Tangled Web We Weave …"' esp 175 sqq, 185 and the analysis of the judgment of Davis J in *Mort NO v Henry Shields-Chiat* 2001 (1) SA 464 (C); Louw, 'Yet another Call for a Greater Role for Good Faith in the South African Law of Contract' 44; Bhana and Pieterse, 'Towards a Reconciliation of Contract Law and Constitutional Values' 891–892.

indirectly as an underlying value that guides the courts in developing the South African law of contract.

Such an increased role of good faith is in turn supposed to give greater meaning and effect to underlying values and rights, most notably dignity. Unlike the traditionalists, who are said to rely on dignity to justify individualist outcomes, i.e. to serve 'empowerment', constitutionalists emphasise that dignity also requires concern for others, i.e. they support its 'constraint' function.[55] Crucially in the present context, *ubuntu* is referred to by some constitutionalists as a value which supports the interpretation of dignity that highlights this 'constraint' function.[56] The implication is therefore that good faith and *ubuntu* are not on an equal footing, or do not perform similar functions in the law of contract: good faith is afforded a more prominent role, which is clearly reflected in statements such as that it is '*the* ethical ideal that undergirds the law of contract'.[57]

With these overviews of the meaning of *ubuntu* and debates on promoting fairness behind us, we can now try to obtain a clearer picture of the role that *ubuntu* could play in developing the South African law of contract.

Synthesis: *ubuntu* and promoting fairness in the South African law of contract

Ubuntu and the public policy rule

As we have seen, South African law allows courts to refuse to recognise or enforce a term if it would be contrary to public policy. In applying this 'public policy rule' South African courts, after years of trial and error, nowadays wisely do not draw watertight distinctions between public policy, public interest, and public morality, and use these concepts interchangeably. Given their broad nature, courts naturally consider a host of specific policy considerations, interests, and values when applying this rule. Crucially in the present context, the Constitutional Court has recognised that public policy is (also) 'informed' by the concept of *ubuntu*.[58]

55 See Barnard-Naudé, '"Oh What a Tangled Web We Weave ..."' 202–206. Further see Hawthorne, 'Constitution and Contract'. On the distinction between the personal 'empowerment' aspect of the right to dignity and its role as 'constraint', which requires that individuals must also recognise each other's dignity, see G F Lubbe, 'Taking Fundamental Rights Seriously: The Bill of Rights and its Implications for the Development of Contract Law' (2004) 121 *SALJ* 395,421–422

56 See Barnard-Naudé, '"Oh What a Tangled Web We Weave ..."' 202.

57 Ibid., 201 (own emphasis). Also see Barnard-Naudé, 'Of Dorothy's Dog' 473 (where good faith is described as *the* primary transformative ethical device of the general law of contract).

58 *Barkhuizen* (n 31) [51]. Also see Bennett, Munro and Jacobs, *Ubuntu – An African Jurisprudence*, 115–120. Cornell and Muvangua suggest that in *Barkhuizen* 'it is through *ubuntu* that good faith comes more to the fore as a value that is applied indirectly in contract law, and instead is now used to develop good faith so as to allow it to be a principle that can be invoked directly to attack a contractual provision' (*Ubuntu and the Law*, 24). However, the passage by Ngcobo J they rely on indicates that it is through informing *public policy* (not good faith) that *ubuntu* comes to the fore.

The implications of this view are not explored, but *ubuntu* clearly cannot simply be regarded as a synonym for public policy, or be equated to the community's general moral outlook or views.[59] This accords with the conclusion earlier that *ubuntu* has a more specific meaning, which focusses on mutual interdependence and respect,[60] and it also reflects that *ubuntu* is not a competing standard or rule on which parties can rely directly, but, a constitutional value which guides courts in applying the public policy rule.

This role of *ubuntu* as a concept or value, which informs the public policy rule (or standard) can be illustrated by applying it to some prominent cases. Thus, the court's refusal in *Sasfin (Pty) Ltd v Beukes*[61] to enforce a finance agreement that essentially deprived a doctor of financial autonomy, or the refusal in *Basson v Chilwan*[62] to enforce a restraint of trade clause could be explained on the basis that the plaintiff's reliance on these terms displayed a fundamental lack of respect for the interests or dignity of a contracting party, without the plaintiff being able to point to countervailing interest worthy of protection.

To this some traditionalists may respond that explaining these cases in terms of *ubuntu* is unnecessary if fair outcomes could in any event be reached without doing so; *ubuntu*'s effect would indeed be only to 'legitimise' the South African common law. However, the potential exists for *ubuntu* as a constitutional value to influence the application and development of the public policy rule in a variety of new contexts by focussing the court's attention on whether enforcement would undermine the value of displaying sufficient concern or respect for the other party. Recent case law, consumer legislation and comparative perspectives,[63] suggest that room exists for developing the public policy rule to ensure greater fairness in a variety of circumstances where a party relies on certain contractual terms. These include a term that excludes or limits liability for breach (especially if this would have the effect of not complying with the most basic duties they contracted to fulfil),[64] a term that allows a party to accelerate performance, exercise

59 See English, '*Ubuntu*' 647. If *ubuntu* were to be defined in this way, the related danger would arise of the 'community' being interpreted in narrow, nationalistic terms. On the dangers subverting *ubuntu* in aid of identity politics see Praeg, *A Report on Ubuntu*, especially xi–xii, 187.

60 See note 21.

61 1989 (1) SA 1 (A).

62 1993 (3) SA 742 (A).

63 The Consumer Protection Act 68 of 2008 could provide guidance through its provisions on unfair terms (section 48), prohibited or blacklisted terms (section 51) and terms presumed to be unfair (reg 44(3), Government Notice No. R. 293, Government Gazette 34180, 1 April 2011). For comparative overviews on general provisions on unfair terms and consumer legislation see Hugh Beale et al., *Cases, Materials and Texts on Contract Law* (Hart, 2nd ed., 2010) ch 16; James Gordley and Arthur von Mehren, *An Introduction to the Comparative Study of Private Law – Readings, Cases, Materials* (Cambridge University Press 2009) 486–494.

64 See *Afrox* (n 31), where the hospital effectively sought to escape liability for the very obligation it undertook to perform, i.e. to provide professional medical care.

a right to terminate a contract or maintain that a contract has terminated;[65] and a term that allows a party to escape liability by imposing a very short time period to proceed with a claim.[66]

A willingness to take *ubuntu* into account in these enquires does not mean that the doors are now opened for parties to escape liability merely because a contract may have some detrimental impact on them. As *Savage v Sisters of The Holy Cross, Cape Province*[67] indicates, *ubuntu* requires that the regard for each other's position should be mutual; courts will have to continue displaying sensitivity to the protectable interests of the party seeking enforcement, which is also what the court did in this case, when it allowed a party to enforce its right to sell property to ensure its financial survival, even though this would have a negative impact on the position of the other party.[68]

To accord *ubuntu* the role of an informing value may perhaps appear to be a radical innovation, but there is no need to view it in such terms. After all, it has been recognised for quite some time (also by traditionalists) that good faith could be regarded as a value which is fundamental to the South African law of contract.[69] And good faith, like *ubuntu*, requires that when a party seeks to rely on a contractual right, some degree of concern or respect must be shown for the impact it would have on the other party. This meaning of good faith or *bona fides* is reflected in modern formulations: Lubbe for example states that 'a party to a contract, in the pursuit of self-interest, must display a degree of recognition and respect for the interests of the other party',[70] whereas Whittaker and Zimmermann refer to a 'standard of honest, loyal and considerate behaviour, of acting with due regard for the interests of the other party'.[71]

However, this does not mean that *ubuntu* and good faith are merely two sides of the same 'other-regarding' coin, or, viewed more broadly, that both are simply ways of defining a general standard of reasonableness. This is apparent when reflecting on their respective origins. The standard of *ubuntu* reflects a way of

65 See *Combined Developers v Arun Holdings* 2015 (3) SA 215 (WCC); *Dula Investments (Pty) Ltd v Woolworths (Pty) Ltd* (1994/2013) [2013] ZAKZDHC 17 (8 May 2013) [51]-[52]; *Beadica 231 CC and Others v Trustees, Oregon Unit Trust and Others* 2018 (1) SA 549 (WCC), and *Botha v Rich NO and Others* 2014 (4) SA 124 (CC) (albeit that the case concerned a rather unusual statutory regime regulating the sale of land on instalments). However, the reversal of *Mohamed's Leisure Holdings (Pty) Ltd v Southern Sun Hotel Interests (Pty) Ltd* 2017 (4) SA 243 (GJ) on appeal in *Mohamed's Leisure Holdings (Pty) Ltd v Southern Sun Hotel Interests (Pty) Ltd* 2018 (2) SA 314 (SCA) is a setback for this line of authority. Also see *Roazar CC v The Falls Supermarket CC* 2018 (3) SA 76 (SCA) [24].

66 See *Barkhuizen* (n 31), and especially the forceful dissent of Moseneke DCJ at [92]–[119].

67 2015 (6) SA 1 (WCC).

68 See especially [36] and [40]. Also see *Dula Investments* (n 64) [51]–[52].

69 See e.g. Brand, 'The Role of Good Faith, Equity and Fairness in the South African Law of Contract: The Influence of the Common Law and the Constitution' 81.

70 G. F. Lubbe, 'Bona Fides, Billikheid en die Openbare Belang in die Suid-Afrikaanse Kontraktereg' *Stellenbosch LR* 1 (1990) 7, 20 and 24.

71 Zimmermann and Whittaker, *Good Faith in European Contract Law* 31.

life, of how members of a community should accord each other mutual respect.[72] In earlier civil law the standard of *bona fides* in turn served to limit an attempt by one person to enforce a contractual right when this would be contrary to notions of fidelity and honesty; this standard developed from the Roman virtue of *fides*, which (like *ubuntu*) was central to preserving early social structures.[73] When we define good faith so broadly that it is simply regarded as synonymous with fairness or reasonableness, these nuances in meaning are lost.[74]

Ultimately, good faith and *ubuntu* could therefore have a mutually reinforcing effect as values that may guide the courts in applying and developing specific rules to promote contractual fairness. Since both values can perform this role independently as counterweights to freedom of contract and *pacta servanda sunt*, it does not appear to be necessary, or indeed even meaningful, for the one to vie for supremacy over the other. A public policy rule bolstered by these constitutional values can be a particularly powerful tool for promoting fairness in a broad range of contexts.

This conclusion has important implications. It calls into question the need, in these circumstances, to accord good faith the role of a competing *standard*, which parties can rely on directly when seeking to escape contractual liability.[75] It suggests that the courts, and the Constitutional Court in particular,[76] have rightly proceeded with caution in exploring potentially more extensive roles of good faith in our law of contract. In this context, a comparative perspective could be quite instructive. South African law is hardly alone in trying to identify the most effective instruments to ensure greater fairness in the law of contract. Some legal systems have had extensive experiences in applying good faith standards, more specifically good faith clauses in private law codes. These clauses are used for a variety of functions, which include preventing parties from exercising rights in an improper manner.[77] Comparative analysis reveals that these systems may have been compelled to apply a good faith clause to fulfil this 'limiting' function because there are no other provisions or rules that could potentially be used towards this end.[78] In South African law, however, we have seen that the public policy rule may be used to prevent a party from exercising or enforcing an

72 See note 2.

73 See Martin Schermaier, '*Bona Fides* in Roman Contract Law' in Zimmermann and Whittaker (eds) *Good Faith in European Contract Law* (Cambridge University Press 2000) 63, 77–83; Paul du Plessis, 'Good Faith and Equity in the Law of Contract in the Civilian Tradition' (2002) 65 *THRHR* 397, 399.

74 See G. F. Lubbe, 'Taking Fundamental Rights Seriously: The Bill of Rights and its Implications for the Development of Contract Law' (2004) 121 *SALJ* 395, 420.

75 Also see Lubbe, 'Bona Fides, Billikheid en die Openbare Belang in die Suid-Afrikaanse Kontraktereg' 19–25.

76 See e.g. *Barkhuizen* (n 31) [82] on the role of good faith.

77 See Jacques du Plessis, 'Giving Practical Effect to Good Faith' (2018) 3 *Stellenbosch LR* 51–54; Whittaker and Zimmermann, 'Good Faith in European Contract Law' 24–25; Jan Smits, *Contract Law – A Comparative Introduction* (Edward Elgar Publishing 2014) 140.

78 See Du Plessis, 'Giving Practical Effect to Good Faith' 225.

otherwise valid contractual right in a variety of circumstances. There is no need to adopt a competing or overlapping good faith standard to fulfil a similar function. The challenge is rather to apply and develop the public policy rule to ensure a more equitable law of contract.[79] And, as argued above, in this regard *ubuntu* can play an important role as an informing, underlying value.

Ubuntu and rules on procedural fairness

Apart from the public policy rule, South African law also combats unfairness by way of a number of rules that provide relief when one party obtains another's consent in a manner which renders it questionable whether the contract really is an expression of the latter's free will; in other words, when there is procedural unfairness. Traditionally, these rules deal with misrepresentation (which includes fraud), duress, and undue influence, and allow the victim remedies such as a right to rescind the contract, obtain restitution, and claim damages. In determining whether relief should be provided, the courts sometimes also consider whether the victim suffered a loss, but this is a secondary requirement; the focus is on the defective consent. The uncertainty as to whether parties really have exercised their autonomy indicates that in these circumstances enforcement cannot be justified by invoking the (constitutional) value of *pacta servanda sunt*.[80] But these established categories could also be explained as cases where one party, through seeking to enforce a contract which was not freely concluded due to its own improper conduct, displays a lack of concern or regard for the latter as a person; in other words, it could be said that such a person fails to act with the mutual respect that is characteristic of the value of *ubuntu*.[81] Support for this type of linking between serious cases of defective consent and *ubuntu* is even discernible among traditionalists.[82]

It has become increasingly apparent, however, that the established categories of defective consent may be too narrow, and that they do not adequately deal with a variety of cases of taking excessive advantage of a contracting party's weakness.

79 Ibid., 5212.

80 *Barkhuizen* (n 31) [57]; See Jacques du Plessis, 'Illegal Contracts and the Burden of Proof' (2015) 132 *SALJ* 664, 683. Also see Bhana 'The Law of Contract and the Constitution: *Napier v Barkhuizen* (SCA)' (n 49) 277; Barnard-Naudé, '"Oh What a Tangled Web We Weave ..."' 186–187.

81 See Cornell and Muvangua, *Ubuntu and the Law – African Ideals and Post-apartheid Jurisprudence*, 25–26 (*ubuntu* demands justice between individuals, an examination of circumstances of each individual, and whether there was an expression of free will). Metz comments as follows: 'Actions such as deception, coercion and exploitation fail to honour communal relationships in that the actor is distancing him from the person acted upon, instead of enjoying a sense of togetherness' (540). Also see Minette Nortje 'Unfair Contractual Terms – Effect of Constitution – *Breedenkamp v Standard Bank of South Africa Ltd*' (2010) 73 *THRHR* 517.

82 See e.g. Wallis, 'Commercial Certainty and Constitutionalism: Are they Compatible?' 18 (referring to fraud and misrepresentation).

These circumstances include various forms of lack of bargaining power (typically present when standard terms are presented on a take-it-or-leave-it basis), economic distress, or weakness or vulnerability due to ignorance or inexperience. In this regard, it is remarkable that even model rules drafted for application in international commercial environments, where more resilience can be expected of parties than when contracting in a domestic context, contain provisions that are markedly more progressive in their protection of weak contracting parties than that provided by the South African common law.[83] This should be a cause of some discomfort for those traditionalists who question in what way South African law really is defective in its ability to promote fairness in contract law.

Structurally, South African law can face the challenge of accommodating these cases in at least two ways. The first would be to expand the list of typical cases of improperly obtained consent. This happened in the past when undue influence was recognised as a new category, inter alia by pointing out that it amounted to a form of *dolus* (or action contrary to the value of *bona fides*).[84] But there is also a second route, which enjoys some support in case law. Certain cases of procedural unfairness, especially inequality of bargaining power, are traditionally (and indeed universally, and understandably) not regarded as serious enough *on their own* to warrant relief. In this regard, case law has recognised, for example, in the restraint of trade cases, that a combination of procedural unfairness *and* substantive harshness of the terms of the contract could tip the scales in favour of the victim by indicating that enforcement would be contrary to the public policy rule considered in the previous section.[85]

However, South African law has clearly not developed as far as it could, at least not when measured by international standards. Some further impetus is required for change. Again a similar facilitating or justificatory function for developing the uncodified, local common law could be fulfilled by the constitutional value *ubuntu*, with its emphasis on mutually respecting the dignity of others. In this context, it especially implies that those who want to take full advantage of having exercised their will freely should not be allowed do so if it is questionable that their contracting partners have done the same.[86] When *ubuntu* fulfils this function of informing the development of the law of contract, it can again stand side by side with good faith as complementary and mutually reinforcing values

83 See UNIDROIT PICC Art 3.2.7, and for comment Jacques du Plessis, 'Art 3.2.7' in Stefan Vogenauer (ed.) *Commentary on the UNIDROIT Principles of International Commercial Contracts* (OUP 2nd ed., 2015) 511–518. On comparable local consumer legislation, especially section 40 of the Consumer Protection Act 68 of 2008, see Du Plessis, 'Illegal Contracts and the Burden of Proof' 664, 684.

84 See *Preller v Jordaan* 1956 (1) SA 483 (A) 489–493; Du Plessis, 'Art 3.2.7' 685.

85 See e.g. *Barkhuizen* (n 31) [59].

86 See Cornell and Muvangua, *Ubuntu and the Law – African Ideals and Post-apartheid Jurisprudence*, 25–26.

that guide the courts in developing South African law to enable the protection of weak contracting parties.[87]

Furthermore, given that both the routes of expanding the categories of improperly obtained consent and the public policy rule are open for development, it is also not readily apparent in this context why the need would exist for allowing victims of procedural unfairness to invoke good faith directly as an independent standard or ground for relief. We return to the point made at the end of the previous section: South African law could avoid duplicating and confusing applications of competing standards by developing specific rules that combat unfairness. In this regard it is not without significance that some modern civilian systems, faced with the challenge of giving effect to the constitutional imperative to protect weak parties who provided security for the liability of others, have gone the route of extending the field of application of public policy rules, rather than to invoke the good faith standard.[88]

Ubuntu as a general equitable norm giving rise to an independent cause of action

This brings us to a final aspect of the relationship between *ubuntu* and the South African common law that remains to be considered. We have seen that *ubuntu* as constitutional value could promote the development of common law rules to ensure a more fair or equitable law of contract. However, could *ubuntu* also exert its influence in a more direct manner? The answer, at least as our law currently stands, is clear. *Ubuntu* does not accord a party an independent cause of action. A plaintiff cannot argue, for example, that the defendant might have validly exercised a right of termination in terms of the common law of contract, but that *ubuntu* as (equitable) norm demands that the court should nonetheless hold that termination is ineffective. In this regard, *ubuntu*'s role therefore differs from the function that a 'meta-norm' like equity traditionally played in English law.[89]

This is the position at present. What the future holds we do not know. But it is difficult to avoid the impression that it is doubtful whether South African law should follow the route of allowing *ubuntu* to act as an independent cause of action, as opposed to taking the alternative, potentially less disruptive path of using *ubuntu* to develop existing instruments and rules aimed at ensuring equitable or fair outcomes. Historically, English law developed the law of equity from a separate institution (the Chancery), because parties felt there was no hope

87 For reliance on good faith to expand the ambit of cases of procedural unfairness see e.g. C-J Pretorius and R Ismail, 'Compromise, Undue Influence and Economic Duress' (2012) 33 *Obiter* 681; Graham Glover, 'Good Faith and Procedural Unfairness in Contract' (1998) 61 *THRHR* 328, 331–335. As indicated above, the concept of *dolus* has been used to justify recognition of undue influence, but it could also guide further expansion of the boundaries of cases of improperly obtained consent – see Du Plessis, 'Art 3.2.7' 682–686.

88 See Whittaker and Zimmermann, 'Good Faith in European Contract Law' 30.

89 Bennett, Munro and Jacobs, *Ubuntu – An African Jurisprudence*, 122.

of attaining justice by developing the common law in the ordinary courts of law. However, as we have seen in the previous sections, *ubuntu* as a constitutional value could influence the incremental development of the South African law of contract, in conjunction with other values, such as good faith. *Ubuntu* does not have to serve the drastic and unpredictable purpose of a general overriding corrective, which, if the English experience is anything to go by, results in a highly problematic competition between parallel sets of rules.

Conclusion

Views on how South African law should promote greater fairness in the law of contract diverge considerably. The debates traditionally focus on common law doctrines such as the rule that the content or enforcement of a contract should not be contrary to public policy, or the principle of good faith, which underlies the law of contract. However, awareness has grown that the customary law concept of *ubuntu* deserves greater recognition when developing the legal system in general, and the law of contract in particular. The courts, and especially the Constitutional Court, have indicated that one direction which such a development could take is to recognise *ubuntu* as a constitutional value, which may guide them when applying and developing the rule that the content and enforcement of contracts should not be contrary to public policy. The potential also exists for *ubuntu* to act as an informing value when determining the scope of the various categories of improper ways of obtaining consent, such as misrepresentation, duress, and undue influence, and when developing further categories where relief is provided to weak contracting parties.

In this development, good faith could stand next to *ubuntu* as constitutional values, the one African and the other Western, which, due to their focus on the interests of others, could act as counterweights to the values of individualism and personal autonomy. This has important implications. If the courts were willing to use *ubuntu* and good faith creatively as such values to guide the development of the rules on public policy and improperly obtained consent, less need would exist for further recognising *ubuntu* and good faith as independent standards, which parties could rely on directly for relief. In this way, an undesirable and confusing duplication of broad standards for relief could be avoided.

However, for *ubuntu* to fulfil the function of a value which guides the development of our modern law of contract, and not to be relegated to a hollow legitimation of pre-existing conclusions, it would have to be interpreted in a way which is fully responsive to the demands of a complex, heterogeneous society, characterised by wide-ranging differences in wealth and bargaining power, and in which consideration need not only be shown to the interests of private individuals, but for all types of entities engaged in contractual interaction. Furthermore, and it is conceded that this may appear somewhat paradoxical, to ensure that *ubuntu* realises this potential, it may be beneficial to draw on the experiences of legal systems which also had to grapple with challenges of developing concrete rules to promote a less individualistic and more 'other-regarding' law of contract. We may quibble about how many of these positions are worthy of emulation, and there will naturally be situations where foreign experiences would be irrelevant to, or indeed incompatible with, local value systems. But there is no inevitable conflict. Unusual and complex mixes are nothing new. In seeking to promote fairness in the South African law of contract we are able to draw on a true diversity of sources, with a richness that Esin Örücü would appreciate.

Selected bibliography

Jaco Barnard-Naudé, 'Of Dorothy's Dog, "Post-structural" Fairy Tales … and the Real: Power, Poverty and the General Principles of the South African Law of Contract' (2013) 29 *SAJHR* 467.

T. W. Bennett, assisted by A R Munro and P J Jacobs, *Ubuntu – An African Jurisprudence* (Juta 2018).

Deeksha Bhana, 'Contract Law and the Constitution: Bredenkamp v Standard Bank of South Africa (Ltd)' (2014) 29 *SAPL* 508.

Fritz Brand, 'The Role of Good Faith, Equity and Fairness in the South African Law of Contract: A Further Instalment' (2016) 27 *Stellenbosch LR* 236.

Drucilla Cornell, 'uBuntu, Pluralism and the Responsibility of Legal Academics to the New South Africa' (2009) 20 *Law and Critique* 43.

Dennis Davis, 'Developing the Common Law of Contract in the Light of Poverty and Illiteracy: The Challenge of the Constitution' (2011) 22 *Stellenbosch LR* 845.

Dennis Davis, 'Where is the Map to Guide the Common-Law Development?' (2014) 25 *Stellenbosch LR* 3.

Patrick Donlan, 'Remembering: Legal Hybridity and Legal History' (2011) 2 (1) *Comparative Law Review* 1.

Jacques du Plessis, 'Comparative Law and the Study of Mixed Legal Systems' in Mathias Reimann and Reinhard Zimmermann (eds) *The Oxford Handbook of Comparative Law* (OUP 2006).

Jacques du Plessis, 'Giving Practical Effect to Good Faith' (2018) 3 *Stellenbosch LR* 379.

Rosalind English, 'Ubuntu: The Quest for an Indigenous Jurisprudence' (1996) *SAJHR* 641.

Graham Glover, 'Good Faith and Procedural Unfairness in Contract' (1998) 61 *THRHR* 328.

Luanda Hawthorne, 'Concretising the Open Norm of Public Policy: Inequality of Bargaining Power and Exploitation' (2014) 77 *THRHR* 407.

Luanda Hawthorne, 'Constitution and Contract: Human Dignity, the Theory of Capabilities and Existenzgrundlage in South Africa' (2011) 2 *SUBB Jurisprudentia* 27.

Joos Hefer, 'Billikheid in die Kontraktereg' (2004) 29 *JJS* 1.

Irma Kroeze, 'Doing Things with Values II: The Case of Ubuntu' (2002) 13 *Stellenbosch LR* 252.

Carole Lewis, 'The Uneven Journey to Uncertainty in Contract' (2013) 76 *THRHR* 80.

Andre Louw, 'Yet another Call for a Greater Role for Good Faith in the South African Law of Contract: Can we Banish the Law of the Jungle, while Avoiding the Elephant in the Room?' (2013) 16 *Potchefstroom Electronic LJ* 44.

G. F. Lubbe, 'Taking Fundamental Rights Seriously: The Bill of Rights and its Implications for the Development of Contract Law' (2004) 121 *SALJ* 395.

Thaddeus Metz, 'Ubuntu as a Moral Theory and Human Rights in South Africa' (2011) 11 *AHRLJ* 532.

Yvonne Mokgoro, 'Ubuntu and the Law in South Africa' in Drucilla Cornell and Nyoko Muvangua (eds) *Ubuntu and the Law – African Ideals and Post-apartheid Jurisprudence* (2012) 317. Fordham University Press

Minette Nortje, 'Unfair Contractual Terms – Effect of Constitution – Breedenkamp v Standard Bank of South Africa Ltd' (2010) 73 *THRHR* 517.

Esin Örücü, 'What is a Mixed Legal System: Exclusion or Expansion?' (2008) 12 (1) *EJCL*, http://www.ejcl.org/121/art121-15.pdf.

Leonhard Praeg, *A Report on Ubuntu* (University of Kwazulu-Natal Press 2014).

Dire Tladi, 'One Step Forward, Two Steps Back for Constitutionalising the Common Law: Afrox Health Care v Strydom' (2002) 17 *SAPL* 473.

Gardiol J. van Niekerk, 'Amende Honorable and Ubuntu: An Intersection of Ars Boni et Aequi in African and Roman-Dutch Jurisprudence?' (2013) 19 *Fundamina* 397.

Malcolm Wallis, 'Commercial Certainty and Constitutionalism: Are They Compatible?' (2016) 133 *SALJ* 545.

5 On kites and ships

Climate changes in comparative law and judicial navigation

Werner Menski

Introduction: kites, ships, and navigational skills

In October 2005, Professor Esin Örücü, then a fresh Emerita, gave the Vote of Thanks after my Inaugural Lecture at SOAS, University of London, on 'The Law of Laws'. Her memorable annual guest lectures on Turkish law in 'Legal Systems of Asia and Africa', the flagship first-year SOAS law course, created a productive climate for developing our ideas about mixed legal systems, legal pluralism, and diversity management in different jurisdictions. In 2005, we talked jokingly about law as an Indian or Turkish onion, whose rings, influenced by the local climate, would provide a particular flavour and generate the specific identity, values, or 'legal postulates' that infuse any legal order.[1]

Neither of us perceived 'law' merely as state law, and we were increasingly aware of the various effects of globalisation. Envisaging various patterns of connectivity, we both constructed different triangles,[2] the latter notably more state-centric. Professor Örücü, trained as a positivist lawyer, but also an active sailor and captain, also spoke from direct experience of commanding a ship.[3] This model of law, constantly subject to various pushes and pulls, exposed to winds from Europe, the Middle East, and faraway New York, was tested in our Turkish law lectures. The Turkish ship's main aim involved staying on course to follow the post-Ottoman Turkish Kemalist vision of modern development. The article on 'Judicial navigation' explains how this was 'symbolised by "Six Arrows": nationalism, laïcism, republicanism, populism, statism and

1 Masaji Chiba (ed.), *Asian Indigenous Law in Interaction with Received Law* (KPI 1986).

2 Werner Menski, *Comparative Law in a Global Context: The Legal Systems of Asia and Africa* (2nd rev ed., Cambridge University Press, 2006) 612; Esin Örücü, 'Judicial Navigation as Official Law Meets Culture in Turkey' (2008) 4(1) *International Journal of Law in Context* 35–61, 43.

3 Much later (see further below), I would contribute anecdotal impressions from a Japanese simulation centre for training captains. See W. Menski, 'Legal Simulation: Law as a Navigation Tool for Decision-Making' (2014) 59(2.1) *Report of Japan Coast Guard Academy*, 1–22. http://harp.lib.hiroshima-u.ac.jp/jcga/metadata/12172?l=en.

reformism'.[4] My own recent work explores similar patterns for the national vision of Bangladesh as a 'wish kite'.[5]

Both of us are retired now, but actively carrying on our respective research, so it seems fitting to provide some reflections here that may lay the foundations for future generations to learn from our experiences, similar to how we learnt from earlier scholars. In this spirit, the present chapter compares and contrasts the methods of presenting legal navigation through the image of a ship[6] or a kite.[7] Both models facilitate a deep plurality-conscious analysis of law. Both methods of presenting decision-making processes bring out varied power structures and influences in this constantly moving, and always somewhat liquid,[8] structure we conceptualise as 'law'.[9] Related theoretical studies of legal transplants, or transpositions,[10] are connected to applied legal studies that seek to make sense of legal conflicts in specific scenarios and contexts. In *Comparative Law: A Handbook*,[11] I provided some insights into how states beyond Europe, specifically India, demonstrate that constructive use of legal pluralist realities can bring about better justice also for minorities. Ten years later, I assess here specifically what further progress has been made in securing rights to post-divorce maintenance for Indian women in the aftermath of the world-famous, much-misunderstood Shah Bano case of 1985.[12]

This account also shows how politicised scholarship and media interventions constantly hold us back in making heuristic progress. It remains therefore necessary to counter allegations that comparative legal studies lack practical relevance and, more specifically, that studies on legal pluralism have so far failed to theorise issues of political power,[13] and risk generating chaos in real life. I rather suggest the opposite, namely that the epistemic violence of partial theorising and giving undue weight to legal centralist doctrine clouds the skies of hope and rolls out the barbed wire that causes a lot of damage. Failure to pick up positive climate changes in comparative law theorising restricts plurality-conscious

4 Örücü (2008), 40.

5 W. Menski, 'Bangladesh in 2015: Challenges of the *Iccher Ghuri* for Learning to Live Together' (2015) 1(1) *Journal of Law and Politics*, 9–32.

6 Örücü (2008).

7 Menski (2014; 2015). See also W. Menski, 'Ancient and Modern Boundary Crossings Between Personal Laws and Civil Law in Composite India' in Joel A. Nichols (ed.), *Marriage and Divorce in a Multicultural Context* (CUP 2012), 219–252.

8 See on this theme the Special Issue of *Jura Gentium*, Vol. XI: *Pluralismo Giuridico*. Annuale 2014 edited by Mariano Croce, http://www.juragentium.org.

9 On this see Seán Patrick Donlan and Lukas Heckendorn Urscheler (eds.), *Concepts of Law. Comparative, Jurisprudential, and Social Science Perspectives* (Ashgate, 2014).

10 Örücü (2008), 37.

11 See W. Menski, 'Beyond Europe' in Esin Őrűcű and David Nelken (eds.) *Comparative Law. A Handbook* (Hart Publishing, 2007), 189–216.

12 Reported as *Mohd. Ahmed Khan v. Shah Bano*, AIR 1985 SC 945.

13 Gad Barzilai, 'Beyond Relativism: Where Is Political Power in Legal Pluralism?' (2008) 9(3) *Theoretical Enquiries in Law*, 395–416.

perceptions and hinders creativity in the search for better justice, especially through deeper theorising of activist judicial creativity in interaction with progressive law-making.[14]

The relevance of comparative analysis and legal pluralism

Various other images for pluralist endeavours, such as comparing apples and oranges, are theorised in *Concepts of Law*.[15] At the launch of that book in Lausanne, it was accepted as a useful visual image to envisage law as a basket of fruit. Indeed, comparative law has meanwhile progressed much further than rhetorically critical commentators recognise.[16] Hence not only does Europe, faced with mass migration from the Global South, need to pluralise,[17] global legal scholarship has meanwhile been irrevocably changed by legal pluralism as 'one of the most salient and influential academic trends in law and society scholarship since the 1970s'.[18] We should now examine how far these climate changes have extended.

Since the present chapter ultimately aims to provide an update on recent pluralist developments in Indian laws, with specific reference to Muslim law, it is also pertinent to highlight precarious tensions in the interplay of the secular Indian state and Indian Muslims; a vast internally plural group of now around 180 million people, 14.23% of the Indian population according to the Census of 2011. Muslim or Islamic laws are thus an important element of Hindu-dominated India as an internally plural nation. While anti-religious and state-centric scholarly perceptions continue to block understanding of such intensely plural legal scenarios, we know that one can describe the phenomenon of law itself through many different words and images.[19] After a long academic journey, I found that seeking to define 'law', or to identify what it is not, is far less productive than analysing how this intensely plural phenomenon actually works in practice.[20] This approach is now finally confirmed, after much partial theorising.[21] While state-centric discourses about 'law' remain dominant, and the more recent prominence of international law and human rights concepts has brought a further climate change in positivism-centric theorising, notable everywhere, it remains pertinent to observe that 'the model of state law has impoverished our professional and public discourses on law for much of the last two centuries'.[22]

14 W. Menski, 'Still Asking for the Moon? Opening Windows of Opportunity for Better Justice in India' (2016) 49(2) *Verfassung und Recht in Übersee*, 125–147.
15 Donlan and Urscheler (2014).
16 See Barzilai (2008).
17 Örücü (2008), 41.
18 Barzilai (2008), 396.
19 Örücü (2008), 35.
20 Menski (2006).
21 Brian Z. Tamanaha, C. Sage and M. Woolcock (eds.) (2012) *Legal Pluralism and Development. Scholars and Practitioners in Dialogue* (CUP 2012).
22 Donlan and Urscheler (2014), 2.

Today, however, one cannot ignore other law-related phenomena, mainly social norms and ethical principles, as well as religious assumptions, which do not immediately need to raise the monsters of theocracy. This immediately means that, in legal systems beyond Europe, the continued presence of personal status laws is not an antiquarian irritant or a relic waiting to be removed, but an integrally interconnected living reality that must then be made productive for strengthening justice, especially for those many millions of people for whom the central state and its laws and agents remain remote. Recognition of such personal laws, even if they are not official law, and the respective constitutional structures as interconnected entities, provides one of the reasons for a growing agreement today that judges, among the most important creative actors in managing 'the accommodation of cultural diversity and multiple normative orders',[23] remain so crucial in the new age of plurality-conscious analysis. The era of big codification projects is long gone. The key task now is to make the existing hybrid legal structures produce meaningful justice for local citizens, if necessary by providing exceptions and making case-by-case allowances. This constant systemic tension between the much-cherished principles of legal certainty or uniformity and situation-specific justice manifests not only in modern unitary nation-states of the Western-type but much more so beyond Europe.

In practice, the highly dynamic volatile element of making decisions, not merely by following precedents but working from case to case and thus constantly generating new patterns of cultural defence,[24] reflects multiple levels of asserting political power within the vastly complex realms of legal systems and their internally pluralist structures. That is why lately I speak of 'POP', law as a 'plurality of pluralities'. Various bureaucratic and judicial acts of utilising discretionary power, ideally wisely, manifest in decision-making processes at all levels of any plural ship, triangle, or kite of law we may imagine. My earlier critique of Hart's socio-legal positivist methodology, and his failure to address problems of cultural and value pluralism in relation to legal analysis,[25] was evidently not explicit enough in highlighting this element of power in such processes, which Hart so clearly recognised. Hence the recent argument that 'a theoretical concept of political power has significantly been missing in research on the plurality of legal practices in various jurisdictions',[26] it seems, is merely a strategically posited claim by a scholar who then still proceeds in the ensuing critique by largely overlooking the potential power of individual legal actors. These may be not only Hart's state officials or, today, various global legal actors, but more or less charismatic spokespersons of their own personal convictions, and/or agents or mouthpieces of a community. They exercise political and legal power, too. My argument below therefore becomes that by factoring in such added pluralities of

23 Örücü (2008), 61.
24 Alison Dundes Renteln, *The Cultural Defense* (Oxford University Press, 2004).
25 Menski (2006), 103.
26 Barzilai (2008), 395.

individual holders of political power (among which I shall later explicitly include also voters) in already structurally pluralist scenarios, we will be able to understand better what today troubles complex entities like the state-nation of India, the present Turkish Republic, or current Japanese or Bangladeshi law, with which this article is not centrally concerned.

As recent troubles of the Turkish state with governance and diversity management confirm, absolute state control remains constantly challenged and undermined in various ways, not only by international legal pressures and – often, also directed at Turkey – outright bullying but by communities, individuals, and their value systems. If a state, and those humans who manage or govern it, tend to ignore such basic conditions of multiple conflicts within normative and legal pluralist structures and processes, various kinds of opposition to state-centrality will arise; hardly a conducive climate for peacefully navigating national legal systems.[27] If there are diversity management failures, an entire nation may collapse in turmoil, the ship may sink, and the kite in the sky of hope is bound to crash. That such complex acts of navigation require immensely hard work and contain multiple irritants contributes to the very nature and *mentalité* of comparative law and of legal pluralism as contested fields. Respect for diversity, albeit within tolerable limits for all stakeholders, becomes an energising asset, providing encouragement to do better, rather than generating control-freakism or violent dogmatic disagreement, even blind rage manifesting in terrorist activities. Whether we gaze at Turkey or the various South Asian states, however, this is easy to say, and much more difficult to manage in practice.

The living law of good governance can, also in Turkey, be symbolised through kite flying,[28] but more about that later. If basic elements of law's connectedness and dynamism are simply forgotten, and the axiom of law's ever-contested inner nature is ignored, any orchestra – to use another useful image employed by Örücü in 2008 – will not produce a high-quality concert; ships of law facing storms, no matter how strong the captain may claim to be, may be pushed in precarious directions, and kites of law may just crash and reach the end of their working life. Turkey seems to have hit partly self-generated rough waters recently, while to the constant amazement of the world, India's uniquely messy and highly flexible model of managing its various diversities, as a state-nation rather than a nation-state,[29] looks as durable and solid as the more muscular model of Turkish legal navigation. In both scenarios, tensions between different forms of governance, between 'tradition' and 'modernity', 'secularism' and 'religion', and not only 'Islam', remain a hugely important factor.

27 See Ihsan Yilmaz, *Muslim Laws, Politics and Society in Modern Nation States: Dynamic Legal Pluralisms in England, Turkey and Pakistan* (Ashgate, 2005).

28 I refer here to press reports that during 2016, some people in Turkey started flying kites as a symbolic protest action.

29 Domenico Amirante, *Lo Stato multiculturale* (Bononia University Press 2015).

The power of memory and the strength of convictions and experience

Professor Örücü grew up in Kemalist Turkey and recounted in her fabulous SOAS lectures how her mother, a school teacher and thus a state employee, came home one day in a chic new haircut, with a cute hat that perfectly matched the desired image of 'the New Turkish Woman'. She remembers, thus, the time when Ottoman Turkey changed through intensive top-down legal intervention, without direct influences of colonialism, into Kemalist Turkey. While that intervention was not experienced in the same way in Anatolian villages, it would be misguided to imagine that current uproar over modalities of governance in Turkey is unconnected to continuing disagreements over the direction and depth of socio-legal reforms within this modern Muslim majority country. As a South Asia specialist, I see similar irritations brought about by climate changes in the public sphere not only in Hindu-dominated India,[30] but most dramatically in Bangladesh today.[31] We also find such tensions in Pakistan,[32] and of course in Afghanistan. Clashes of laws and values, especially when 'religion' is involved, are today again a worldwide phenomenon. But it is far too simple to just blame 'religion' or 'tradition'.

In the 1920s, the Turkish ship of law changed direction and appearance.[33] Numerous innovations were, prominently, codified legal transplants from various European countries, translated into Turkish, which itself raises crucial questions about the precise nature of such European transplants. The stressful, exciting process of a new nation-state exercising state-centric sovereign powers over its citizens through guided social engineering, steering the nation's ship into a new climate, partly gently, yet also with some force, was completed, so one thought. Subsequent fine-tuning was indeed largely left to the nation's judiciary. Hence 'the navigator steersman judge must be alert at all times',[34] to ensure that the ship stays on the 'intended track',[35] and moves 'in the direction of the "charted route" of the Republic',[36] following the nation's vision. That this is a matter of utmost public interest requires little discussion. Whether India, Turkey, Pakistan, Japan, or Bangladesh, the need to manage the pluralities of huge, internally diverse countries and their cultures and religions, even if negotiated under different labels, is everywhere going to be stressful, and the fit between the aspirations of universalising trends and pluralising tendencies 'is always uncomfortable'.[37]

30 Menski (2016).
31 Menski (2015).
32 Mudasir Nazar, 'Pakistan's Frontline Status, War on Terror and the Jama'at E-Islami Response' (2016) 36(2) *South Asia Research*, 143–66.
33 Örücü (2008), 39–40.
34 Ibid., 43.
35 Ibid., 48.
36 Ibid., 56.
37 Ibid., 36.

Notably, the situation in Turkey is quite unlike Japan, which had in the 1890s copied Prussian laws, but not the socio-cultural values attached to it. While Japanese legal developments have raised important questions for legal philosophy in terms of 'rights translation',[38] Turkey evidently wanted deeper socio-religious reforms to impact directly on people's lives and thought patterns. That this has not completely succeeded, despite the perceived muscularity of Kemalist Turkish law, is reflected in Professor Örücü's lifetime work as a comparative lawyer, despite her initial inclination to view law as a state-centric instrument. Excellent examples of the continuing tense dynamics and diverse lived experience of plurality-conscious navigation in response to different winds are provided by such work.[39] Indeed, there is meanwhile a notable climate change also in comparative legal theorising, affecting the movements of all key stakeholders. I suggest that this relates closely to growing democratisation, itself a pluralising factor rather than a uniformising trend, which may partly explain the current turmoil in Turkey where presidential ambitions constitute a conceptual contradiction.

The changing climate for the movement of ships and kites

My recent work has theorised the plural entity of 'law' explicitly as a kite with four corners.[40] In brief, at the top, corner 1 represents various forms of traditional natural law, ethics and values. On the right-hand side, corner 2 signifies various social normativities as well as economic sustainability. On the left-hand side, corner 3 represents the various familiar forms and manifestations of state law, while at the bottom corner 4 concentrates on the new natural law of human rights and international law.

As indicated, in today's democratic environments, the typical traditional focus on state structures hides that 'law' is not only a matter of political top-down power but also involves the power of the ballot box. Within dominant scholarly contexts, the recent remarkable shift of emphasis in academia and activism specifically towards international law and human rights, corner 4 of the kite, has tended to overlook this localising, diversifying dimension. While William Twining critiqued globalisation,[41] the paradigmatic shift towards strengthening international laws has generated new power structures and discourses that specifically put states (corner 3 of the kite) on the defensive, while privileging international norms and powers. This resulted in more neglect for the continuing importance of corners 1 (natural law, ethics/values) and 2 (social normativities). In current bipolar adversarial scenarios of conflict, various powerful lobbies arising from corner 4 of the kite are now bullying states to follow so-called international standards. A simple

38 Ko Hasegawa, 'Normative Translation in the Heterogeneity of Law' (2015) 6(3–4) *Transnational Legal Theory*, 501–517.

39 See Örücü and Nelken (2007); Örücü (2008).

40 For this see Menski (2014).

41 *Globalisation and Legal Theory* (Butterworths 2000).

example is recent pressure, both on India and Turkey, to implement gender-neutral minimum age limits of 18 years for legally valid marriages. Proponents of such internationally standardised patterns are frequently unaware of, or are unwilling to acknowledge, that specific social and normative structures infuse the connected 'legal postulates', ethical entities characterised as closely related to identity construction, with key issues like 'honour' and status.[42] The rationale underpinning such local normative systems that suggest differentiated benchmarks and solutions is often brusquely brushed aside as violating international standards of human rights and gender justice, without any respect or concern for situation-specificity and local forms of precariousness.[43]

Both Turkey and India, having faced strong gusts of wind from corner 4, have reacted to such pressures in their own, historically conditioned ways. Turkey's earlier experience and memory of the Ottoman Empire being forced by international powers to accept many externally imposed rules generated strong nationalism, which still underpins continuing convictions within Turkey that the nation must be protected against such external pressures. Such resentful memories act together with the ambivalent geostrategic positioning of Turkey, its desire to be as close to Europe as possible and its inevitable connectedness to the Middle East as well as proximity to Russia. All of this generates various navigational turbulences, which now again include massive refugee movements. Like India, which faces similar volatilities, Turkey's ship thus cannot sail in isolation. It is pushed and pulled by events elsewhere in the world, specific developments closer to home, and problems at home itself.

For India, the traumatic experience of falling prey to colonial rule over centuries, not to speak of the cruelties around Independence in 1947, generated a proclivity towards non-alignment and also grounds strong latent resistance to international meddling in national affairs. Presently, ideological critiques of certain excesses by a Hindu nationalist government fail to remember that such historically grounded convictions about protecting the national public interest and the nation's integrity are perceived as higher values than following internationally dictated norms. Here, too, various refugee movements, earlier and today, add significant complications and more hidden agendas. In such volatile environments, pitting one sense of self-righteousness against another generates potentially poisonous conflict scenarios, with rational debate as a casualty. While attempted international interventions in Indian governance are not the main focus of this article, our analysis must account for the fallouts of this precarious conflict scenario. Additionally, when religion is involved, as we shall see,

42 See Chiba (1986).

43 The most recent example is the current introduction in Pakistan of a long overdue marriage law for the Hindu minority, based on international law benchmarks, as the gender-neutral age limit of 18 years for legally valid marriages indicates. As this overlooks local legal problems, this will soon generate new legal issues.

the intensity of feelings quickly rises, generating multiple distortions in discourse management on all sides.

As indicated, national governments these days are more accountable to a voting public which in turn shows increasing sophistication in spotting abuses of power and self-serving politicians' lies and pretensions. As people's power becomes a legally more relevant factor, national governments concerned about their own survival and the nation's safe future will now not only gaze at international law in corner 4 of the power kite structures, but also have to account today, more than earlier, for expectations arising from corners 2 and 1. Notably, the 'silent revolution',[44] brought about by the electorally critical masses of low-caste Dalit voters and their agenda, has become crucial in post-millennium India and will spearhead further democratic upsurges.[45] New research identifies that India's female voters now demand more attention through the ballot box.[46] Current struggles faced by Turkey, too, given such electoral concerns, may lead to further people-driven revisions of ambition and policy. However, we turn now to South Asian methods of managing legal diversity.

Memory power and diversity management in South Asian laws

My biography includes experience of kite flying during a certain spring festival when the skies over many parts of South Asia are full of kites. Intriguingly, I saw in January 2015 that one can now buy kites with the Prime Minister's picture on them.[47] Now it is part of the fun to crash the kite of a leader who promised India a better future.[48] Indians as passionate kite flyers intuitively understand the impossibility of having complete control over kites, however. This does not mean they sympathise with their leaders, but this understanding perhaps adds to the charisma of those who dare put themselves forward as captain for a mega-nation ship. India's new visionary leader, unlike Kemal Atatürk at first sight, actually shares many elements of Atatürk's aspirations, though India's visions seem far less state-centric and more focused on identity politics, particularly the Hinduness (*Hindutva*) agenda of the current BNP regime. While Muslim majoritarian

44 Christophe Jaffrelot, *India's Silent Revolution: The Rise of Low Castes in North Indian Politics* (Permanent Black 2003).

45 Suhas Palshikar and Sanjay Kumar, 'Participatory Norm: How Broad-Based Is It?' (2004) 39(51) *Economic and Political Weekly*, 5412–5417.

46 Praveen Rai, 'Women's Participation in Electoral Politics in India: Silent Feminisation' (2017) 37(1) *South Asia Research*, 58–77.

47 Narendra Modi was elected in 2014 as India's Prime Minister in a landslide victory for the Hindu nationalist BNP (Bharatiya National Party).

48 Recent accounts of Turkish kite flying as a symbolic form of protest did not surprise me, for I have been training many young Turkish scholars in comparative law and diversity management and know that some of them were involved in recent protest movements, risking the ire of those in authority.

Turkey still struggles to balance nationalism and secularism, and different Muslims fight against each other, for Hindu-dominated India secularism has never meant French-style laïcism, but denotes a plurivocal policy of equidistance between all religions, under a strong Constitution that combines acknowledgement of Hindu domination with respect for all religious and other minorities.[49] India thus insists, to the chagrin of those who hate 'religion' and 'tradition', that Hindu-influenced majoritarianism plays a legitimate role. Yet as a nation-state with a plural DNA, India cannot be a Hindu state, which its Constitution makes very clear. Moreover, 'Hinduism' itself is a collection of loosely connected religions, literally a basket of sects, depending on regional origin, language, caste, and, importantly, individual choice. Additionally, more than 180 million Muslims plus substantial communities of Christians of various kinds, Parsis, Jews, and numerous tribal communities co-exist. Such tribals, living largely in borderland regions, prominently in India's Northeast, with cousins across national borders, like the Kurds of Turkey, often resent the demands of the central state. In such sensitive scenarios, the nation-state's integrity becomes a self-harming irritant when it seeks to dominate the often violent contentions too aggressively.[50]

Thus, whether we envisage law like a ship or a kite, the entity we perceive is always composed of different interacting components. This plurality is so complex that different perspectives of the whole, like looking at an Indian elephant, do yield different perceptions. While the Turkish state and its leadership took a forceful state-centric approach, India has always been less certain that this is the right approach and has experimented with different methods to engage centrifugal dissent, including the creation of new states. India meanwhile has 29 states within its massive federation and operates a unique multicultural governance policy.[51] Persistent claims for leaving space to local, unofficial legal regulation have, however, agitated many modernist, state-centric scholars.[52] While both state-centric perspectives and more anthropologically oriented approaches co-exist, which is hardly new, many commentators on South Asian laws constantly choose to forget that law everywhere comprises of not only rules but also values and processes, always within dynamic time-space-context frameworks. Ultimately, this highly dynamic interaction between rules, processes, and values makes the ship sail, causes kites to stay in the air, or somehow tells the elephant to move ahead. While law involves a constant journey, to what extent the various movements actually need state control remains everywhere contested. Obviously,

49 The reverse picture, with Muslim domination and Hindus as the main minority, prevails now in secular Bangladesh, to the consternation of many myopic observers even in Bangladesh itself. See Menski (2015).

50 Thangkhanlal Ngaihte, 'Armed Forces in India's Northeast: A Necessity Review' (2015) 35(3) *South Asia Research*, 368–385.

51 Amirante (2015).

52 For example, Vasudha Dhagamwar, in *Towards the Uniform Civil Code* (N.M. Tripathi Pvt. Ltd 1989), demanded introduction of such a code, despite doubts whether this would ever be feasible without major public opposition.

a ship without a captain easily becomes a hazard, yet putting it this way does not unconditionally endorse command theories of law. It merely reflects recognition of close connections between law and order, particularly in crowded conditions. As indicated earlier, I experienced this first-hand in the simulation centre of the Japanese Naval Academy in Kure in 2014. Guiding a boat into Tokyo harbour, a crowded space with many simultaneous movements, highlighted within seconds the crucial importance of navigation skills and the need for constant, instant decision-making.[53] Captains of ships and judges are thus correctly identified as key decision-makers in navigational scenarios.[54] Kite flying is even more of a high-risk activity, as kites are rather infirm structures attached to strings, which somehow connect all the different corners. This reinforces a major methodological point about the necessarily intense interdisciplinary and interconnected nature of all law. The rather flimsy, yet powerful and strong kite structure is constantly guided through the air by a more or less skilful kite flyer, often assisted by someone who holds a reel with extra string, allowing the kite to soar higher if the conditions are right. All sorts of law-related conclusions are possible for such observations regarding kite choreography and legal management.[55]

The kite imagery and its dramatic potential also teach us about people's law-related interactions. In Indian games, with so many kites in the sky, strings will get entangled. Indeed, part of the fun is to cut others' kites and/or retrieve crashed kites. Intriguingly, one of my predecessors at SOAS, Professor Sir Norman Anderson, an expert on Anglo-Mohammedan laws, used the kite image decades ago to describe law reforms in Pakistan.[56] Examining to what extent Pakistan was an Islamic state, Anderson concluded by comparing the people of Pakistan with boys flying a kite on a misty day: 'They cannot see it; they cannot tell where it is going; but they certainly feel the pull'.[57] While Pakistan has meanwhile banned kite flying as an un-Islamic activity with Hindu cultural roots,[58] the deeper symbolism of banning social practices of skilful navigation in a spirit of friendly competition seems to bypass the nation's lawmakers – or maybe not. Where a theocratically imagined version of traditional reliance on Qur'an and Sunna is sought to be imposed on a diverse population of various Muslims and non-Muslims, a deeper message is wrapped into patriarchal state-centric *Grundnorms*: Pluralism

53 Menski (2014).

54 See Örücü (2008).

55 Popular spectacles of European beach-based kite flying competitions as entertainment miss the key point of law-related kite methodology, which is admittedly rather boring, namely to achieve sustained stability. This lacks the performative drama (*tamasha*) of beach kites, which may, however, still be part of certain legal processes to identify the right direction for legal development.

56 Menski (2006), 373; See also W. Menski, 'Flying Kites in Pakistan: Turbulences in Theory and Practice' (2009/10) 1(1) *Journal of Law and Social Research*, 41–57, 41.

57 J.N.D. Anderson, 'Pakistan: An Islamic State?' in R.H.C. Holland and G. Schwarzenberger (eds.), *Law, Justice and Equity* (Sir Isaac Pitman and Sons 1967) 127–136.

58 Menski (2009/10), 42.

and negotiation of co-existence are bad, only the voice and singular authority of the dominant male counts. We learn from Khaled Hosseini's (2003) *The Kite Runner* how disastrously this worked out in Afghanistan,[59] related closely to local legal practices and norms. Kabul seems to have witnessed a brutal game in the skies over the city if, at the end of the day, there is supposed to be only one kite remaining in the sky, and the owner of that kite wins this game. Hosseini's novel indicates the ensuing trouble if the winner is the wrong kind of person.[60] This is not just fiction; there is no respect for pluralism and diversity; the game's higher purpose is to assert autocratic domination. Combined with religious doctrinal rigidity, this yields extreme danger through intrinsic intolerance of any form of diversity. Related plurality-phobic approaches explain why Bangladesh currently risks similar self-destruction. The powerful Islamist opposition to the current Awami League leadership of Bangladesh, whose vision, not unlike Turkey, is based on the wish kite of nationalism, democracy, socialism, and secularism,[61] sees respect for pluralism and secularism which involves an acknowledgement of various forms of local religion, virtually as instruments of the devil.

Turning to India now, which experiences similar struggles of diversity management, the key difference is Hindu domination, which structurally precludes, despite loudly voiced fears of many observers, a rigidly uniformising Hindu agenda. In the clashes over various gods, the real story is indeed immensely complex.[62]

India's national struggle over pluralist sustainability

This section now provides the promised update on the so-called Shah Bano episode in Indian law, showing how an integrated perspective of plurality-conscious legal analysis can invigorate both theory and practice and can assist in securing better forms of justice, following Amartya Sen.[63] This may help to make better sense of complex socio-legal developments in intensely plural nations beyond Europe. In Chapter 9 of Örücü and Nelken's *Comparative Law*, I provided some insight into how Hindu-dominated Indian law had, in my view,[64] skilfully managed to ensure that India's many divorced Muslim women would not be deprived of the firm basic rights guarantees in the Constitution of 1950. This topic must be seen in combination with the protective maintenance provisions of section

59 Khaled Hosseini, *The Kite Runner* (Bloomsbury 2003).

60 In this instance, a Shia boy from the minority Hazara community helps his employer's son (who he does not know is his half-brother) to win, only to be promptly captured and raped by those authoritarian Muslims who also claim to control the skies over Kabul.

61 Menski (2015).

62 Marco Ventura, *From Your Gods to Our Gods* (Cascade Books 2014).

63 Amartya Sen, *The Idea of Justice* (Penguin 2009).

64 See Menski, 'Beyond Europe' (2007), while the strategy chosen is still depicted as 'utterly unsatisfactory' by Ventura (2014) 26.

125, Criminal Procedure Code of 1973.[65] Meanwhile, though, the focus of activist energy in India has somehow shifted to the hotly debated issue whether an instantaneous triple *talaq* by a Muslim husband is legally valid. This diverts attention away from the practically much more important Shah Bano issue concerning the extent of obligation that divorcing Muslim husbands should have towards their ex-wives under Islamic law as well as Indian law.

Significantly, one of India's leading legal activists, the founder-director of the Majlis Legal Centre, has recently complained that the media continues to do significant damage by endorsing the view that, after divorce, India's Muslim women are stripped of all rights.[66] Indeed, Muslim men continue to claim the widely known 'religious' right to unilaterally divorce their wives, also instantly, and are then frequently tempted to avoid any responsibility for such women's subsequent welfare. This strategy is arguably a common human temptation, hardly unique to Muslims. In India, however, such private nastiness and selfishness clashes directly with the country's gender-sensitive and welfare-oriented formal legal system. The resulting struggles are not fully resolved today, as new cases will come up whenever individual couples cannot agree about their modalities of divorce and asset distribution. Apparently, a good Muslim husband should be kind also to the woman he divorces, given that divorce is 'the worst of all permitted things' for pious Muslims. While bitter cases concerning post-divorce maintenance claims will continue to come before the courts, evidently not only from Muslims, what is India's current official law on this subject? What is it that the media are not telling Muslim women, as Flavia Agnes rightly claims, about their rights as so laboriously secured from India's courts by many Muslim women?

This story needs to be told here in great brevity, which might actually produce more clarity, as the key points are actually simple, but truly dramatic and far-reaching.[67] Significant progress had been made by 2007 to curtail 'religious' patriarchal reasoning, to redress gender imbalances and to secure post-divorce maintenance rights for Indian Muslim women.[68] Today, India's Muslim men of course still have the right to divorce but are required, by an alert judiciary relying on sophisticated statutes and their own sense of justice, to make reasonable maintenance arrangements for their ex-wives, who have been guaranteed instant access to the courts. Such developments are remarkably progressive.[69] However, the problem remains that if the media, other women, most Muslim men, but even experts who should know better, continuously claim that divorced Muslim wives have no rights, an individual woman at household level would struggle

65 Menski, 'Beyond Europe' (2007).

66 See Flavia Agnes, 'Muslim Women's Rights and Media Coverage' (2016) 51(20) *Economic and Political Weekly*, 51(20), 13–15.

67 Sushmita Nath, 'Accommodating Religious Demands and Gender-Justice Concerns: Indian State Practices After the Shah Bano Judgment' (2013) 126 (January) *Asien*, 45–67, conveys this well.

68 Menski, 'Beyond Europe' (2007).

69 See, with some surprise, Nath (2013).

to ascertain her legal rights and articulate any claims against a deviant husband. Before the end of the so-called *iddat* period, he should simply make reasonable arrangements for her future welfare, and then there would be no need for a court case.

In fact, by 1979, India's activist Supreme Court had firmly established that a divorcing Muslim husband had to provide reasonable and adequate means for her dignified survival to an ex-wife.[70] This underpinned my argument that non-Western legal systems 'seem inherently more attuned than Western legal systems and scholars to the intellectual and practical challenges of comparative law and legal pluralism'.[71] The realisation that law is 'first of all a culturally embedded phenomenon and is specific to particular people who are interlinked at many levels'[72] is matched with a clearly visible shift to the courts.[73] While this clear-cut Indian stance remains half-hidden, there continues to be considerable pressure on India today, largely globally driven, to legislate for a Uniform Civil Code (UCC) and to abandon personal laws, which are not trusted to deliver gender justice. Such an activist agenda, however, diverts attention from the fact that divorced Muslim wives in India have already secured formally endorsed maintenance rights both under the country's general and personal law systems. Muslim women, in fact, have had a better legal position than all other divorced Indian women in this regard for some decades now.[74] Yet, politicised pressure for a UCC, while quite old in principle,[75] has found fresh support in the current Hindu nationalist government, though with a different and in my view completely misguided and dangerous agenda. Introducing a UCC for India will never get rid of Muslim law, as many Hindu fundamentalists are dreaming. Uniform codification with such an agenda would simply create violent chaos for multicultural India.

In my view, anyway, India already has a uniform civil law, only it does not dare tell its people.[76] Uniformising codification, rather than the currently operative mirror image of a harmonised structure which maintains the personal law system, would disrupt the well-working, current, uniquely plural legal order, which I explained earlier.[77] Indian lawyers and politicians know of such analyses but are studiously trying to ignore them. Since the developments discussed here primarily concern fiscal prudence and only secondarily the curtailing of Islamist patriarchal excesses, the blind spot is increasingly obvious: What should Hindu-dominated

70 *Bai Tahira v Ali Hussain Chothia*, AIR 1979 SC 362. As has also been made clear, however, if both parties are completely destitute, the courts cannot magically create money.
71 Menski, 'Beyond Europe' (2007), 189.
72 Ibid., 194.
73 Ibid., 200.
74 See also Agnes (2016).
75 J. Duncan and M. Derrett, *The Death of a Marriage Law* (Vikas 1978).
76 Menski (2016).
77 Menski, 'Beyond Europe' (2007), 205–212. See also W. Menski, 'The Uniform Civil Code Debate in Indian Law: New Developments and Changing Agenda' (2008) 9(3) *German Law Journal*, 211–250.

India do about securing rights to maintenance for all its numerous divorced wives, not just Muslim wives? Raising such agenda would touch many raw nerves, for India struggles ideologically and sentimentally with admitting its huge problems with marital instability.[78] Here again, though, there is uniformity, as both Muslim and Hindu traditions are emotionally and sociologically opposed to divorce, clinging to idealising visions of marital bliss; a nice ideal, but rather often not reality.

This particularly large blind spot in the Indian psyche again confirms, for me, that there is nothing wrong with legal pluralism itself in relation to India. Trouble arises for those who claim powers to suggest solutions, but cannot manage the existing conflicts and contradictions in a realistic sustainable manner. Worse, this deliberate blindness misleads a somehow still unsuspecting electorate, in the world's largest democracy, to believe that following a Western model of law will benefit the country and its people! Much of the blame for this obfuscation lies not actually with the nationalist Indian government, but with elitist modernist academics and journalists who meddle in politics, playing political football with India's laws and lives, risking the crashing of kites and the sinking of the national ship.

Hence it becomes necessary here to provide a fuller updated picture of the kite battles in the Indian skies of hope.[79] When the world-famous Shah Bano case came up,[80] a storm broke loose after the ex-husband, a Supreme Court lawyer, opposed Shah Bano's claims for decent maintenance payments. She was, of course, not a slum dweller and had grown-up sons who could maintain her. Basic legal principles were at stake in this power game between Indian state law and Muslim law, given the Supreme Court's clear-cut verdict of 1979, mentioned above. The Shah Bano case brought no legal innovation, since the ex-husband's claim, doomed to failure, was simply that, as a Muslim, he should be exempt from India's general law relating to post-divorce maintenance. Since the Shah Bano case was actually the husband's strategic appeal and not her case, the naming of this case itself turns out to be an obfuscating factor.

The Supreme Court also suggested that it would be better if India had a UCC, so that problems over Muslim law application would cease. Instant riots ensued all over India. The government's reaction, focused on calming the rioters, produced the sophisticated, very short Muslim Women (Protection of Rights on Divorce) Act, 1986. This is not, as many misguided authors have claimed, a badly drafted act. We know today, contrary to what Indian informants will still tell foreign researchers,[81] that its intended job was done rather well. Firstly, it calmed the rioters, now believing that Muslim men could still divorce unilaterally and then

78 Derrett (1978: 194) observed much earlier that the public 'are *not* interested in dissolution of marriage' (italics in the original).

79 See Menski (2016).

80 *Mhd. Ahmad Khan v. Shah Bano*, AIR 1985 SC 945.

81 See Ventura (2014), 26.

refuse any further responsibility for the woman. While that is certainly not what the 1986 Act provides, nobody was told, deliberately, for the riots might otherwise have continued. Instead, cleverly engineered legal discourse management, as 'politicised gossip',[82] provided fodder for the ongoing myths about Muslim divorced wives in India still having no rights.

Yet this story did not end here. A prominent secular Muslim, Danial Latifi, and other activists instantly challenged the constitutionality of the 1986 Act in the Supreme Court, which then sat on this petition for 15 years,[83] testing the waters through various *obiter dicta*.[84] Meanwhile, numerous 'progressive' scholars ruthlessly milked the Shah Bano/1986 Act mythology, while India's High Courts laboured hard to protect the rights of many divorced Muslim wives.[85] When the Supreme Court finally gathered the courage to pronounce its *Danial Latifi* verdict on 28 September 2001,[86] soon after 9/11, there were no riots. Rather stunned silence,[87] from gender activists but also from Muslims who were powerfully reminded by this verdict of their constitutional obligations as Indian citizens, indicates that nobody wanted to admit publicly that Shah Bano's ex-husband's Islam-inspired test case had badly misfired; only Flavia Agnes raised this.[88]

While legal pluralism in India had won a resounding battle, nobody seemed to rejoice. More tellingly, the Indian state kept strategically silent about the positive impact, in terms of fiscal prudence, of this legal outcome.[89] Here we see the major blind spot again, the key message being assiduously hidden from the Hindu majority, for how does one tell one's majority voters that the Indian welfare state actually expects all Indian men, and not just bad Muslims, to make sustainable provisions for divorced wives, as well as elderly parents? The only sustainable way to achieve this involves throwing such welfare obligations into the lap of the able-bodied man's family, thus holding society, here specifically the ex-husband, accountable for welfare burdens. Almost nobody has picked up that this matches new European welfare policies.[90]

Through later research on Muslim divorce cases,[91] I found highly experienced High Court judges quietly applying a basically equitable, justice-focused formula.

82 W. Menski, 'Law, State and Culture: How Countries Accommodate Religious, Cultural and Ethnic Diversity. The British and Indian Experience' in Marie-Claire Foblets, Jean-François Gaudreault-Desbiens and A.D. Renteln (eds.), *Cultural Diversity and the Law. State Responses from Around the World* (Bruylan 2010), 403–446.
83 Menski, 'Beyond Europe' (2007), 207.
84 Menski (2010), 430.
85 Menski, 'Beyond Europe' (2007), 206–209.
86 *Danial Latifi v. Union of India*, 2001(7) SCC 740.
87 Menski, 'Beyond Europe' (2007), 207.
88 Menski (2010), 433, n. 95.
89 Ibid., 434.
90 Edward L. Rubin, *Soul, Self & Society: The New Morality & the Modern State* (OUP 2015).
91 See W. Menski, 'Double Benefits and Muslim Women's Postnuptial Rights' 2007(2) *Kerala Law Times*, Journal Section, 21–34 and W. Menski, 'Literate Kerala, Bribes and a New Case

Ascertaining the monthly needs of a divorced Muslim wife, one multiplied this sum by 12, and then again by seven, to obtain a lump sum for seven years of reasonable provision for a divorced wife, probably allowing her to rebuild her life during that period. At the Family Court level, it transpired in 2015, in complete contrast to earlier fieldwork evidence from 2004, that judges were awarding destitute divorced women of any community the maximum amounts they could squeeze out of recalcitrant ex-husbands, while middle-class women found their claims rejected on the ground that securing 'lipstick money' was not the Court's task. This is further evidence of what I have elsewhere called 'slumdog law', gender-sensitive affirmative action for the benefit of destitute divorced wives in Indian courts today.[92]

Seen in this light, current discourses over the legal validity of the instant triple *talaq* seem devised to maintain the momentum of a deliberately engineered focus on alleged deficiencies in traditional Indian Muslim law. This gender politicking also maintains the call for a UCC, but cleverly distracts from the predicaments of India's general national policy about protection of all divorced Indian wives. This deliberately cultivated blind spot, a rather massive patch, indicates the continued conspiratory engagement of Indian state elites and various 'progressive' sets of scholars and commentators in frying their own small fish at the cost of better justice for all of India's divorced women. Neither continued Muslim-bashing nor the introduction of a UCC would offer destitute divorced women any realistic remedies. The hard task ahead is the painstaking development of a context-sensitive, balanced approach to gender justice which offers divorced Indian women the fullest possible protection through an indirect welfare state system that actually turns to the divorcing husband rather than opening state coffers.

Almost unnoticed, India's Family Courts have started implementing that massive process. We now urgently need socio-legal research to see how this works at the various court levels. The right balance should, I suggest, avoid a scenario in which Indian men would no longer wish to marry in the first place (as already happens more and more), given the progression of the laws on post-divorce maintenance risks being unfairly weighted against men. In view of earlier warnings about a trend for 'insurance by divorce',[93] and the prediction that, like in England, 'disposal of the property will be the prime topic for dispute, not the grounds for divorce',[94] this writing has been on the wall for some time.

---

of *Mata*: On the Limits of Judicial Patience and Legal Realism' 2008(4) *Kerala Law Times*, Journal Section, 21–31.

92 Menski (2012), 245.

93 Tahir Mahmood, *Personal Laws in Crisis* (Metropolitan 1986), 127–130.

94 Derrett (1978), 16.

Conclusions

What the almost forgotten nineteenth-century German jurist Rudolf Stammler (1856–1938) called 'the right law' remains a key concept also for current analyses of skilful judicial kite flying in India while securing sustenance for distressed and economically disempowered, divorced wives. That such notions of 'justice' and 'the right law' remain heavily contested could be documented in much more detail. Today's overpowering global focus on human rights and international law has blown ships of law, and also India's kites of law, into an aggressive claims-focused direction in well-meaning yet often unrealistic efforts to improve gender justice. Exaggerated gender rhetoric and excessively one-sided blaming of men for marital breakdown will not assist impoverished women, who still need activist, gender-sensitive court support in many contested cases. Where self-controlled ordering at individual and family level has failed and divorced women face destitution, while the divorcing man has resources that he could be expected to share, a welfare state that promises its people basic justice, whether directly or indirectly, must step in with activist zeal to raid the pockets of ex-husbands. India's official law on this subject is in place, powerful and sophisticated. The Shah Bano saga and its convoluted aftermath teach us that, typical for a state beyond Europe, India is deeply aware of the necessarily plural legal engagements required to handle this enormous challenge in a massive country where many people still go hungry. India is not Finland or Switzerland. Suitable sustainable remedies are not found, despite well-meaning assertions to the contrary,[95] through the magic of producing more state law or uniformising reforms. The bottleneck of balanced justice, not only for Muslim divorced wives, can manifestly be removed by better practical implementation of the existing laws. That laborious but doable task requires continued judicial alertness in the new climate of plurality-conscious navigation, by multiple legal actors, including women who know their rights and can fly their own kites responsibly.

Selected bibliography

Flavia Agnes, 'Muslim women's rights and media coverage' (2016) 51:20 *Economic and Political Weekly* 13.

Domenico Amirante, *Lo stato multiculturale* (Bononia University Press 2015).

J.N.D. Anderson, 'Pakistan: An Islamic state?' in R.H.C. Holland and G. Schwarzenberger (eds), *Law, justice and equity* (Sir Isaac Pitman and Sons 1967).

Gad Barzilai, 'Beyond relativism: Where is political power in legal pluralism?' (2008) 9:3 *Theoretical Enquiries in Law* 395.

Masaji Chiba (ed.), *Asian indigenous law in interaction with received law* (Chipa 1986).

Vasudha Dhagamwar, *Towards the uniform civil code* (NM Tripathi Pvt. Ltd 1989).

95 See Leila, *Talking of Justice. People's Rights in Modern India* (Aleph 2014), written by a retired senior female Judge.

Seán Patrick Donlan and Lukas Heckendorn Urscheler (eds), *Concepts of law. Comparative, jurisprudential, and social science perspectives* (Ashgate 2014).

J. Duncan and M. Derrett, *The death of a marriage law* (Vikas 1978).

Ko Hasegawa, 'Normative translation in the heterogeneity of law' (2015) 6:3–4 *Transnational Legal Theory* 501.

Khaled Hosseini (2003) *The kite runner* (Bloomsbury 2003).

Christophe Jaffrelot, *India's silent revolution: The rise of low castes in North Indian politics* (Permanent Black 2003).

Tahir Mahmood, *Personal laws in crisis* (Metropolitan 1986).

Werner Menski, *Comparative law in a global context: The legal systems of Asia and Africa* (CUP 2006).

Werner Menski, 'Beyond Europe' in Esin Örücü and David Nelken (eds) *Comparative law. A handbook* (Hart Publishing 2007) 189.

Werner Menski, 'Double benefits and Muslim women's postnuptial rights' (2007) 2 *Kerala Law Times*, Journal Section 21.

Werner Menski, 'The uniform civil code debate in Indian law: New developments and changing agenda' (2008) 9:3 *German Law Journal* 211.

Werner Menski, 'Literate Kerala, bribes and a new case of mata: On the limits of judicial patience and legal realism' 2008(4) *Kerala Law Times*, Journal Section 21.

Werner Menski, 'Flying kites in Pakistan: Turbulences in theory and practice' (2009/10) 1:1 *Journal of Law and Social Research* 41.

Werner Menski, 'Law, state and culture: How countries accommodate religious, cultural and ethnic diversity. The British and Indian experience' in Marie-Claire Foblets, Jean-François Gaudreault-Desbiens, and A.D. Renteln (eds.) *Cultural diversity and the law. State responses from around the world* (Broylan 2010) 403.

Werner Menski, 'Ancient and modern boundary crossings between personal laws and civil law in composite India' in Joel A Nichols (ed.) *Marriage and divorce in a multicultural context* (CUP 2012) 219.

Werner Menski, 'Legal simulation: Law as a navigation tool for decision-making' (2014) 59:2.1 *Report of Japan Coast Guard* Academy 1.

Werner Menski, 'Bangladesh in 2015: Challenges of the iccher ghuri for learning to live together' (2015) 1:1 *Journal of Law and Politics*, University of Asia-Pacific 9.

Werner Menski, 'Still asking for the moon? Opening windows of opportunity for better justice in India' (2016) 49:2 *Verfassung und Recht in Übersee* 125.

Sushmita Nath, 'Accommodating religious demands and gender-justice concerns: Indian state practices after the Shah Bano judgment' (2013) 126 (January) *Asien* 45.

Mudasir Nazar, 'Pakistan's frontline status, war on terror and the Jama'at E-Islami response' (2016) 36:2 *South Asia Research* 143.

Thangkhanlal Ngaihte, 'Armed forces in India's Northeast: A necessity review' (2015) 35:3 *South Asia Research* 368.

Esin Örücü, 'Judicial navigation as official law meets culture in Turkey' (2008) 4:1 *International Journal of Law in Context* 35.

Suhas Palshikar and Sanjay Kumar, 'Participatory norm: How broad-based is it?' (2004) 39:51 *Economic and Political Weekly* 5412.

Praveen Rai, 'Women's participation in electoral politics in India: Silent feminisation' (2017) 37:1 *South Asia Research* 58.

Alison Dundes Renteln, *The cultural defense* (OUP 2004).

Edward L., Rubin, *Soul, self & society: The new morality & the modern state* (OUP 2015).

Amartya Sen, *The idea of justice* (Penguin 2009).
Leila Seth, *Talking of justice: People's rights in modern India* (Aleph 2014).
Brian Z. Tamanaha, C. Sage and M. Woolcock (eds), *Legal pluralism and development: Scholars and practitioners in dialogue* (CUP 2012).
William Twining, *Globalisation and legal theory* (Butterworths 2000).
Marco Ventura, *From your gods to our gods* (Cascade Books 2014).
Ihsan Yilmaz, *Muslim laws, politics and society in modern nation states: Dynamic legal pluralisms in England, Turkey and Pakistan* (Ashgate 2005).

6 On lifelong and fixed-term marriage

A study in estrangement

Jan M. Smits

Introduction

The work of Esin Örücü abundantly shows the great value of the comparative approach towards law. This value lies primarily in its potential to shift horizons and thus provide a different angle to a certain topic or question. Put in her own words, legal comparison permits 'to keep the communication and conversation going and allows cross-fertilisation'.[1] Although this is indeed a prominent feature of good comparative work, the discipline of comparative law is not unique in providing alternatives to existing outcomes. The law must always take into account alternative modes of thinking, no matter whether these are based on experience with a foreign law or are coming from other sources. The law will always benefit from *estrangement*, meaning that the familiar is compared with existing or untried solutions in order to clarify what the law ought to be.[2] This is why, among other fields, economics, empirics, psychology, ethics, and literary and cultural studies all offer approaches to law that are just as valuable as comparative analysis.[3] They confront us with the unfamiliar and thus allow for a better grounding, or rejection, of long-accepted rules.

True to this feature of legal analysis as estrangement, this chapter questions the long-standing rule that marriage is concluded for an indeterminate period of time. Few rules are more accepted than the one that, when partners enter into a marriage, they do so for life. Notwithstanding the possibility to divorce one's partner after marriage – accepted in all secular jurisdictions except the Philippines – marriage must be concluded as a lifelong bond or, in contractual

1 See e.g. Esin Örücü, *Critical Comparative Law: Considering Paradoxes for Legal Systems in Transition* (Kluwer 1999) 132–133.

2 See e.g. Shai Lavi, 'Turning the Tables on "Law and …": A Jurisprudential Inquiry into Contemporary Legal Theory' (2010) 96 *Cornell Law Review* 811, 817 and Jan M. Smits, 'Law and Interdisciplinarity: On the Inevitable Normativity of Legal Studies' (2014) 1 *Critical Analysis of Law* 75.

3 This does not mean that comparison with an existing solution adopted elsewhere has no distinct advantage compared to the exploration of some isolated idea: it offers the value of experiment. See Jan M. Smits, *The Mind and Method of the Legal Academic* (Edward Elgar 2012) 74 ff.

terminology, for an indeterminate term. This means that it is impossible to agree upon matrimony for, for example, only two or five years. The question is whether this is indeed the most appropriate rule to adopt. To this end, this chapter first attempts to establish the origins of marriage as a permanent bond. This traditional view is subsequently contrasted with an alternative propagated in Islamic law. Next, it provides an overview of recent proposals to introduce fixed-term marriage, followed by the presentation of the normative case for accepting temporary marriage before the chapter concludes.

Finding the origins of lifelong marriage

Anthropologists regard marriage as an institution that is common to all human cultures.[4] Although this does not mean that matrimony has taken the same form or served the same purpose throughout history, all modern secular jurisdictions regard it as a bond concluded for life. This is seen as so self-evident that legislators do not even take the trouble of putting this into explicit wording. Civil codes only tend to state that marriage is dissolved by way of death or divorce,[5] thus implying that any other way of terminating marriage is not possible. However, explicit references to marriage for life can still be found in Christian marriage vows (such as the 'till death us do part' formula used in the Anglican and Catholic churches).

As is often the case with age-old institutions, it is not easy to trace the motives of why a marriage must be concluded for an indeterminate term. It is possible that the existence of this rule can be explained historically, but that convincing reasons for its continued existence no longer exist. In the Western legal tradition, marriage as a lifelong bond seems based on an amalgam of religious, moral, and economic motives. Its religious background is that in medieval Europe it was Canon law that governed marriage, subsequently influencing the notion of civil marriage in later times. In Canon law, marriage was (and still is[6]) a bond which by its nature is perpetual and exclusive, no doubt based on several passages in the Bible that refer to marriage as an eternal and indissoluble institution.[7] This fits in nicely with the views of early Christian theologians who made the argument that the indissolubility of marriage is not only a legal rule but also a moral virtue. To Augustine, for example, one of the reasons why marriage is good is because it restrains sexual promiscuity, prevents procreation outside of matrimony, and would offer the optimal environment for the raising of children.[8]

4 See e.g. Donald Brown, *Human Universals* (McGraw Hill 1991).

5 Cf Art 227 French Code Civil, § 1313 German BGB, Art 1:149 Dutch BW and Art 161 ff Turkish Civil Code.

6 Thus, literally Art 1134 Code of Canon Law.

7 As the later Protestant doctrine could rely on e.g. Mark 10:9 and Matthew 19:6.

8 Augustine, *The Excellence of Marriage* (*De bono conjugali*, written around 401), in John E. Rotelle (ed.), *The Works of Saint Augustine: A Translation for the 21st Century* (New City Press 1999), Vol I–9: Marriage and Virginity) 5.5, 37.

It has been argued that the underlying rationale of lifelong marriage is surprisingly modern: at the risk of anachronistic interpretation, the impossibility to dissolve a marriage (mostly associated with the prohibition of divorce, but its ratio also applies to marriage for a determinate time) would be a means to protect women from being set aside by their husband and children to be protected within the family.[9] The evolution of marriage from a private contract to a public institution (first through the Church and later through the State) can be seen in this light: it allows those in power to have control over marriage and thus make it an instrument of achieving a public goal. As any deviation from the standard model of marriage should come about through contracting among the marriage partners, this would open up all the risks usually associated with unequal bargaining power: the more powerful spouse could contract away the protection that the law offers to his less potent partner. But as long as marriage is a *status*, this risk does not materialise: the partners are bound as soon as they 'say "yes" to the pre-packaged relationship'.[10] This is well captured in the old United States Supreme Court's qualification of marriage as an institution that cannot be modified, restricted, enlarged, or released upon the consent of the parties.[11]

This emphasis on the importance of marriage as a status, and not as a contract of which the terms are at the free disposal of the parties, can also be put in economic terms. One aspect of this lies in the clear signal it sends to society about the marital status of people if marriage is only possible for an indeterminate term.[12] If for any type of marriage the two spouses have the intention to stay together for better or for worse, and until death does them part, this conveys a much clearer message to the outside world than the existence of different types of marriage bonds of varying length. Another aspect is that, despite romantic ideals about true love, marriage is an economic device in that it allows for swapping. Cohen puts it like this:

> Men and women have much that they can exchange with one another. Each has sex to offer ... Each had procreation to offer ... Then there is physical protection and income (and) homemaking and child-rearing ... The central point is that men and women each desire the other as providers of vital services.[13]

9 Masha Antokolskaia, *Harmonisation of Family Law in Europe: A Historical Perspective* (Intersentia 2006) 133.

10 Marjorie Schultz, 'Contractual Ordering of Marriage: A New Model for State Policy' (1982) 70 *California Law Review* 207, 232.

11 *Maynard v Hill*, 125 US 190, 211 (1888). See in more detail Jan M. Smits, *Elgar Advanced Introduction to Private Law* (Edward Elgar 2017), Chapter 5.

12 Eric A Posner, *Law and Social Norms* (Harvard University Press 2000) 71.

13 Lloyd R. Cohen, 'Marriage: the Long-Term Contract' in Anthony W. Dnes and Robert Rowthorn (eds) *The Law and Economics of Marriage and Divorce* (Cambridge University Press 2000) 13; see Smits (2017), Chapter 5.

Marriage thus enables the spouses to pool resources and share the costs of cohabitation and child-rearing. Economic analysis thus emphasises the gains from marriage compared to remaining single.[14]

Marriage as a swapping device clearly also serves an evolutionary goal. Anthropologist Helen Fisher spoke about the 'sex contract': because compared to other species the raising of a human child is a long and costly process, women gave sexual exclusivity in exchange for food hunted by men and protection of both her and her child.[15] Marriage was in this respect a social support system.[16] The faint shadow of this in today's society is one partner specialising in earning the family income and the other partner doing more in the household. Marriage for an indeterminate term could be seen as an instrument to realise this: the services that partners exchange remain important during a lifetime and it would therefore be undesirable if they were able to escape from the bond with their current partner. In other words, each of the partners is only willing to make the investment if it can rely on the other partner staying with him or her.

There is much to say about the adequacy of these motives. As said before, they may explain why the current rule on marriage duration has come about, but this does not mean that they still offer convincing arguments against a fixed-term marriage in today's context. The religious argument is already unconvincing because there is no reason why a religious, or any other personal, view of matrimony should inform the state's concept of marriage. It is not because Christians or Muslims have a particular view of matrimony that the law must share it. The same can be said of the moral argument, one that is never decisive in the law. The need for protection of the weaker marriage partner is clearly an important motive, but it seems obvious that the rule against short-term marriage is not the only means of realising such protection. The mere existence of divorce procedures is already evidence of this. This calls for an exploration of alternatives. The first step in this exploration is to contrast the familiar Western view of marriage with the fixed-term marriage contract known as *nikah mutah* in Islamic law.

Temporary marriage in Islamic law: *nikah mutah*

It was argued in the above that estrangement could help us to better understand and think through familiar solutions. Probably the greatest contrast with lifelong marriage, as we know it in the Western legal tradition, is provided by an institution in Islamic law known as *nikah mutah*.[17] Of this 'pleasure marriage' based on

14 Cf Gary S. Becker, 'A Theory of Marriage' in Theodore W. Schulz (ed.), *Economics of the Family* (University of Chicago Press 1974).

15 Helen E. Fisher, *The Sex Contract: The Evolution of Human Behavior* (William Morrow 1982), 89.

16 Cf Robin Fox, *Reproduction & Succession: Studies in Anthropology, Law, and Society* (Transaction Publishers 1997) 48.

17 On which see e.g. John L. Esposito (ed.), *The Oxford Dictionary of Islam* (Oxford University Press 2003) 221.

the Quran[18] the duration can be agreed upon by the parties themselves. In practice its length ranges from one hour to 99 years. There is no need for a *mullah* to be present upon concluding the marriage, but the prospective wife must utter a set formula with which she declares to marry the prospective husband for a set period of time and against a counter-performance the latter has to agree upon (the *ajr*, usually consisting of a sum of money).[19] Although at present *mutah* is only accepted in the Twelver Shia Islam, and practised in particular in Iran,[20] it was once applied in the entire Muslim world. The prophet Muhammad is supposed to have allowed it for men while travelling, for example when on pilgrimage. The current requirements for *mutah* to be valid are that the bride is not married, is a Muslim, and is preferably either divorced or no longer a virgin. After expiration of the fixed-term marriage the woman needs to abstain from sexual intercourse for two months (the period of *iddah*) before she can marry somebody else, thus allowing to identify the father of the child in case of pregnancy.

Mutah is a much-debated institution in the Muslim world. On the one hand, it is seen as a means to have legitimate sexual intercourse without having to enter into a 'real' permanent marriage. This explains why *mutah* has come to play an important role in Iran, where, under the conservative regime of the ayatollahs, sexual intercourse before marriage is strictly prohibited. *Mutah*, actively promoted by the Iranian authorities, allows young couples more freedom in having the love life they desire.[21] It would also allow widows and divorced women to enter into a legitimate relationship. On the other hand, *mutah* is often qualified as a form of legalised prostitution. It is said to lead to exploitation of vulnerable young women without any obligation on the part of the man. Men who are regularly married (or even entered into all four marriages that Muslim law allows) can have as many temporary marriages as they desire.

It is important to emphasise that, although obligations of maintenance vis-à-vis the spouse or ex-spouse during or after the temporary marriage do not exist (unless agreed upon in the marriage contract), children born out of *mutah* must be recognised and supported by the man. These children formally have equal status (also as to inheritance rights) as children born out of a permanent marriage. In practice, however, it will be easier for men to deny fatherhood in cases where the child was born from *mutah*.[22] The community is also likely to regard the child as second rank compared to children born from a permanent marriage.

18 According to the Shia Verse 4:24 allows *mutah*, but the text is interpreted by Sunnites to mean the exact opposite, namely that Muhammad prohibited *mutah*. Some Sunnites, however, do accept the somewhat similar *misyar* marriage.

19 See, also for a detailed description of *mutah* on other points, Shahla Haeri, *Law of Desire: Temporary Marriage in Shi'I Iran* (Syracuse University Press 1989) 50 ff.

20 Where it is called *sighe* (in Farsi).

21 Robert Tait, 'Iranian Minister Backs Temporary Marriage to Relieve Lust of Youth' *The Guardian* (London, 4 June 2007); Haeri (1989) 8.

22 Ann Black, Hossein Esmaeili and Nadirsyah Hosen, *Modern Perspectives on Islamic Law* (Edward Elgar 2013) 124; Haeri (1989) 2.

With this, *mutah* serves different goals. It not only legalises sexual intercourse (whether paid for or not) but also offers some protection to children born out of the temporary relationship.[23] However, it is doubtful whether this protection is very effective in practice. Together with the lack of maintenance obligations towards the (ex-)wife in case of a longer-lasting *mutah*, this explains the controversial nature of the institution. *Mutah* thus confronts us with both the potential and the boundaries of fixed-term marriage. It appears problematic for the law to accept a relationship in which a partner only enjoys the benefits and does not carry the burdens, as in a case where children are born from the relationship or one of the partners' financial position is unduly affected by it. But nothing stands in the way of a temporary marriage in cases where such burdens do not arise. And if they do, it is the task of the law to provide effective protection.

Testing the waters: proposals to introduce fixed-term marriage

Until now, little has been said about societal views on the appropriate duration of marriage. This contribution cannot aim for an empirical survey, but it can test the waters by describing some recent proposals to introduce fixed-term marriage.[24] These proposals all stem from one common idea, namely that the law must better reflect the current reality that approximately half of all marriages end in divorce. It is therefore no longer apt to expect a marriage to last a lifetime. In addition, fixed-term marriage can de-stigmatise divorce and thus reduce the emotions among ex-partners and the impact it has on children. It could also lead to a more amicable separation if the marriage is to end anyway. From the economic perspective fixed marriage would also simply be more efficient: it is less costly to decide on separation ex ante (and renew the vows if desired) than to pay for it ex post.[25] Finally, the advantage of taking the ''till death us do part' vow out of marriage may be that spouses can try out the institution as well as each other, although this argument may carry less weight in those jurisdictions where cohabiting before tying the knot is a common thing to do.

Several of these motives are taken up in a recent book written by Susan Pease Gadoua and Vicki Larson. Psychologist and relation therapist Gadoua and journalist Larson argue that lifelong marriage is an outdated and unrealistic ideal that leads to 'blaming, shaming, and sense of failure' in a case where the partners are

23 Black (2013) 124.

24 The idea is not as new as one might think: see for an anecdotal overview of 19th century authors on this topic: Vicky Larson, 'A Temporary Marriage Makes More Sense than Marriage for Life' (*Aeon.co*, 16 November 2015), https://aeon.co/ideas/a-temporary-marriage-makes-more-sense-than-marriage-for-life.

25 Stefania Marcassa and Gregory Ponthiere, 'Until Death Do Us Part? The Economics of Short-Term Marriage Contracts' (2014) 53 *Population Review* 19.

not able to live up to it.[26] They call upon people to marry more consciously and creatively and upon the legislator to provide alternatives to the one-size-fits-all model of marriage for life. Examples of this creativity can already be seen in relationships such as commuter marriage, open marriage, and swing marriage. Legislative intervention took place in some American states that introduced the possibility of a covenant marriage that only allows divorce in cases of fault. Next to other types of 'do-it-yourself marriages', Gadoua and Larson propose that the legislator should also introduce a 'starter marriage', a marriage that is renewed or terminated after the period the parties have agreed upon.[27] In such a marriage, the wedding partners can agree upon a range of different things, including finances, homemaking, pet care, and holidays. Although Gadoua and Larson limit their proposal to cases in which the partners do not intend to have (or already have) children, it is not difficult to see that a starter marriage is not incompatible with having children as long as mandatory rules offer sufficient protection to the latter.

In the last few decades, various legislators around the world have also proposed to introduce marriages with an expiry date. In 1971, Maryland legislator Lena King Lee proposed a 'Marriage Contractual Renewal' Bill that would allow partners to conclude a marriage for three years with an option to renew for successive periods of three years.[28] German politician Gabriele Pauli made a similar proposal in 2007 when she argued that marriage should be limited to seven years as the average time a marriage tends to last before divorce.[29] Her main reasoning was that marriage must be seen as a documentation of love and is therefore to be re-evaluated every once in a while. Yet another proposal was made in 2011 by the biggest party in the Legislative Assembly of Mexico City (a town that has its own competences in the area of family law and already introduced same-sex marriage in 2010). This proposal was primarily motivated by the wish to allow newlyweds to exit their marriage after two years in a way other than through a tedious divorce procedure: better to renew a harmonious relationship than to go through a painful and expensive divorce with all the hassle this involves in cases where the relationship fails. The contract was to include provisions on how to deal with children and property in case of a split.[30]

Despite the fact that none of these proposals was turned into law, they did stir discussion and inspired various writers to argue in favour of fixed-term marriage as

26 Susan Pease Gadoua and Vicki Larson, *The New 'I Do': Reshaping Marriage for Skeptics, Realists and Rebels* (Seal Press 2014) 5.

27 Ibid., 45 ff.

28 Maryland, General Assembly, 1973, LR3, filed 10 April 1972, www.law.umaryland.edu/marshall/specialcollections/lenaleepapers/marriagecontractbill.pdf.

29 Wahlprogramm Gabriele Pauli 19 September 2007, on which Karsten Polke-Majewski, 'Sieben Jahre für Frau Pauli' (*Zeit Online*, 19 September 2007), http://www.zeit.de/online/2007/38/pauli-csu-ehe-probezeit.

30 'Proponen en México matrimonios temporales de dos anos' (*Pijamasurf*, 30 September 2011), http://pijamasurf.com/2011/09/proponen-en-mexico-matrimonios-temporales-de-dos-anos.

well. In one op-ed Paul Rampell, who uses the term 'marital lease' or 'wedlease', describes how this could work:

> Two people commit themselves to marriage for a period of years – one year, five years, 10 years, whatever term suits them. The marital lease could be renewed at the end of the term however many times a couple likes. It could end up lasting a lifetime if the relationship is good and worth continuing. But if the relationship is bad, the couple could go their separate ways at the end of the term. The messiness of divorce is avoided, and the end can be as simple as vacating a rental unit.[31]

The contract would have to describe what is owned by each of the spouses and in case a child is born during the wedlease it automatically continues until the child is 18 years old.[32] This need to accommodate children within the statutory regulation of wedlease led another writer, Matt Richtel, to argue that the initial marriage term must be 20 years, the average time of marriage before the children leave the nest.[33]

Opposite these adherents of temporary wedlease stand those who still believe in wedlock or marriage for life. They have not only the ideal of romantic love on their side, but can also point at the fact that in most Western jurisdictions divorce has become much easier than it was in the past, in particular if a couple has no children. And if they do have children, a fixed-term marriage may not help as extensive arrangements about maintenance and visitation rights need to be made anyway. In cases where such agreements were already made in the marriage contract itself, they are likely to be disputed at the time of divorce. Also, stigmatisation through divorce is at present much less of a problem than in the past and in so far as it is still a stigma, not renewing the wedlease (or even the decision to enter into the temporary marriage) is likely to be as much of a dishonour as divorce itself. But, as will be set out in the next section, this still leaves space for temporary marriage.

From wedlock to wedlease?

The above shows that marriage, with the many forms it takes at different times and locations, is very much a functional institution serving a public goal in a certain social and cultural setting. Marriage reinforces the social and cultural norms of a society. It is clear that marriage today is no longer the marriage of 100 or even 25 years ago. Does this also mean that the time is ripe for accepting fixed-term

31 Paul Rampell, 'A High Divorce Rate Means It's Time to Try "wedleases"' *The Washington Post* (Washington, 4 August 2013).

32 Rampell (2013).

33 Matt Richtel, 'Till Death, or 20 Years Do Us Part' *New York Times* (New York, 28 September 2012).

marriage? This is ultimately a question of how far we wish to go with the contractualisation of family relationships. True to Frederick William Maitland's qualification of contract as 'that greediest of legal categories',[34] there has been in the last few decades a constant trend towards a bigger role for contracting in family law. Prenuptial agreements and agreements about, for example, cohabitation, sperm donation, adoption, co-parenting, and surrogacy are increasingly concluded. The fact that these 'deals' are not always enforceable does not make them less influential in helping people to create and sustain families.[35]

The duration and contents of marriage have so far escaped this trend towards more private autonomy. Spouses have to say 'yes' to a fixed package in which the conditions for entry and exit and benefits and responsibilities of the spouses are strictly defined. Family law thus continues to put severe limits on marriage formation and maintains the importance of marriage status rather than allowing a contract to prevail.[36] It was seen above that this seems motivated by a wish to protect the weaker marriage partner and potential children. But if one regards marriage as an egalitarian liberal community of two equal people,[37] it is not clear why the spouses should not be allowed some more autonomy. This fits the current norm that there should not be only one single family model to which everyone must conform, but instead a greater diversity of different models each to be supported by the law.[38] Seen from this perspective, nothing stands in the way of introducing a fixed-term marriage.[39] Despite the doubts discussed above, one argument firmly stands in favour of such an arrangement: it allows the spouses to better think through the consequences of their marriage (because of the need to draft specific agreements about the contents of the relationship and its ending) and to reassess their commitment on a regular basis. This is a better legal framework for a bond that is unlikely to last for life than the current lifelong marriage. In those jurisdictions where divorce is costly and complicated, it also provides an easy and efficient exit from an unhappy relationship.

This raises the question of how such wedlease should be regulated by the legislator. This is a matter of both the length and renewability of the marriage and the protection of potential children. As to the length of the wedlease, the legislator could offer a set menu of various options, ranging from a two-year trial marriage to a seven-year contract and traditional lifelong marriage. Reassessment

34 F.W. Maitland, 'Introduction' to Otto Gierke, *Political Theories of the Middle Age* (Cambridge University Press 1900), xxiv.
35 Martha M Ertman, *Love's Promises: How Formal & Informal Contracts Shape All Kinds of Families* (Beacon Press 2015), xii.
36 Cf. Jill Elaine Hasday, 'The Canon of Family Law' (2004) 57 *Stanford Law Review* 825, 837.
37 Carolyn J Frantz and Hanoch Dagan, 'Properties of Marriage' (2004) 104 *Columbia Law Review* 75.
38 See in more detail Ertman (2015), Part IV.
39 This conclusion is also reached by Marjorie M Shultz, 'Contractual Ordering of Marriage: A New Model for State Policy' (1982) 70 *California Law Review* 204, 223.

of the temporary marriage and its terms will have to take place at the end of the two- or seven-year period. The partners then have three options: renew the existing term, turn their wedlease into a permanent marriage or end their relationship in conformity with what was agreed upon in the wedlease.

The other concern of the legislator must lie with providing for the risks of automatic termination of the marriage. The reason why current family law tends to dislike a quick and easy exit from marriage and requires court intervention for divorce is the wish to protect the more vulnerable partner and potential children. This is obvious in so far as children are concerned: if the former spouses are not able to agree upon child custody, visitation rights, and maintenance (or their arrangements are not in the child's best interests), the court must intervene for the sake of protecting the child's interest. The criterion of the child's best interests is such an overriding factor that it is in fact quite irrelevant what the type of relationship the parents previously had.

Insofar as the spouses themselves are concerned, present family law protects the weaker spouse by reorganising income and assets upon divorce. This follows from the already mentioned nature of marriage as a swap contract: spouses swap financial support for care of home, hearth, and children.[40] They make their career decisions together: one gives up a job or works fewer hours, the other makes a career. In the eyes of the law, care, feeding, and cleaning are just as important to this partnership as bringing in the family income. Divorce does therefore not end the legitimate expectation of the spouse (in traditional families the wife) to be compensated for her investment. This view of marriage as a common project with financial solidarity is even more important now that women suffer higher costs than men when exiting marriage as it will usually be more difficult for them to find a suitable job (in cases where they did not work or only worked part-time) or a new partner.

The question is whether this motive also applies to fixed-term marriage, which typically contains an agreement about the consequences of marriage for the spouses' finances. One reason why the law has long[41] been reluctant to respect the spouses' well-considered agreement about what happens to property, pension rights, and spousal maintenance upon divorce is that choices made at the time of marriage are often insufficiently informed about what the parties' financial position will be at the time of separation. But this is different in the case of fixed-term marriage, which not only lasts for a shorter period but also requires the spouses to reconsider their financial arrangements at the time of marriage renewal. In this sense, a wedlease can leave more space for the couple's individual autonomy.

40 Martha M Ertman, 'Marital Contracting in a Post-*Windsor* World' (2015) 42 *Florida State University Law Review* 479, 481; see Smits (2017), chapter 5.

41 This is naturally dependent on the jurisdiction involved: seen as less problematic in civil law jurisdictions, English law now also provides more room for prenuptial agreements: see *Radmacher v Granatino* [2010] UKSC 42, 75.

Conclusions

The law benefits from estrangement. Confrontation of existing rules with new insights from other jurisdictions or non-legal sources can help to improve the law. The above offers an example of how confrontation of a longstanding and seemingly self-evident rule with insights from Islamic law, relation therapy, and public opinion can lead to statutory innovation. It shows that lifelong marriage is not self-evident at all. If this rule is seen as fulfilling the function of protecting spouses and children, fixed-term marriage is a viable alternative if it offers similar protection. The current rules on divorce, guaranteeing reasonable arrangements on property, pension rights, and spousal maintenance and providing for child custody, visitation rights, and child maintenance, offer inspiration for how to regulate wedlease. Apart from saving the high financial and emotional costs of divorce, its introduction will have the distinct advantage that (future) spouses have to better think through the consequences of their marriage and reconsider their commitment at set intervals. This calls for a legislative experiment introducing wedlease next to marriage for life. This is the comparative method in action: estrangement leading to a concrete proposal to make the existing law better suited for today's reality.

Selected bibliography

Gary S. Becker, 'A Theory of Marriage' in Theodore W. Schulz (ed.), *Economics of the Family* (University of Chicago Press 1974).

Lloyd R. Cohen, 'Marriage: The Long-Term Contract' in Anthony W. Dnes and Robert Rowthorn (eds), *The Law and Economics of Marriage and Divorce* (CUP 2000) 13.

Martha M. Ertman, *Love's Promises: How Formal & Informal Contracts Shape All Kinds of Families* (Beacon Press 2015).

Susan Pease Gadoua and Vicki Larson, *The New 'I Do': Reshaping Marriage for Skeptics, Realists and Rebels* (Seal Press 2014).

Shai Lavi, 'Turning the Tables on "Law and …": A Jurisprudential Inquiry into Contemporary Legal Theory' (2010) 96 *Cornell Law Review* 811.

Stefania Marcassa and Gregory Ponthiere, 'Until Death Do Us Part? The Economics of Short-Term Marriage Contracts' (2014) 53 *Population Review* 19.

Esin Örücü, *Critical Comparative Law: Considering Paradoxes for Legal Systems in Transition* (Kluwer 1999).

Marjorie Schultz, 'Contractual Ordering of Marriage: A New Model for State Policy' (1982) 70 *California Law Review* 207.

Jan M. Smits, 'Law and Interdisciplinarity: On the Inevitable Normativity of Legal Studies' (2014) 1 *Critical Analysis of Law* 75.

7 What is the role of norms and values in the reception of law?

Richard De Mulder and Helen Gubby

Introduction

In examining law as transposition, Esin Örücü concluded that the '[i]nternalisation of norms and standards by the people in a recipient system is crucial if there are to be fruitful developments'.[1] The difficulty in transposing law from one legal system to another does not so much concern the structure and substance, the techniques and forms, 'but the transposition of values and content'.[2] Certainly, norms and values play a role in legal systems. However, it is argued here that it is not the norms and values of the recipient system that guide the success of a reception of law, but simply whether the importation fulfils a need, or in other words is useful, in that system at that particular moment in time. What works, what is effective, generates norms and values. In this sense, the law is pragmatic.

Concepts of law

In the philosophy of law, the concept of law has rather changed over time.[3] Four periods in the development of the understanding of law can be distinguished:

1. Natural law – given by God
2. Natural law – given by nature
3. Laws of physics
4. The conventionalistic (or 'nominal') concept of law.

In periods 1 and 2, from 1500 to 1800, the concept of natural law is dominant. This concept of law is based on the idea that the laws of social life can be derived by contemplating the essence of human nature and society. The concept of law in these first two periods is normative: natural law reflects the ideal order of society. In period 1, it is normative in the sense that the laws of social life are ascribed

1 Esin Örücü, 'Law as Transposition' (2002) *The International and Comparative Law Quarterly*, 205–223, 221

2 Ibid., 222.

3 J.M.M. de Valk, *De evolutie van het wetsbegrip in de sociologie* (Van Gorcum- Assen 1979) 129.

to a higher legislator, i.e. God. If God is seen as an almighty powerful and good entity, how could his creation not be perfect? In period 2, the concept of natural law changes as reason takes God's place. In natural law theories, therefore, factual and normative statements are not distinguished from each other.

Period 3 extends from 1800 to 1900, and is the period in which the physical law concept is dominant; social science looks for general laws for society as a whole. The physical concept of law is a factual one. No norm for behaviour is given, but a factual pattern is established. The basic idea is that the laws of the physical world and society can be discovered by perceiving the regularities in physical and social phenomena. Reality is of a strongly deterministic character; it is not possible to deviate from the laws.

Period 4 is the period after 1900. During this period, the conventionalistic, or nominal, concept of law is dominant. This concept of law is based on the assumption that it is human beings themselves who create order in what they perceive in the world. Whether there is, or is not, a fixed order in reality is an open question. Laws are always of a hypothetical character and are only valid for a limited group of phenomena during a limited period.

Gutter was not convinced that social scientists, and particularly sociologists, had really considered these developments.[4] In particular, he expressed concern that lawyers had adopted the outdated natural law ideas from sociologists and believed that norms, based on religious or 'natural' values could control human behaviour. He consequently regarded the legal discipline as unscientific. It had not taken on the changes in the understanding of law in the third and fourth periods as referred to above.

For our argument here, it is particularly important to notice that in empirical sciences, 'laws' have been stripped of their values and have lost their normative content. In the legal discipline,[5] however, laws are still normative in the sense that they prescribe behaviour; they express the will of a person or a construct (such as the state, the sovereign, or the legislator). This is not a problem as long as those who are supposed to adhere to these laws have somehow accepted them. However, many sociologists and legal scholars, adhering to the outdated natural law concept of law, will still be certain that they perceive deeper values in those laws. Their legal and philosophical arguments are often based on the values that they perceive.

In Figure 7.1, an analytical scheme of the four concepts of law is given. This kind of analysis will be explained in the following section.

4 Cor Gutter, *Niet weten wat men niet weet* (Rotterdam, public lecture 30 November 1972,) 13, Retrieved 10 October 2016 from http://hdl.handle.net/1765/30556.

5 It would be confusing to call it 'science' precisely because of the concept of law that is used in the legal discipline.

Concepts of law

	Given by some intelligence	Given by nature
Norms and facts mixed	God-given natural law	Natural law given by nature
Facts	Conventionalistic laws	Laws of physics

Figure 7.1 Concepts of law.

Legitimation of state power according to Weber

An important issue is whether the exertion of state power, such as the enforcement of legal norms, will be accepted by citizens. In other words, do those citizens perceive the use of this power to be *legitimate*?[6] If state power is legitimised (accepted by the citizens) it is more than mere power; it is authority. Weber is a leading scholar with respect to this subject and it is useful to analyse his ideas about this concept a little further here.[7] This will also provide an opportunity to introduce a useful technique for analysing some of the concepts that are crucial in this paper.[8]

Weber provides a three-fold divide (or 'trichotomy') for the legitimacy of power: charismatic power, traditional power, and rational power.[9] The terms used in this three-fold division may be defined as follows. Charismatic leaders derive their authority from 'impulses', the emotions of those who acknowledge their authority. Traditional authority is power wielded by either an individual or a group, which is accepted because the individual or the group wielding that power is felt to have always had that power.[10] The acceptance of power can also be rational: power is accepted because citizens are conscious of the fact that chaos could result if that power is not exercised, or that power is useful in some other, more specific, way.

6 A.D. Belinfante and J.L. de Reede, *Beginselen van het Nederlandse staatsrecht* (Wolters Kluwer 2015)

7 Max Weber, *Wirtschaft und Gesellschaft* (Köln, Kiepenheuer & Witsch1964).

8 Johan Goudsblom introduced this technique. J. Goudsblom, *Balans van de sociologie* (1st edn, Sun1974).

9 In the former section, an example was the divide between natural law concepts, physical laws and conventionalistic laws.

10 'Durch eingelebte Gewohnheit', according to Weber.

Weber's concepts of 'charismatic', 'traditional', and 'rational' authority, at first glance, appear to be unclear. However, these concepts become clearer through establishing two relevant aspects: (1) whether a person accepts the authority over him in a conscious or unconscious way and (2) whether he or she would or would not be prepared to accept this authority if it were exercised by someone else. The rational forms of legitimacy, and particularly the 'pragmatic' kind, appear to be more modern than charisma and tradition.

Legitimation of state power

	less conscious	**more conscious**
not flexible	traditional	rational?
flexible	charismatic	rational?

Figure 7.2 Legitimation of state power.

Weber uses a four-fold division to explain his statements on legitimacy (Figure 7.2).

1. Goal rational; considered and calculated
2. Value rational; conviction and principle
3. Affective; impulse, emotion
4. Traditional; '*durch eingelebte Gewohnheit*'

This produces the following scheme (Figure 7.3):

Legitimation of state power

	less conscious	**more conscious**
not flexible	traditional ("conservative")	value-rational ("principled")
flexible	charismatic ("spontaneous")	goal-rational ("pragmatic")

Figure 7.3 Legitimation of state power: refined.

The modern requirement of goal rational legitimacy for the activities of authorities is probably responsible for much of the tension in the modern, democratic constitutional state. It is increasingly often demanded that state activities should be in themselves useful. Legitimation on the grounds of charisma, tradition, or simply because 'one should have law and order' is not as easily accepted as it once was.

Models of man

After the development of the conventionalistic concept of law, there have been new developments within the field of economics. The fourth period acknowledged laws as a product of the human mind, and therefore not immutable. This new understanding of empirical laws as a product of human intellectual activity provided empirical disciplines with a certain freedom to move from one paradigm[11] to another. The success of market economies has coincided with the acceptance of a new basic paradigm, which is used to study human behaviour and hence to explain, predict, and attempt to direct it.[12]

As pointed out before, many social scientists and most lawyers base their approach on a sociological, natural law way of thinking. They use a model of man often referred to as the sociological model of man, *homo sociologicus.* According to this theory, man's behaviour will conform to the norms of the group to which he or she belongs. However, in modern economic theory, it is the *homo economicus*, or a somewhat more sophisticated form of this model, the REMM (Resourceful, Evaluating, Maximising Model) which now provides the prevailing model of man in economics and managerial science. Processes are studied from the point of view of methodological individualism. In other words, processes are described, explained, and predicted on the basis of the behaviour of individuals. In *homo economicus*, the idea is that monetary values can always be attributed to goods and services and that that is what people maximise. The REMP (Resourceful, Evaluating, Maximising Person) maximises whatever he or she appreciates as desirable or useful, even if no monetary value can be measured. Likewise, the REMP is able to take costs into account even if their value is not precisely known, such as the costs of information. Furthermore, the 'Resourceful' aspect not only means that the REMP is creative in finding new ways of maximising utility, but he or she also *anticipates* future circumstances and/or effects of his or her behaviour.[13]

11 In the sense of Thomas Samuel Kuhn, *The Structure of Scientific Revolutions*, University of Chicago Press 1970.

12 Michael C. Jensen and William H. Meckling, 'The Nature of Man' (1994) 7 *Journal of Applied Corporate Finance* (Summer 1994) 4–19.

13 Richard De Mulder, 'Introduction. Some Remarks on Rationality' in Richard V. De Mulder (ed.) *Mitigating Risk in the Context of Safety and Security. How Relevant Is a Rational Approach?* (Rotterdam ESL/OMV 2008).

The REMP wants all his or her decisions to be of maximum use to him or herself. Ideologically, this may sound rather denigrating. The REMP would at first sight appear to be a 'calculating citizen'. Yet, in practice, this selfishness is not necessarily negative because REMPs realise that their own interests are better served by taking other people into account. Negotiation is the lifeblood of the REMP.

The modern science of economics (and in its wake business studies) has influenced marketing, production management, and finance. Rational decision-making, as Jensen and Meckling meant it, has become the norm. Modern managers talk in terms of expenditure and profit, and of the probability of occurrences taking place. Decisions are made based on knowledge of these variables in the past and the expectations about them in the future. This approach in economics is also referred to as 'agency theory', as it provides powerful insights into the sometimes problematic relationships between agents and principals in all kinds of organisations.[14] It is interesting to see that the Sveriges Riksbank Prize in Economic Sciences in Memory of Alfred Nobel 2016 was awarded jointly to Oliver Hart and Bengt Holmström for their contributions to *contract theory*. Contract theory is based upon the REMM and analyses, among other things, how problems associated with measuring costs and revenues could lead to different arrangements in contracts. It provides, for example, an explanation for the success or failure of the privatisation of services or public/private cooperation. This shows how scientifically relevant the new REMM is. For the subject matter of this article, however, it is particularly interesting to note that the theories of the Dutch legal scholar Paul Scholten are consistent with this new approach in the modern social sciences. He was a contract theorist *avant la lettre*. [15]

The law cannot be applied if rationality is ignored

Social and economic interests drive the behaviour of people and must be taken into account by the law in order to be effective. The determining factor is rationality. Paul Scholten's legal scholarship is highly respected within the Netherlands but is little known in common law jurisdictions. Scholten saw the law as embedded within society. Every law is based upon an appreciation of social interests,[16] and is aimed at exerting an influence on what happens in that social reality. For Scholten, law is an open system, for the law is never complete, not only because it is the imperfect product of human beings, but also because it is constantly being added to. As every law is based on an appreciation of social interests, Scholten argued that the meaning of a law could, therefore, only be understood in the

14 Michael C. Jensen and William H. Meckling, 'Theory of the Firm: Managerial Behavior, Agency Costs and Ownership Structure' (1976) 3 *Journal of Financial Economics* (October) 305–360.

15 Paul Scholten, *Asser's Handleiding tot de Beoefening van het Nederlands Burgerlijk Recht: Algemeen Deel* (Zwolle 1974).

16 As in the REMP model, these interests are not just financial.

context of human relations and that requires a place to be made for sociological or teleological interpretation. Whether the grounds for applying a rule in a particular way are considered to fit will depend upon whether they appear consistent with the legal order as a whole.[17]

Illustration: rape within a marriage

There is no better illustration of Scholten's argument that laws are based upon an appreciation of social interests, than the decision of the Supreme Court of the United Kingdom, at that time the House of Lords, in the case of *R* v *R* 1992.[18] The matter at issue here was the long-standing common law rule that a husband was immune from prosecution for raping his wife. The question was whether the Sexual Offences (Amendment) Act 1976 altered this long-standing rule, and this depended upon the interpretation of the word 'unlawful' in the Act. The court declared that:

> we do not consider that we are inhibited by the Act of 1976 from declaring that the husband's immunity as expounded by Hale no longer exists. We take the view that the time has now arrived when the law should declare that a rapist remains a rapist subject to the criminal law, irrespective of his relationship with his victim. … This is not the creation of a new offence, it is the removal of a common law fiction which has become anachronistic and offensive, and we consider that it is our duty having reached that conclusion to act upon it.[19]

In other words, the old rule was out of step with the social reality of British society and the role of women in that society in the 1990s. The old rule simply did not work anymore; it was no longer socially useful. As it was no longer socially useful, it was no longer rational and hence lacked legitimation.

This shift sees the beginning of a move to generate stronger norms concerning individual sexual rights, not just for women. Until 1994, English law meant that the offence of rape could only be committed against a woman. A few years later the description of the law on rape was amended in the Criminal Justice and Public Order Act 1994 to make it possible not only for women to be seen by the criminal law as the victims of rape but also men. This provision later became part of the new description of the *actus reus* of rape in the Sexual Offences Act 2003.[20]

Were these changes the result of the norms and values of British society as a whole at that point in time? Or were these changes simply an answer to a new

17 Scholten, *Asser's Handleiding tot de Beoefening van het Nederlands Burgerlijk Recht*, 2–4, 34–35, 75–76, 130–131.

18 *R v R* [1992] 1 AC 599 (HL).

19 Ibid., 611.

20 Sexual Offences Act 2003, s 1 (1).

social reality in which the homosexual voice would no longer be repressed, and homosexual men and women refused to be treated as second class citizens? A strong interest group had emerged, a group that intended to negotiate decisions of maximum use to themselves. It would go on to generate new norms and – according to some – values. One sign of that is the passing into English law of the Marriage (Same Sex Couples) Act in 2013.

Does the same apply to an importation of a law? Is the determining factor of success not the existing norms and values of the recipient society, but simply whether the imported law works well in the context of the given social reality at that time? An interesting case study is the shift in patent law in the United States from the indigenous first-to-invent system to the first-to-file system.

Illustration: patent law

Where more than one person has worked upon developing a patentable invention, the first-to-file system awards the patent to the inventor who is the first to file a patent application, regardless of the date of invention. The patent system in the USA prior to the America Invents Act (AIA) 2011 was based on a first-to-invent doctrine. This first-to-invent doctrine meant that where there were competing inventors for the same invention, the patent would be granted to the inventor who first conceived of the invention and then diligently reduced it to practice by filing a patent application (or actual reduction to practice). In the event of a dispute as to who was the first inventor, the case was adjudicated by the US Patent and Trademark Office (USPTO) in a process known as interference proceedings. In the interference proceeding, there would be a review of the evidence of conception, reduction to practice, and diligence. Upon completing the review, the USPTO would determine who had actually made the invention first.

Almost every other country in the world had a patent system based on the first-to-file doctrine already. The use of the first-to-invent doctrine meant, therefore, that the USA was out of step with most other patent jurisdictions, including the European patent system. One of the few other countries that used a first-to-invent system, its neighbour Canada, changed to a first-to-file system in 1989. The Philippines, which had been influenced by American patent law, switched in 1998. The USA finally followed suit by including this provision in the AIA in 2011. The switch applies to all patent applications filed in the USA on or after 16 March 2013. The shift in legal doctrine raises interesting questions: does the move to a first-to-file system represent a change in norms in the USA? Will the first-to-file system be successful in the USA or, to paraphrase Örücü, can a 'living law' fed and fertilised by the specific nutrients and conditions of a foreign soil' take root or grow new roots when implanted elsewhere?[21]

In the case of the first-to-file doctrine, its roots are to be found in British soil. It was in the latter part of the eighteenth century, during the early stages

21 Örücü, 'Law as Transposition' 211.

of the industrial revolution in Britain, that the foundations of pre-modern patent law were being laid. A number of patent disputes heard by the common law courts concerned the matter of who was 'the true and first inventor', one of the requirements for a patent grant under the Statute of Monopolies 1624. There are few reported patent cases in the eighteenth century. Determining the court's attitude to the term 'inventor' in this period, therefore, must be gleaned from what evidence has remained. One of the earliest cases which considered the matter is the case of *Dollond v Champney* 1766. Dollond brought several actions for the infringement of a patent granted to his father in 1758 for making achromatic lenses. The case brought against Champney was not reported, but it is probably this 1766 case that is referred to in *Boulton and Watt v Bull* in 1795.[22]

In *Boulton and Watt v Bull*, Buller, J. observes that the objection to Dollond's patent at the time appears to have been that he was not the first inventor. It had been argued that a certain Dr Hall had made the same discovery before him, but this Dr Hall had 'confined it to his closet'. It was held in Dollond's case that, as Dr Hall had not made his discovery public, Dollond was to be considered the first inventor.[23] It would appear, at least from this reading of Dollond's case, that the term 'first inventor' was taken to mean the one who first made an invention public, whether or not he was the original creator. For the purposes of the Statute of Monopolies, the first person to disclose the invention to the public, even if he was not chronologically the first inventor was the 'true and first inventor' and therefore had the right to the patent grant.

In *Forsyth v Riviere* 1819, it was again confirmed that what was important in the eyes of the law was not who was the original inventor, but who first published or introduced the invention to the country. In the words of Abbott, CJ:

> if several simultaneously discover the same thing, the party who first communicates it to the public, under a patent, is entitled to the benefit of it; the law not requiring that the patentee should be literally the first inventor, or finder-out of something new, but that it was sufficient if the patentee be the first publisher or introducer of the invention.[24]

Original creativity was secondary to disclosure. The patent monopoly was the price paid by society for the disclosure of the invention to the public. In the eighteenth century, judges were often uncomfortable with the notion of awarding monopolies but, in the case of new inventions, the justification expressed for this monopoly was that the invention had not been known before, hence it took nothing away from the public, if the invention was successful it would be good for trade and commerce, and that the inventor's knowledge would be freely available to the public upon the expiry of the patent. Lord Eldon even rejected

22 *Boulton and Watt v Bull* 1795, 2 H Black.
23 Ibid., 470.
24 *Forsyth v Riviere* 1819, 1 HPC 788/1 CPC 404.

the notion that a patent should be seen in the light of a monopoly, for it was a bargain with the public and hence the patent specification was of a contractual nature.[25] While inventors could be awarded for their ingenuity, time and costs incurred in developing the invention, the benefit to society was the paramount consideration. The first-to-file, the first therefore to make the knowledge available, had the right to the patent.[26]

In the USA, on the other hand, the patent system has been traditionally linked to the first-to-invent principle. The US Code of Patents states:

> Whoever invents or discovers any new and useful process, machine, manufacture, or composition of matter, or any new and useful improvement thereof, may obtain a patent therefor, subject to the conditions and requirements of this title.[27]

Constitutional arguments have been put forward to interpret this provision as embedding the first-to-invent principle: it is 'whoever invents' who 'may obtain a patent'. The inventor is, then, by definition, the one who invented that particular invention first. The US Constitution grants Congress the power:

> To promote the Progress of Science and useful Arts, by securing for limited Times to Authors and Inventors the exclusive Right to their respective Writings and Discoveries.[28]

Proponents of the first-to-invent principle interpret this as the power to grant patents to inventors, not to 'winners of the race to the Patent Office'. The change to the first-to-file provision has met with some resistance. In 2014, MadStad Engineering even filed a constitutional challenge to the AIA, on the grounds that the first-to-file provision of the AIA was unconstitutional. The case was dismissed on appeal by the Federal Circuit Court, although on the ground that MadStad Engineering lacked standing.[29]

An equally deep-seated objection to the first-to-file system is quite simply that it was unfair. US proponents of the American first-to-invent principle have seen the first-to-invent principle in a normative context: it is only morally right that the patent should be awarded to the one who invented the technology first, not to the first patent applicant.[30] The original inventor is further protected in the American system by a grace period of one year. Unlike the European patent system, this allows an inventor to file for a patent even if the subject matter has

25 *Harmar v Playne* 1807, 1CPC 257.
26 Helen Gubby, *Developing a Legal Paradigm for Patents* (Eleven 2012).
27 35 US Code § 101.
28 United States Constitution, Article I, Section 8.
29 *MadStad Engineering, Inc v U.S. Patent & Trademark Office* 756 F.3d 1366 (Fed Cir 2014).
30 Martin J. Adelman et al., *Patent Law* (Thomson/West 2008) 80.

been already disclosed to the public, if the inventor files for a patent within 12 months. Certain disclosures will not be seen as prior art. The AIA has maintained this grace period, although commentators argue that the grace period under the new law does not give as robust protection as under the previous law.

An attachment to the traditional first-to-invent principle, with its grace period, and a rejection of the first-to-file system, as unfair, could generate emotions. This was alluded to by David Kappos when he was the director of the USPTO. He disclosed that people could become quite angry during discussions on this issue and even walk out of meetings.[31] Nonetheless, even opponents of the first-to-file system had to acknowledge one major advantage of that system: it was simple and efficient.

It is argued here that the first-to-file system will become accepted in American law, not because it feeds into the existing norms and values of that society, but because it works. It is the answer to a new social reality: the globalisation of patents, the ever-increasing number of patent applications and the need to find an effective way to administrate the system.

The number of patents filed has been steadily increasing globally. In the year the AIA was passed into law, 2011, there were more than 535,000 patent applications made to the USPTO.[32] The pressure of work and time constraints placed on patent examiners have led to complaints of poor quality control concerning the USPTO.[33] Backlogs have been the inevitable result.

The first-to-invent system entailed a costly and lengthy interference proceeding to determine in disputed cases who, of the two inventors claiming the invention, conceived of the invention first. Although such interference proceedings were certainly not an everyday occurrence for the USPTO, the first-to-file system makes these proceedings superfluous. The administration becomes simpler. Given the pressures all patent offices are under these days, this type of streamlining becomes attractive.

Furthermore, there is continuing international pressure to harmonise patent law. Filing a patent application for many businesses is not restricted to filing for protection in the domestic market, but patent protection is sought in all jurisdictions relevant to their business. Having a greater degree of uniformity is in the interests of business. The USA, with its first-to-invent system, was out of step with other major patent systems.

In time, it might even be the case that the norm will shift in the USA to seeing the first-to-file system as a fair system. As patent litigation in the USA is notoriously expensive, the cost of a patent interference proceeding could prove

31 David Kappos during the American Chamber of Commerce in the Netherlands seminar, Amsterdam, 2 April 2012.

32 USPTO Patent Statistics, https://www.uspto.gov/web/offices/ac/ido/oeip/taf/us_stat.htm, accessed 10 October 2016.

33 Warren K. Mabey, 'Deconstructing the Patent Application Backlog' (2010) 92 *Journal of the Patent and Trademark Office Society* (Spring), 212–214.

prohibitive for a small inventor, quite possibly leading to the abandonment of the patent application. The first-to-file system does not put small inventors at a disadvantage because, if they have filed their application first, this will be the determining factor and not who has the financial assets to initiate interference proceedings. However, this is not the only reason that the first-to-file system will become embedded in American law. The first-to-file system will be accepted because it answers a social need; a more effective and easier way of dealing with patent applications in an era in which the number of patent applications is constantly growing and markets have become global. This system is more rational; it is more useful to individuals as well as society as a whole.

Conclusion

Örücü poses the question of whether a living law, fed and fertilised by the specific nutrients and conditions of a foreign soil, can take root or grow new roots elsewhere. She considers that the internalisation of norms and standards by the people in a recipient system is crucial to successful growth. It is argued here that the most crucial factor determining success is not the internalisation of foreign norms and standards by the recipient system, but quite simply whether the law meets a social need because it is useful.

This approach based on social reality is built upon a number of fundaments. The first fundament is that the natural law concept is obsolete. The second fundament is Weber's theory that acceptance of power can also be rational: the enforcement of norms by the state is accepted as legitimate because citizens are conscious of the fact that chaos could result if that power is not exercised ('value rationality') and furthermore, most particular forms of exertion of power will only be accepted if they are useful per se ('goal rationality'). The third fundament is Scholten's theory that the social functionality of the law is the basis for legal decision-making. This is supported by the fourth fundament, the replacement of the old sociological model of man by the model of man developed in the field of economics: the REMM – the Resourceful, Evaluating, Maximising Model. Social and economic interests drive the behaviour of people. Using that model, a legal norm will be successful if it is useful in a certain society; it works well and becomes embedded in the norms of that society because it responds to a social need and furthers individual interests. It is the utility of an imported law that is the primary factor in determining the successful transference of that law to foreign soil.

Selected bibliography

Martin J. Adelman et al., *Patent Law* (Thomson/West 2008).
A.D. Belinfante and J. L. de Reede, *Beginselen van het Nederlandse staatsrecht* (Wolters Kluwer 2015).
Johan Goudsblom, *Balans van de sociologie*, (1st edn, Sun 1974).
Helen Gubby, *Developing a legal paradigm for patents* (Eleven 2012).

Cor Gutter, *Niet weten wat men niet weet* (Rotterdam, public lecture 30 November 1972,) 13, Retrieved 10 October 2016 from http://hdl.handle.net/1765/30556.

Michael C. Jensen and William H. Meckling, 'The nature of man' (1994) 7 *Journal of Applied Corporate Finance* (Summer) 4–19.

Michael C. Jensen and William H. Meckling, 'Theory of the Firm: Managerial Behavior, Agency Costs and Ownership Structure' (1976) 3 *Journal of Financial Economics* (October) 305–360.

Thomas Samuel Kunh, *The Structure of Scientific Revolutions* (1970).

Warren K. Mabey, 'Deconstructing the patent application backlog' 92 (2010) Journal of the Patent and Trademark Office Society (Spring) 212–214.

Richard De Mulder, 'Introduction. Some Remarks on Rationality in Richard V. De Mulder (ed.), *Mitigating Risk in the Context of Safety and Security. How Relevant Is a Rational Approach?* (Rotterdam ESL/OMV 2008).

Esin Örücü, 'Law as Transposition' (2002) 51 *International and Comparative Law Quarterly* 205.

Paul Scholten, *Asser's Handleiding tot de Beoefening van het Nederlands Burgerlijk Recht: Algemeen Deel* (Zwolle 1974).

J. M. M. de Valk, *De evolutie van het wetsbegrip in de sociologie* (Van Gorcum-Assen 1979) 129.

Max Weber, *Wirtschaft und Gesellschaft* (Köln, Kiepenheuer & Witsch 1964).

8 The Influence of the *trias politica* of Montesquieu on the first Dutch Constitution

Emese von Bóné

Introduction

This chapter is about the influence of the *trias politica* on the first Dutch Constitution of 1798, a typical example of French legal transplant.[1] It deals with the ideas of a great French lawyer and with a typical French 'product' which was introduced in the Netherlands during the period of the Batavian Republic (1795–1806).[2] The *trias politica* had a great impact not only in France but also in the former Dutch Republic. The theory of dividing powers was a new phenomenon in the eighteenth century and is still considered as one of the most important basics for the rule of law. In this chapter, I will explain the creation of the Batavian Republic as this period is important for the Netherlands because of the introduction of the first Dutch Constitution. I will show the influence of the *trias politica* of Montesquieu on the first Dutch Constitution. I will end the chapter with an epilogue and a conclusion.

The creation of the Batavian Republic

The Batavian Republic came into existence through the Batavian Revolution which had a prologue, before the French Revolution broke out, in the so-called Patriot movement.[3] In the Republic of the Seven Sovereign States the governing patricians, who were called the regents (*regenten*) and especially those of the province of Holland, started to co-operate with the middle-class (patriot) democratic movement against the Stadholders. The rise of the middle-class emancipation movement had its roots in eighteenth-century Rationalism.[4] The Patriot

1 This focus on legal transplant echoes the work of Esin Örücü in the project of *Transfrontier Mobility of Law and Legal Transplants*, based at the Legal History, Comparative Law and Computer Science Department, Erasmus University of Rotterdam.

2 Since 1795 the Netherlands was a vassal state of France and since 1811 it was part of the French Empire.

3 Simon Schama, *Patriots and Liberators, Revolution in the Netherlands, 1780–1813* (Collins 1977).

4 Willem Verkade, *Democratic Parties in the Low Countries and Germany, Origins and Historical Developments* (Universitaire Pers Leiden 1965) 37.

movement was directed against the regent oligarchy because the latter did not allow the middle-class to take part in the city councils. The so-called Patriots, however, attacked not only the regent class but also the Stadholder.[5] William V was deprived of several offices, but the Orangists, with the support of England and Prussia, launched a counter-offensive. This so-called Revolution was stopped in mid-course in 1787 when a Prussian army acting on behalf of Prince William's wife Wilhelmina, who was the sister of the King of Prussia, invaded the country and re-established Prince William V in his function as Stadholder in The Hague.[6]

In the Northern Netherlands, the Republic was ruled once again by the Orangist party from 1787 until 1795.[7] In 1795, the restored Orangist party, called the Prinsgezinden, was overthrown by the new regime of the Patriots. The Orangist party, which was faithful towards the Stadholder, was dedicated to a policy of no-change. The Orangists were afraid because of the ruling Dutch middle-class Patriots who were earlier (when they emigrated in 1787 to France) witness of the French Revolution.

The French Revolution was a result of the suppression of the ordinary people, the load of taxes for the '*tiers état*' and the financial crisis. The works of philosophers and lawyers of the Age of Enlightenment, such as Rousseau and Montesquieu, also played a role. It was the period of rapid advance in print culture and publishing, in world exploration, and in the rapid growth of science and technology. All of this had a profound impact on the political and cultural landscape. At the end of the century of the Age of Enlightenment, the American Revolution and the French Revolution set in motion developments that dominated political life also in the Netherlands.

The intervention of French revolutionary troops in the Netherlands changed the situation anew and the final victory of the 30,000 'Patriots' was secured in 1795.[8] In 1795, the old structure of the Republic of the Seven United Provinces

5 The Stadholder had formerly been the provincial representative of the territorial prince in the Republic of the Seven Sovereign Provinces. The Stadholder was the servant of the provincial states, who appointed him. In the course of the Republic the authority of the Stadholder increased. He was commander-in-chief of the army and navy, he presided over all provincial and general bodies and he appointed most officials. Several provinces appointed the same person as their Stadholder and from 1590 onwards two men, the Prince of Orange and one other member of the Nassau family held all stadholderships. After 1748 the Stadholdership became again heritable.

6 Pieter Geyl, *History of the Low Countries, Episodes and Problems, The Trevelyan Lectures 1963 with Four Additional Essays* (Macmillan 1964) 173.

7 The Republic (1581–1795) was a federal state of seven sovereign provinces. Each province was ruled by the provincial states. The Republic was governed by the States-General, which consisted of representatives of the seven provinces. Some territories were not independent but were governed by the States-General. These so-called Generality lands were Staats-Brabant, Staats-Limburg, Staats-Vlaanderen and Opper-Gelder.

8 These dissident groups, the 'Patriots' and the Orangists or the so called 'Prinsgezinden' cannot properly be described as parties in the modern sense but are better described as factions. Willem Verkade, *Democratic Parties in the Low Countries and Germany, Origins and Historical Developments* (Universitaire Pers Leiden 1965) 37.

was swept away by the Batavian Revolution. This was the Dutch response to the events in France although the Batavian Revolution was not a bloody Revolution.

When the French came to the Batavian Republic, in January 1795, the Orangist regime collapsed, and the Stadholder Prince William V fled to England. The French left the Revolution-making to the Patriots. Then, in one town after another, beginning with Amsterdam, the oligarchic town governments were dismissed and, to the acclamations of the crowd, new men were installed. These new men were well-to-do citizens immediately below the regent class. The revolutionised town councils in each of the seven provinces sent deputies to their respective provincial capitals, and thus the personnel of the provincial state assemblies was changed everywhere. The revolutionised state assemblies sent deputies to compose a new States-General in The Hague, which was still an assembly of delegates from the provinces. The first task was now to reorganise and strengthen the union.

In May 1795, a peace treaty was concluded in The Hague and the Batavian Republic, which became a vassal state of France, was then recognised by the French Republic.[9] The Republic had to give up the territories of Maastricht, Venlo, and Staats-Vlaanderen, which became French. The old, loose confederation was replaced by a real union.[10] The Batavian Republic was divided into eight departments with totally different borders from those of the former Republic. The departments were named after rivers, such as the department of de Schelde, which was the former province of Zeeland. The departmental administrations had very little power and were very different from the former provincial states.

It was especially the province of Holland (which was crushed under the weight of provincial debt) and radicals, also known as Unitarians, who wanted the provinces to be merged into the Republic. The northern provinces such as Groningen and Friesland were composed of Federalists (conservatives) who wanted to maintain the structure of the old Republic and the autonomy of the provinces.[11] Many of the old Patriots (anti-Orangists) also did not want to give up their provincial positions. In the following years, the Batavian Republic became more moderate, but the Constitution of the short-lived radical regime of 1798 was retained. The confederation was replaced by a unified state, the Batavian Republic. The old system of provincial sovereignty was gone for good.

For the first time, there was national unity, i.e. one constitutional and administrative system for the whole country. Long disputes and negotiations were necessary before a National Assembly could be elected by the Batavian people as

9 The peace-treaty between France and the Batavian Republic was concluded in The Hague on 16 May 1795. According to this treaty France recognised the Batavian Republic and an offensive and defensive alliance was concluded with the Republic. The Batavian Republic became the first '*république soeur*' of France.

10 The old republic was a federation of sovereign states.

11 Between the Unitarians and the Federalists stood the Moderates. Pieter Gerbenzon and Nikolaas Algra, *Voortgangh des Rechtes* (6e druk, Samsom H.D. Tjeenk Willink 1987), 187–188.

a whole in the spring of 1796.[12] From then on, no general assembly had to depend on the provincial state assemblies, but instead represented the nation. The first Constitution, which had 918 articles, was called the Thick Book.[13] This Constitution was rejected on 8 August 1797.[14] A second National Assembly was still quarrelling over the new Constitution when the radical minority, made up of Unitarians supported by the French army, carried out a *coup d'etat* on 22 January 1798.[15] The Federalists were removed from the Assembly, and a unitary Constitution was carried through.[16] The State Secretary of France, Delacroix, came solemnly to the National Assembly and gave a speech in which he stressed the importance of a Constitution.[17]

On 23 April 1798, the first Dutch Constitution was accepted in Parliament. The representatives in the National Assembly had to swear that they would reject federalism, aristocracy, and government by a Stadholder.[18] In less than four months, the Batavian people got their first Constitution, which was a reproduction of the French Constitution of 1795.[19]

The first Dutch Constitution of 1798 and the influence of Montesquieu

In August 1789, the *Déclaration des droits de l'homme et du citoyen* was approved by the French Parliament. This document was based on the theory of the social contract and the *trias politica*.[20] In the works of Rousseau and Montesquieu, we

12 *Het Plan van Constitutie van 1796*, bewerkt door Leonard de Gou ('s-Gravenhage 1975), IX.

13 *Het Ontwerp van de Constitutie van 1797*, De Behandeling van het Plan van Constitutie in de Nationale Vergadering met een facsimile uitgave van het ontwerp constitutie, bewerkt door Leonard de Gou, volume III ('s-Gravenhage 1985).

14 *De Staatsregeling van 1798*, Bronnen voor de totstandkoming, volume I, bewerkt door Leonard de Gou ('s-Gravenhage 1988), XII.

15 *De Staatsregeling van 1798*, I, XXXVIII and XLVIII. Dag verhaal van de Constituerende vergadering representeerende het Bataafsche Volk, 22 januari 1798, II, 2. Diederik Verhagen, *L'influence de la Révolution française sur la première Constitution Hollandaise du 23 Avril 1798*, (thèse de droit Paris, pub. Kemink 1949), 24.

16 The first Constitution is of 1798. *Staatsregeling voor het Bataafschen Volks*, Johannes Allart (Amsterdam 1798). Willem-Jan van Hasselt, *Verzameling van Nederlandse staatsregeling en grondwetten*, 16e druk (Alphen aan den Rijn 1987). Diederik Verhagen, *L'influence de la Révolution française sur la première Constitution Hollandaise du 23 Avril 1798* (thèse de droit Paris, pub. Kemink 1949), 22–24.

17 Diederik Verhagen, *L'influence de la Révolution française sur la première Constitution Hollandaise du 23 Avril 1798* (thèse de droit Paris, pub. Kemink 1949), 22, 23. *'Qu'il vous doive une Constitution libre, sage, basée sur les principes qui peuvent seuls fonder la félicité publique.'*

18 Diederik Verhagen, *L'influence de la Révolution française sur la première Constitution Hollandaise du 23 Avril 1798* (thèse de droit Paris, pub. Kemink 1949), 22.

19 DiederikVerhagen, *L'influence de la Révolution française sur la première Constitution Hollandaise du 23 Avril 1798* (thèse de droit Paris, pub. Kemink 1949), 29.

20 *Déclaration des droits de l'homme et du citoyen,* Articles 3, 6, 16.

find the freedom of individuals. The freedom of individuals was based on a social contract and gave the opportunity to form a state. The *Déclaration des droits de l'homme et du citoyen* was not the first declaration of human rights, as it has the same roots as the *Bill of Rights of Virginia* of 1776.[21]

In the Batavian Republic, a Declaration of Human rights was also promulgated on 24 January 1795. This Declaration was based on the French *Déclaration des droits de l'homme et du citoyen.*[22] It is an example of a French transplant in the Batavian Republic.

The first Dutch Constitution was created in 1798 and contained the following principle: *De Bataafse republiek is één en ondeelbaar*, which means the Batavian Republic is one and indivisible. The Dutch Constitution of 1798 contained the sovereignty of the people. In Article 10 of the chapter *Burgerlijke en Staatkundige grondregels* of the first Dutch Constitution, it was stated that the Batavian people choose a government by the people, by representation. As we can see the first Dutch Constitution of 1798, was based on the conception of Rousseau's *Du Contrat Social*:

> *Chacun de nous met en commun sa personne et toute sa puissance sous la suprême direction de la volonté Générale.*[23]

The first Constitution was also inspired by the ideas of Montesquieu. Charles-Louis de Secondat, the jurist and political philosopher was born at the Château de la Brède, near Bordeaux on 18 January 1689. After his father's death in 1713, he inherited the title of baron de la Brède. He was appointed Counsellor of the Bordeaux Parliament (1714), and in 1716 he inherited his uncle's title of Baron de Montesquieu and also his office, serving as the Deputy President of the Parliament. Montesquieu satirised French institutions as we can read in his first major work *Lettres persanes.*[24] Because of the success of his first major work Montesquieu was elected in 1728 to the French Academy. In the same year he set out for a grand tour of Europe, particularly England, where he remained from 1729–1731. Montesquieu's greatest work *De l'Esprit des Lois* (the *Spirits of Laws*) was published in 1748.[25] It is a comparative study of three types of government:

21 BenVermeulen, 'Déclaration des droits de l'homme et du citoyen (1789)' in Hemme Battjes en BenVermeulen (eds), *Constitutionele klassiekers* (Ars Aequi Libri 2007), 102–112.

22 Gerbenzon and Algra, *Voortgangh des Rechtes*, 184.

23 Jean Jacques Rousseau, *Du Contrat Social*, chapitre VI. Each of us puts his person and all his power under the supreme direction of the general will (own translation).See also: Alfons Dölle, 'De Constitutie voor het Koninkrijk Holland van 1806' in Jan Hallebeek and Boudewijn Sirks (eds), *Nederland in Franse schaduw, recht en bestuur in het Koninkrijk Holland (1806–1810)* (Hilversum 2006) 25–45.

24 Montesquieu, *Oeuvre completes*, textes présenté et annoté par Roger Caillois (Bibliothèque de la Pléiade, Gallimard 1949), vol. I, 133–373.

25 Ibid., vol. II.

republic, monarchy, and despotism.[26] Montesquieu held that governmental powers should be separated and balanced to guarantee individual rights and freedom. In his *De l'Esprit des Lois*, we find his theory of the *trias politica*:[27]

> In every government there are three sorts of powers: the legislative; the executive in respect to things dependent on the law of nations; and the executive in regard to matters that depend on the civil law....
>
> When the legislative and executive powers are united in the same person, or in the same body of magistrates, there can be no liberty....
>
> Again there is no liberty, if the judiciary power be not separated from the legislative, and executive. Were it joined with the legislative, the life and liberty of the subject would be exposed to arbitrary control; for the judge would be then the legislator. Were it joined to the executive power, the judge might behave with violence and oppression.
>
> There would be an end of everything, were the same man or the same body, whether of the nobles or of the people, to exercise those three powers, that of enacting laws, that of executing the public resolutions, and of trying the causes of individuals.[28]

In *De l'Esprit des Lois*, we read that there is no freedom if the three powers are reunited in one power. We find this principle of the *trias politica* also in Title III of the first Dutch Constitution of 1798: *de vertegenwoordigende hoogste magt* (the Legislative power), *de uitvoerende magt* (Executive power) and *de regterlijke magt* (the Judicial power). The Legislature was called *het Vertegenwoordigend Lichaam*, which was the House of Representatives and was a kind of Parliament. The Legislative Body chose the Directory, which comprised five directors. The Directory formed the Executive Body. The Executive Body appointed eight

26 Three types of government we see also in the work of Aristotle, *Politeia*, book III, chapter 14: democracy, aristocracy, and monarchy although Montesquieu gives a different interpretation to these governments. Montesquieu puts 'aristocracy' and 'democracy' together and reduces these forms of government to 'republic'. Monarchy is according to Montesquieu a constitutional Monarchy. *De l'Esprit des Lois*, Livre XI, chap 9 and 11.

27 See English translation of Montesquieu, *Spirits of Laws: Great Books in Philosophy* (Prometheus Books, New York).

28 Montesquieu, *De l'Esprit des Lois*, livre XI, 6: *Il y a dans chaque état trois sortes de pouvoirs: la puissance législative, la puissance exécutrice des choses qui dépendent du droit des gens, et la puissance exécutrice de celles qui dépendent du droit civil ... Lorsque dans la même personne ou dans le même corps de magistrature, la puissance législative est réunie à la puissance exécutrice, il n'y a point de liberté. Il n'y a point encore de liberté si la puissance de juger n'est pas séparée de la puissance législative et de l'exécutrice. Si elle était jointe à la puissance législative, le pouvoir sur la vie et la liberté des citoyens serait arbitraire: car le juge serait législateur. Si elle était jointe à la puissance exécutrice, le juge pourrait avoir la force d'un oppresseur. Tout serait perdu si le même homme, ou le même corps des principaux, ou des nobles, ou du peuple, exerçaient ces trois pouvoirs: celui de faire des lois, celui d'exécuter les résolutions publiques, et celui de juger les crimes ou les différends des particuliers.*

Ministers. The Unitarians in the Parliament were very much inspired by the ideas of the Age of Enlightenment and the French Revolution.[29] The separation of powers was a *novum* because in the former Republic of the Seven Sovereign States the three powers were not separated. In the former Republic the administration of justice was extremely divided in the various Dutch countries, although the judges were independent. Centralisation of the administration of justice was not realised before the French period. In the old Dutch Republic, the 'Hoge Raad van Holland and Zeeland' had existed since 1581. This court was the 'supreme court', but this 'supreme court' was only accessible for the provinces of Holland and Zeeland and not for the whole country because the old Dutch Republic was not a unitary state.

But what was the role of the judiciary in the theory of the *trias politica*? According to the text in *De l'Esprit des Lois*, it is possible that the law, which is clear-sighted in one sense, and blind in another, might in some cases be too severe. According to Montesquieu, the national judges are no more than the mouth that pronounces the words of the law ('*la bouche de la loi*'), which means that the judge is merely the mouth-piece of the law.[30] Montesquieu writes in his book *De l'Esprit des Lois*: In a republic, the very nature of the Constitution requires the judges to follow the letter of the law.[31] The national judges are no more than the mouth that pronounces the words of the law, mere passive beings, incapable of moderating either its force or rigour.[32]

The first Dutch Constitution of 1798 was a very long and detailed Constitution.[33] The '*Algemene Beginselen*' (general principles) and '*Burgerlijke en Staatkundige grondregels*' consisted of 72 articles. The '*Acte van Staatsregeling*' contained 308 articles with five appendixes and nine additional articles. The Dutch state looked like a confederation of free people. The Batavian Republic was 'one and indivisible'. In the division of the three powers we see the influence of Montesquieu although the three powers were not totally equal to each other because in Title III of the '*Staatsregeling*' we read the term '*Vertegenwoordigende Hoogste Magt*' which means that the Legislative power had the most (*hoogste* =

29 Jan Willem Schulte Nordholt, 'Het tertium comparationis- De Nederlandse Revolutie tussen de Amerikanen en de Franse in' in Wim Couwenberg (ed.), *Opstand der burgers. De Franse revolutie na 200 jaar* (Kampen 1988) 52–66.

30 Karel Schönfeld, 'Montesquieu en 'la bouche de la loi' (dissertation, University of Leiden 1979) 6. Jos Coopmans, 'Vrijheid en gebondenheid van de rechter vóór de codificatie' in *Rechtsvinding,opstellen aangeboden aan prof. dr. J.M. Pieters ter gelegenheid van zijn afscheid als hoogleraar aan de Katholieke Universiteit te Tilburg* (Kluwer 1970) 71–109. WillemWitteveen, *De triasleer onder spanning*, ed. Paul Cliteur en Mark Rutgers, (Groningen 1990) 29–51. Gerard Wiarda, *Drie typen van rechtsvinding* (Zwolle 1972) 7.

31 Montesquieu, *De l'Esprit des Lois*, livre VI, 3. '*Dans le gouvernement republicain, il est de la nature de la constitution que les juges suivent la letter de la loi*'.

32 Montesquieu, *De l'Esprit des Lois*, livre XI, 6.' *Les juges de la nation ne sont que la bouche qui pronounce les paroles de la loi; des être inanimés, qui n'en peuvent modérer ni la force ni la rigueur*.'

33 Roelof van Haersolte, *Inleiding tot het Nederlandse staatsrecht* (Zwolle 1983) 16–20.

highest) power. So according to the text of the Constitution, the Legislative power had more power than the '*Uitvoerend Bewind*' (the Executive power) and the '*regterlijke magt*', the Judicial power.

Epilogue and conclusion

In the years after the introduction of the first Dutch Constitution of 1798, French politics again influenced the situation in the Netherlands. In France, Napoleon carried out a *coup d'etat* in 1799, and he was the first Consul who took all the power. Under the influence of Napoleon, the Batavian Republic got a new Constitution in 1801, which was a less democratic Constitution than the former Constitution of 1798.[34] The Executive Body proposed the bill without consulting Parliament, and directly to the citizens who were entitled to vote. Parliament protested and was dismissed. Elections were held, but only 68,700 out of 416,000 citizens voted. About 52,000 citizens voted against the Constitution, and only 16,700 citizens voted in favour of a new Constitution.[35] Most of the electorate did not show up because it was disappointed in the political situation. Although so few people voted for the new Constitution it was accepted. Considerable changes were made: the task of Parliament became much more restricted and the Executive Body got much more power. The democratic principles of 1798, with the ideas of Montesquieu, were replaced by the principle of authority, which was carried out by the *Staatsbewind*, meaning Government of the State, which was composed of 12 members.[36] Meanwhile, Napoleon continued the war with England and this war was very expensive. Napoleon decided that, according to the new pact of 1803, the Batavian Republic should contribute to the war expenses.

On 2 December 1804, Napoleon crowned himself as emperor in the Notre Dame of Paris. He wanted more influence in the Batavian Republic. He appointed Rutger Jan Schimmelpenninck as *Raadspensionaris*, a kind of Counsellor of the Batavian Republic. The *Staatsbewind*, which was the Executive Body, was then replaced by the *Raadspensionaris*. The term *Raadspensionaris* was also used in the former Republic. The 'pensionaris' was a lawyer and was appointed by the city. He got a 'pensio' which is a salary. The provincial states of Holland also engaged a 'pensionaris' who was called *Raadspensionaris* or 'Landsadvocaat'.[37] The *Raadspensionaris* in the Batavian Republic was the executive power in the period of the Batavian Republic. A new Constitution was necessary to change the

34 Staatsregeling des Bataafschen Volks, Den Haag, Staatsdrukkerij 1801.

35 Albertus van Hulzen, *Vaderlandse geschiedenis*, volume 2, vierde druk (Wolters-Noordhoff, Groningen 1988) 79.

36 Staatsregeling des Bataafschen Volks, Den Haag, Staatsdrukkerij 1801, Article 29.

37 Emese von Bóné, 'Le pensionnaire municipal et sa double fonction; un homme politique et un acteur en justice souvent négligé' in René Robaye (ed.) *Les acteurs de la justice, magistrats, ministère public, avocats, huissiers et greffiers (XIIe–XIX siècle), Travaux de la Faculté de Droit de Namur* (Presses Universitaires de Namur 2002) 150–162.

executive power of the '*Staatsbewind*' with three directors in the Executive power of one a single person. This time only 4% of the electorate showed up. However, the new Constitution was accepted in 1805 and the *Raadspensionaris* got all the power.

The most important reason for changing the Executive power was that Napoleon wanted more influence in the Batavian Republic. That is why he appointed Rutger Jan Schimmelpennick as *Raadspensionaris*. The power of the Legislative Body became more restricted. In a very short period, namely 1798, in 1801, and in 1805, the Batavian Republic had changed its structure many times and the Constitution has changed many times during the Batavian Republic. However, the *trias politica* was still present in the Constitutions of 1798, 1801, and 1805. In 1801, *het Vertegenwoordigend Lichaam*, which was the House of Representatives, was replaced by *het Wetgevend Lichaam*, which was the Legislative Body, and the *Uitvoerend Bewind*, which was the Executive Body of five directors, was replaced by the *Staatsbewind* of three directors. We see a decrease of the Legislative power and an increase of the Executive power. The Judicial power remained. In 1805, the Legislative power again became less powerful and the Executive Body of the *Staatsbewind*, with three directors, was replaced by a single Counsellor, the *Raadspensionaris*.[38] The Judicial power remained as it was. In Article 69 of the Constitution of 1805, we read that the Judicial power is only practised by judges. We read the same in the Constitution of 1801. It is interesting that Article 69 of the Constitution of 1805 is more elaborated because the article also mentions that no political power can influence the Judicial power. In the Constitution of 1798, we read in Article 260 that the members of the Judicial power will not intervene in the Legislative power nor in the Executive power. Although not only in the first Constitution of 1798, but also in the Constitution of 1801 and 1805, we find the separation of the powers as Montesquieu wrote in *De l'Esprit des Lois*; the Constitution of 1798 was the most democratic Constitution because the Legislative power had the most power.

The period of the Batavian Republic came to an end because Holland became a Kingdom. In the Constitution of 1806, the Judicial power remained independent.[39] The position of the King was stronger than the position of the *Raadspensionaris*. The legislation was drawn up by the King and the Legislative Body together.[40] In this Constitution we hardly recognise Montesquieu's *trias politica*.[41] Napoleon wanted more control over the Batavian Republic and also over the European countries, which were situated on the sea and that is why Napoleon decided in 1806 to replace the Batavian Republic with the Kingdom of Holland (1806–1810). The Constitution had to be changed again. In the

38 Staatsregeling des Bataafschen Volks, Den Haag, Staatsdrukkerij 1805, Article 38.

39 Dölle, 'De Constitutie voor het Koninkrijk Holland van 1806' 25–45.

40 Article 51 Constitution of the Kingdom of Holland 1806.

41 Dölle, 'De Constitutie voor het Koninkrijk Holland van 1806' 25–45.

new Constitution of 1806, a new form of government was defined. The function of *Raadspensionaris* was replaced by heritable royalty, in the form of Louis Napoleon, the brother of Emperor Napoleon.[42] Louis Napoleon was not a very strong administrator. Finally, Louis Napoleon abdicated[43] and the French Empire annexed the Kingdom of Holland. The French were experts at building up a centralised administration and a well organised Judicial organisation. Even after the defeat of Napoleon in 1813 at the Battle of the Nations the Judicial organisation remained. The Dutch statesman Van Hogendorp drew up a draft for a new Dutch Constitution in which the *trias politica* was maintained, and is still visible in the Dutch Constitution of today.

Selected bibliography

Emese von Bóné, 'Le pensionnaire municipal et sa double fonction; un homme politique et un acteur en justice souvent négligé', in René Robaye (ed.) *Les acteurs de la justice, magistrats, ministère public, avocats, huissiers et greffiers (XIIe–XIX siècle)* (Travaux de la Faculté de Droit de Namur: Presses Universitaires de Namur 2002) 150–162.

Jos Coopmans, 'Vrijheid en gebondenheid van de rechter vóór de codificatie', in *Rechtsvinding, opstellen aangeboden aan prof.dr. J.M. Pieters ter gelegenheid van zijn afscheid als hoogleraar aan de Katholieke Universiteit te Tilburg* (Kluwer 1970) 71–109.

Alfons Dölle, 'De Constitutie voor het Koninkrijk Holland van 1806', in J. Hallebeek and A.J.B. Sirks (eds) *Nederland in Franse schaduw, recht en bestuur in het Koninkrijk Holland* (1806–1810) (Hilversum 2006) 25–45.

Pieter Gerbenzon and Nikolaas Algra, *Voortgangh des Rechtes* (6e druk Samsom H.D. Tjeenk Willink 1987).

Pieter Geyl, *History of the Low Countries, Episodes and Problems, The Trevelyan Lectures 1963 with Four Additional Essays* (Macmillan 1964).

Leonard de Gou, *Het Plan van Constitutie van 1796* ('s-Gravenhage 1975).

Leonard de Gou, *Het Ontwerp van de Constitutie van 1797, De Behandeling van het Plan van Constitutie in de Nationale Vergadering met een facsimile uitgave van het ontwerp constitutie*, volume III ('s-Gravenhage 1985).

Leonard de Gou, *De Staatsregeling van 1798, Bronnen voor de totstandkoming*, Volume I ('s-Gravenhage 1988).

Montesquieu, *Oeuvres complètes*, textes présenté et annoté par Roger Caillois, Bibliothèque de la Pleiade, Volume I (Gallimard 1949).

Simon Schama, *Patriots and Liberators, Revolution in the Netherlands, 1780–1813*, (Collins 1977).

Karel Schönfeld, Montesquieu en 'la bouche de la loi' (dissertation Leiden 1979).

42 Louis Verberne, *Schets van de geschiedenis van het Koninkrijk der Nederlanden* (ontwikkelingscentrale van het R.K. Werkliedenverbond in Nederland, Utrecht 1941) 23.

43 K.B. 1sten van Hooimaand van het jaar 1810 (Royal Decree 1 of July 1810).

Jan Willem Schulte Nordholt, 'Het tertium comparationis- De Nederlandse Revolutie tussen de Amerikanen en de Franse in', in Wim Couwenberg (ed.) *Opstand der burgers. De Franse revolutie na 200 jaar* (Kampen 1988) 52–66.

De Staatsregeling van 1798, I, XXXVIII and XLVIII. Dag verhaal van de Constituerende vergadering representeerende het Bataafsche Volk, 22 januari 1798, II.

Staatsregeling voor het Bataafschen Volks (Johannes Allart 1798).

Louis Verberne, *Schets van de geschiedenis van het Koninkrijk der Nederlanden, ontwikkelingscentrale van het R.K. Werkliedenverbond in Nederland* (Utrecht 1941).

Diederik Verhagen, *L'influence de la Révolution française sur la première Constitution Hollandaise du 23 Avril 1798* (these de droit Paris, Utrecht: Kemink 1949).

Willem Verkade, *Democratic parties in the Low Countries and Germany, Origins and historical developments* (Universitaire Pers Leiden 1965).

Ben Vermeulen, 'Déclaration des droits de l'homme et du citoyen (1789)', in Hemme Battjes en Ben Vermeulen (eds) *Constitutionele klassiekers* (Ars Aequi Libri2007) 102–112.

Gerard Wiarda, *Drie typen van rechtsvinding* (Zwolle 1972).

Willem Witteveen, in Paul Cliteur en Mark Rutgers (eds) *De triasleer onder spanning* (Groningen 1990) 29–51.

9 A legal transplant

French law in Dutch shallow waters[1]

Tammo Wallinga

Introduction

Esin Örücü was project leader of the research project 'Traditions and Transitions in Law & Society' of the Faculty of Law of Erasmus University Rotterdam, which ran from 2001 to 2006, and I was one of the participants.[2] The project was a happy symbiosis between the Departments of Comparative Law on the one hand and Legal History on the other. A comparative approach, both in its historical and contemporary form, was applied to achieve a better understanding of legal transplants and phenomena of the reception of law. Given this background, it is not difficult to find a subject for a contribution to the volume in hand: obviously, it should combine legal history and comparative law. And since legal history and comparative law are very close neighbours in the area outside mainstream positive law, subjects with both an historical and a comparative side to them are many. This chapter will study the legal regime concerning alluvion – the phenomenon of land surface increasing through deposits of sediment from either rivers or the sea – in Roman, French, and Old Dutch law. It contains a particular case of a legal transplant, and it will allow us to draw a few modest conclusions about legal transplants in general.

Alluvio in several legal systems

The specific legal figure treated in this contribution is the natural phenomenon of *alluvio*, to give it its Latin name. In many places around the world, the sea or a river leaves sediment on its shore or banks, and this leads to the forming of new land. The legal question that arises, of course, is who will be the owner of the new land. This is a typical example of the continuity of problems: the question poses

1 This article is an adaptation of an article in French ('Terre, droit français et droit néerlandais dans la province de Groningue (1492–1876)'), in Christian Dugas de la Boissonny (ed.), *Terre, forêt et droit*, [Journées internationales d'histoire du droit, Nancy 12–15 Juni 2002], Nancy 2006, 471) that was based on a paper given at the annual congress of the Société d'Histoire du Droit in Nancy in 2002.

2 See https://www.narcis.nl/research/RecordID/OND1288548/Language/en.

itself in all places and at all times – it is just the answer to the question that varies. I will start by studying the phenomenon in Roman, French, and Dutch law.

Roman law

The Roman law concerning alluvion is found especially in title 41,1 of the Digest, *De adquirendo rerum dominio.* Text D. 41,1,7,1 (Gaius, Cott. 2) states that when a river adds to someone's land, the new land becomes the property of the owner of the original land: *Praeterea quod per alluvionem agro nostro flumen adicit, iure gentium nobis adquiritur.*[3] It must be noted that in this title about the acquisition of ownership, the alluvion on the seashore is not directly treated. In all likelihood it must be implicitly excepted, because in the text D. 1,8,2,1 (Marcianus 3 Inst.) the seashore is described as *res communis omnium*: *Et quidem naturali iure omnium communia sunt illa: aer, aqua profluens, et mare, et per hoc litora maris.*[4] It is logical to think that whatever, as a result of alluvion, is added to it, also becomes *res communis omnium.*[5]

The seashore is *res communis omnium* because it is of public interest. This does not exclude the possibility of acquiring temporary ownership of it by putting a small building on it, as the following text shows. But this ownership disappears as soon as the building is taken away:

> D. 1,8,5 (Gaius 2 Cott.) – D. 1,8,6pr (Marcianus 3 Inst.): (5) *Riparum usus publicus est iure gentium sicut ipsius fluminis. itaque navem ad eas appellere, funes ex arboribus ibi natis religare, retia siccare et ex mare reducere, onus aliquid in his reponere cuilibet liberum est, sicuti per flumen ipsum navigare. sed proprietas illorum est, quorum praediis haerent: qua de causa arbores quoque in his natae eorundem sunt. 1. In mare piscantibus liberum est casam in litore ponere, in qua se recipiant, (6) in tantum, ut et soli domini constituantur qui ibi aedificant, sed quamdiu aedificium manet: alioquin aedificio dilapso quasi iure postliminii revertitur locus in pristinam causam, et si alius in eodem loco aedificaverit, eius fiet.*
>
> [The right to use riverbanks is public by *ius gentium* just as is the use of the river itself. And everyone is at liberty to run boats aground on them, to tie ropes on to trees rooted there, to dry nets and haul them up from the sea, and to place any cargo on them, just as to sail up or down the river itself. But ownership of the banks belongs to those whose estates they connect with.

3 Furthermore, what the river adds to our land by alluvion becomes ours by the law of nations.' Translations of Digest fragments are from Watson, *The Digest of Justinian,* revised edition, (Penn Press 1998).

4 'And indeed by natural law the following belong in common to all men: air, flowing water, and the sea, and therewith the shores of the sea'.

5 Another possibility, which I have not researched, would be that the *alluvio* from the sea was not a phenomenon known to the Roman jurists.

> Accordingly, trees growing in them belong to those same proprietors. 1. Those who fish in the sea are at liberty to erect a hut on the shore in which to take shelter.
>
> (6) This principle is taken as far as to the conclusion that people who build there are constituted owners of the ground, but only as long as the building remains there. Conversely, when the building collapses then, as if by right of *postliminium*,[6] the place reverts to its former condition, and if someone builds in that same place, it becomes his.]

There is a fundamental difference between the seashore and the banks of a river. The latter also have a public function, up to a certain point, but are nevertheless subject to private ownership. The owner of the bank must accept a certain amount of public use of his land: landing of ships, fastening of their cables, and drying of nets.

The banks of rivers which border on *agri limitati* form an exception. Since the dimensions of the land are fixed, the *alluvio* is not added to them: D. 41,1,16 (Florentinus 6 Inst.) *In agris limitatis ius alluvionis locum non habere constat.*[7] This is an exception that must be mentioned, since it has left its traces in modern codifications.[8]

French law

For French law, we shall start with the presentation of the *Corps législatif* by Portalis, in which he gives a short historical overview of the rules that apply to alluvion in France.[9]

The feudal system considered the alluvium of navigable rivers as property of the King;[10] that of non-navigable rivers was property of the *seigneurs haut-justiciers*, at least in most of the customary law. In the *pays de droit écrit* – the southern part of France where reception of Roman law was much stronger than in the north – the owners of the riverbanks had generally retained their rights, but in the years just before the Revolution, they were being threatened by the *fisc*. Portalis mentions the Parlement de Bordeaux as a protector of these owners. Concerning the alluvium on the seashore, he says: *Les délaissemens formés par la*

6 The *ius postliminii* regulates the position of a Roman, who had been taken prisoner by the enemy and sold as a slave but later regained his freedom.

7 'In the case of lands measured out, it is generally agreed that the right of alluvion has no place.'

8 For example, the Dutch Civil Code of 1838, Article 651 says that the alluvium becomes the property of the owner of the riverbank, whether or not the exact dimensions of the land are mentioned in the property title (cf. below).

9 P.A. Fenet, *Recueil complet des travaux préparatoires du Code civil* (Videcoq 1827), vol. XI, 112.

10 Ordonnance des eaux et forêts 1669, art. 41 tit. 27, quoted by H.G. Kronenberg, *Rechtsgeschiedenis van den Aanwas* (thesis, University of Groningen, pub. Vilders 1911) 64.

mer sont régis par d'autres principes, parce qu'ils tiennent à un autre ordre de choses: ils sont exceptés des maximes que nous avons établis.[11] This consideration is repeated in the report presented to the Tribunate by the tribune Faure: *La loi n'étend point le droit d'alluvion aux relais de la mer. Les rivages de la mer font partie des limites de l'État. L'intérêt politique exige pour tout ce qui concerne la mer et ses rivages une législation spéciale.*[12]

Portalis says nothing about the *alluvio* from the sea during the *Ancien Régime.* Information about this period seems to be ambiguous. Merlin, in conformity with the summary of Portalis, assures us that the *lais et relais de la mer* have always been part of the public domain: *Les rivages de la mer font incontestablement partie du domaine public*;[13] and he goes on to quote D. 43,8,3; the Ordonnance de la Marine 1681; an edict of Louis XIV of February 1710 (preamble); Article 1 of the law of 22 November–1 December 1790; and finally Article 538 of the *Code Civil.*[14] Incidentally, the Digest text that he quotes for Roman law only speaks of the property of the seashore (which is *res communis omnium*) but says nothing about the alluvion on the shore.

Pothier gives us a different picture in his *Traité de la propriété.*[15] As for the rivers, he makes a distinction between navigable and non-navigable. The alluvium on the banks of the former belongs to the King:

> *Par notre droit français, les alluvions qui se font sur les bords des fleuves et des rivières navigables, appartiennent au roi. Les propriétaires des héritages riverains n'y peuvent rien prétendre, à moins qu'ils n'aient des titres de la concession que le roi leur a faits du droit d'alluvion le long de leurs héritages.*
>
> [In our French law, the deposits that form on the banks of streams and navigable rivers belong to the King. The owners of the lands bordering on the river cannot claim to have any rights unless they have deeds of concessions made to them by the King of the right of alluvion along their lands.]

The alluvium on the banks of the non-navigable rivers follows the Roman rules: *A l'égard des alluvions qui se formeraient le long des bords d'une rivière non*

11 'The deposits formed by the sea are ruled by other principles, because they belong to another order of things: they are excepted from the maxims that we have established'. Fenet, *Recueil complet des travaux préparatoires du Code civil,* XI, 129.

12 'The law does not extend the right of alluvion to the deposits of the sea. The shores of the sea are part of the limits of the State. Political interest requires special legislation for all that concerns the sea and its shores'. Fenet, *Recueil complet des travaux préparatoires du Code civil,* 144.

13 'The shores of the sea are unquestionably part of the public domain.'

14 PhA. Merlin, *Répertoire universel et raisonné de jurisprudence* (Garnerie, vol. 6, 1813), 719 s.v. *lais et relais.* N.b. this is an addition in this edition of 1813, which is not in the first edition of 1777.

15 A.M.J.J. Dupin (ed.), *Oeuvres de R.-J. Pothier contenant les Traités du droit français* (Tarlier, vol. 5, 1831), *De la propriété* nr. 159.

navigable, dont la propriété appartient aux propriétaires des héritages voisins, on doit suivre la disposition du droit romain.[16] And the alluvium which forms on the seashore also belongs, according to Pothier, to the owners of the land adjacent to the sea: *Les alluvions que la mer ajoute aux héritages voisins de la mer appartiennent aussi, par droit d'accession, aux propriétaires desdits héritages, qui peuvent faire des digues pour se les conserver.*[17]

This contradicts Merlin's point of view, and it is a surprising statement, since in a country that has known the feudal system one would rather expect that the seashore and the alluvium on it would belong to the King. Pothier's opinion seems to be an isolated one, and he gives no references. Still, given Pothier's importance, this particular opinion of his merits further investigation – which I cannot undertake here.

It is to be noted that Pothier refers to a process similar to that which has been used for centuries in the Netherlands, in the province of Groningen. From time to time a new dyke was built to consolidate the alluvium in the form of new land. Pothier, therefore, knew of its existence. Apparently, it also exists or existed in certain parts of France.[18]

After the Revolution

After the Revolution it was soon decided (in a law of 2 December 1790) that:

> *les fleuves et rivières navigables, les rivages, lais et relais de la mer ... et en général tous les portions du territoire national qui ne sont pas susceptibles d'une propriété privée, sont considérées comme des dépendances du domaine public.*[19]
>
> [... the streams and navigable rivers, the banks, land deposited and left by the sea ... and generally all the parts of the national territory not subject to private ownership, are considered to be dependencies of the public domain.]

This article was taken over practically without change in Article 538 of the *Code Civil.*

16 'Concerning the deposits that form along the banks of a non-navigable river, whose ownership belongs to the owners of the neighbouring lands, one must follow the provision of Roman law'.

17 'The deposits that the sea adds to the lands close to the sea also belong, by right of accession, to the owners of said lands, who may construct dykes in order to keep them.'

18 Chardon shows that he is familiar with the phenomenon of *alluvio* from the sea, without however mentioning the process of diking: 'On sait qu'Aigues-Mortes, où Saint-Louis s'embarqua, en 1248, est actuellement éloigné de la Méditerranée d'une lieue et demie; la plus grande partie du vignoble d'Agde était, au commencement du 18me siècle, couverte des eaux de la mer.' M. Chardon, *Traité du droit d'alluvion* (Comynet/Tourneux 1830), 40.

19 Quoted by Kronenberg, *Rechtsgeschiedenis van den Aanwas*, 69.

The *Code Civil*

Article 538 of the *Code Civil* contains an enumeration of the things that are not subject to private ownership, but are considered to be *dépendances du domaine public*:

> *Les chemins, routes et rues à la charge de la nation, les fleuves et rivières navigables ou flottables, les rivages, lais et relais de la mer, les ports, les havres, les rades, et généralement toutes les portions du territoire national qui ne sont pas susceptibles d'une propriété privée, sont considérés comme des dépendances du domaine public.*
>
> [The roads, ways, and streets paid for by the nation, the navigable and floatable streams and rivers, the banks, land deposited and left by the sea, the ports, harbours, roadsteads, and generally all the parts of the national territory not subject to private ownership, are considered to be dependencies of the public domain.]

Here we find a distinction between public and private that formed a solid principle during the composition of the *Code Civil*. One finds it time and again, at all stages of the legislative process; it has never been discussed. The article contains no surprises as regards the seashore, given the tradition, in which only Pothier appears to have entertained a different opinion.

The *Motifs* of the *Code Civil* say[20] that already in Roman law there existed a fundamental distinction between the things that belong to all (*res communes omnium*), among which is the seashore; the things that belong to no-one (the *res nullius*; in reality this is the Roman category of *res extra commercium* – the definition of the *Motifs* is a bit confusing): in this category we encounter the things destined to be used in religious ceremonies, or which belong to collective bodies of persons, e.g. theatres; and finally the category of the *res singulorum*. Civil law ought to occupy itself exclusively with the last category. As far as the others are concerned, civil law should only say that these come under a different regime.

The alluvion is also treated in Articles 556 and 557 of the *Code Civil*:

> 556: *Les attérissemens et accroissemens qui se forment successivement et imperceptiblement aux fonds riverains d'un fleuve ou d'une rivière, s'appellent alluvion.*
>
> *L'alluvion profite au propriétaire riverain, soit qu'il s'agisse d'un fleuve ou d'une rivière navigable, flottable ou non; à la charge, dans le premier cas, de laisser le marchepied ou chemin de halage, conformément aux réglemens.*
>
> 557: *Il en est de même des relais que forme l'eau courante qui se retire insensiblement de l'une de ses rives en se portant sur l'autre: le propriétaire de la rive découverte profite de l'alluvion, sans que le riverain du côté opposé y puisse venir réclamer le terrain qu'il a perdu.*
>
> *Ce droit n'a pas lieu à l'égard des relais de la mer.*

20 Book II title I, 9.

[556: The deposits and accretions that form imperceptibly over time on the lands bordering on a river are called alluvium.

The alluvium benefits the owner of the bank, whether it concerns a stream or a river, navigable, floatable or not; as long as, in the former case, a path or towpath is left, in accordance with the regulations.

557: The same applies to the deposits that running water makes when it imperceptibly moves itself away from one of its banks and carries itself to the other: the owner of the uncovered bank benefits from the alluvium, without his neighbour on the other side being able to come and reclaim the terrain he has lost.

This right does not apply to the land uncovered by the sea.]

Article 556 states that the alluvium of a river (navigable or not) is the property of the owner of its bank, who has to accept the existence of a public road or a towpath. This implies that the seashore has a different regime, which is confirmed by Article 557: it states explicitly that the regime of Article 556 does not apply to alluvion on the seashore.

Ancient Dutch law

During the Middle Ages, the seashore and the rivers of Holland belonged to the local lord. This is the normal principle of feudal law, in which at least the rights on the rivers were considered to be *regalia*.[21] But it is impossible to describe a single system that would have applied to the entire territory of the present Netherlands.

Traditionally, the Netherlands consisted of several provinces which show sometimes profound differences; for instance, where their law is concerned. And a single province like Groningen could contain different legal regimes within its boundaries. The two northernmost provinces of the Netherlands, Groningen and Friesland, share an important characteristic: they had never really been part of the feudal system. Friesland, for instance, accepted, or rather chose, the Duke of Saxony as its lord only as late as 1498. It seems that after that, there were some attempts by the lords of Friesland to acquire property rights over the alluvium from the sea, but without any lasting success.

Ancient law in the province of Groningen

Whatever the situation in Friesland, in the province of Groningen, the law concerning alluvion has always been crystal-clear. There is a Constitution of 1492 by the highest court in the province, in which the court concludes that the alluvia generally become the property of the owner of the adjacent land. This

21 Hugo Grotius says that the *regalia* of hunting and fishing belonged to the counts of Holland: *Inleidinge in de Hollandse Regtsgeleerdheid*, II, 1 and *De Jure Belli Ac Pacis* Lib. II, cap. viii, § 5 (quoted by Kronenberg, *Rechtsgeschiedenis van den Aanwas*, 1).

Constitution is the oldest rule that is known for this province. The application of the rule to the City and Environs (*Stad en Ommelanden*) of Groningen was confirmed in 1518 by Charles of Guelder, and once again by Charles V in 1536:[22] they confirmed their intention to respect the ownership within and outside the dykes. The rule was codified in the laws of the Environs of Groningen in 1601, and it stayed in force until the nineteenth century. Its application was general, without being limited to either rivers or the sea.[23]

It was under this legal regime that the landscape in the north of the province of Groningen slowly shaped itself. Every 50–100 years, an amount of alluvium formed that was large enough to be profitably dyked by the owners of the adjacent lands. They would pay the cost of constructing the dyke. As a result of this process, long and narrow properties were formed, extending from south to north.

The Netherlands between 1811 and 1838

The ancient private law of all the provinces of the Netherlands was abrogated on 1 May 1809 by King Louis Napoléon – the brother of Napoléon who had become King of the Netherlands in 1806 – by the introduction of the *Wetboek Napoleon ingerigt voor het Koningrijk Holland* (the *Code Napoléon*, as the *Code Civil* was called since 1807, adapted for the Kingdom of Holland – the latter term used in the wider sense of 'the Netherlands'). Its Article 433 is an almost literal translation of Article 538 of the *Code Civil*:

> WNH 433. *De wegen, rij- en gangpaden, die tot laste van het rijk zijn, de bevaarbare stroomen en rivieren, de stranden van de zee, de havens en reeden, en in het algemeen alle gedeelten van Hollands grond, welke voor geenen uitsluitenden eigendom vatbaar zijn, worden onderhoorig geacht aan de publieke domeinen.*
>
> [The roads, drive-, and walkways which are at the expense of the state, the navigable streams and rivers, the beaches of the sea, the harbours and roadsteads, and generally all those parts of Holland's land, which are not susceptible to any exclusive ownership, are considered to be subject to the public domain.]

The seashore generally forms part of the public domain. But there is an important difference with the *Code Civil*: one has not translated the words *lais et relais*. This would suggest that the law concerning alluvion was not changed. I would suppose – but I have not been able to verify it – that this was a conscious decision.

22 It was customary for the feudal Lord of the land to confirm certain privileges to cities during their first visit after the start of their reign.

23 R.A. Vos, 'De kwelderkwestie' in *Pro Excolendo Iure Patrio 1761–1961* (JB Wolters 1961), 157, 158.

There is a single article in the *Wetboek Napoléon* that rules the matter of alluvion from a river:[24] these alluvia belong to the owner of the riverbank. Probably significantly, there is no parallel article to 557 of the *Code Civil* which excludes alluvion from the sea.

After Louis Napoléon abdicated in 1810, his brother introduced the original *Code Civil* in 1811. As a result, a change was introduced in the regime concerning the alluvium from the sea: this would in future also form part of the public domain. There is even a Decree of 11 January 1811 which gives detailed regulations for the Netherlands:[25]

Titre I.

art.1 *Les schoores, ou terres en avant des polders, qui sont couvertes et découvertes par la marée, sont, comme lais et relais de la mer, aux termes de l'article 538 du Code Napoléon, des dépendances du domaine public.*

art.2 *Tous particuliers, corps ou communautés qui prétendraient droit à des terres de la nature définie par l'article 1.er, dans les départemens … seront déchus de leurs droits sans nulle formalité préalable, si, dans le délai d'un an, à compter de la publication du présent décret, ils ne forment leur demande et ne justifient de ces droits devant notre maître des requêtes directeur des polders, ou devant le préfet de leur département.*

[Title I.

art.1 The *schorren*, or lands in front of the polders, which are covered and uncovered by the tide, are, as *lais et relais de la mer* in terms of article 538 of the Code Napoléon, dependencies of the public domain.

art.2 All private persons, bodies or communities who claim to have rights to any lands of the nature defined by art.1, in the departments … will be stripped of their rights without previous formalities, unless within one year after the publication of this Decree they deposit their claim and justify their rights before our master of requests director of the polders, or before the prefect of their department.]

24 Art. 448: '*De aanwassen, welke eene rivier, ongevoelig, en van langzamerhand, aan de aanpalende landen heeft aangespoeld, komen als een accessoir aan den eigenaar van die landen* = The alluvia that a river has imperceptibly added over time to the properties on its banks, belong to the owner of these properties as accessories'. The project for a Civil code by Van der Linden, strongly inspired by the Code Napoleon, also limits itself to regulating the alluvion from rivers (II,2,2 art. 8): JTh. de Smidt (ed.), *Joannes van der Linden, Ontwerp Burgerlijk Wetboek 1807–1808* [Fontes Iuris Batavi rariores, 1] (Graphic 1967).

25 C.J. Fortuijn (ed), *Verzameling van wetten en besluiten en andere regtsbronnen van Franschen oorsprong, in zooverre deze ook sedert de invoering der nieuwe wetgeving in Nederland van toepassing zijn*. Derde deel (1808–1813) (Bij Johannes Müller, 1840), 253.

Titre VI.

art.43 *Les dispositions du titre I.er sont applicables aux départemens du Zuyderzée, des Bouches-de-la-Meuse, des Bouches-de-l'Yssel, de Frise, de l'Ems-Occidental et de l'Ems-Oriental.*

[Title VI.

art.43 The dispositions of the first title apply to the departments of the Zuyderzee, the Mouths of the Meuse, the Mouths of the IJssel, Frisia, Western Ems and Eastern Ems.]

Article 2 abolishes all rights to the alluvia for those who have not presented and proved their claim within a year. Article 43 states that this regime applies, among other areas, to Friesland and the mouth of the river Ems. The consequence of this Decree was that the landowners in the north of the Netherlands could maintain their ownership of the existing alluvium, but that any future alluvium would form part of the public domain. As far as we know, there has been little or no registration of existing rights in conformity with Article 2.

After 1814 French law remained in force in the Netherlands, but efforts to produce a national codification continued. In a draft version of 1820, there is an article which still regulates alluvion *à la française*, but in 1823 it was proposed to make a modification concerning the alluvion from the sea. Undoubtedly one intended to return to the situation of before 1811 as far as the alluvion on the Groningen coast was concerned.[26]

After the revolt of the southern Netherlands in 1830, the draft – which would now only apply to the north – was fundamentally modified in 1832. The result of this was Article 577 of the Dutch Civil Code of 1838. One explicitly considered that the public domain did not extend to the *lais et relais de la mer*. The corresponding words of Article 620 of the draft of 1830 were deleted.[27] The intention was to protect the rights of the owners of the adjacent properties. Articles 651 and 652 give a more detailed regulation:

BW 1838, 651: *De aanslijkingen en aanwassen, welke natuurlijk, langzamerhand en ongemerkt aan de landen, bij een loopend water gelegen, aangroeijen, worden aanspoelingen genaamd.*

De aanspoeling komt ten voordeele van de eigenaars van den oever, zonder onderscheid of in den titel van eigendom al of niet melding worde gemaakt van de hoegrootheid der landen; behoudens de wetten en verordeningen opzichtelijk voet- en jaagpaden.

26 J.C. Voorduin, *Geschiedenis en beginselen der Nederlandsche wetboeken, volgens de beraadslagingen deswege gehouden bij de Tweede Kamer der Staten-Generaal (...)*, III. Deel. Burgerlijk Wetboek, art. 385–876 (Robert Natan, akademie-boekhandelaar 1838), 339.

27 G. Diephuis, *Het Nederlandsch Burgerlijk Regt*, Zesde deel (Wolters 1886), 60; N.K.F. Land, *Verklaring van het Burgerlijk Wetboek*, Tweede deel (Bohn 1901), 159.

> [The deposits and accretions which grow naturally, slowly and imperceptibly on to the lands that lie next to running water, are called alluvia.
>
> The alluvium goes to the profit of the owners of the bank, without distinction whether or not the size of the lands is mentioned in the property title; and without prejudice to laws and regulations concerning foot- and towpaths.]
>
> BW 1838, 652: *De bij het tweede lid van het vorige artikel gemaakte bepaling is ook toepasselijk op aanspoelingen, welke aan de oevers van bevaarbare meeren plaats hebben.*
>
> *Dezelfde bepaling is eindelijk ook toepasselijk op aanwassen, gorsingen en schorren, door de zee aan de stranden en aan de oevers der rivieren, alwaar ebbe en vloed gaat, aangespoeld, het zij de oever aan den staat, of wel aan bijzondere personen of gemeenschappen, toebehoort.*
>
> [The provision made in the second clause of the previous article also applies to alluvia which take place on the shores of navigable lakes.
>
> The same provision finally also applies to accretions, mudflats, and salt marshes which the sea washes on to the shores and banks of tidal rivers, whether the banks belong to the State or to particular persons or communities.]

The practice in Groningen in the nineteenth century

Let us now look at the problem that presented itself in the province of Groningen. The new lands of course represented a considerable value in which, around 1838, the Department of the Public Domain became particularly interested. From that year on, this branch of the government started legal proceedings against the owners – the city of Groningen among them – of coastal properties, in order to acquire ownership of the alluvia.[28]

The Department of the Public Domain used the following reasoning. After 1811, a certain quantity of alluvium had been formed which, according to the French *Code Civil* which was then in force, became property of the State. This did not concern a large surface, but the consequences for the future were tremendous. If the Department was right, all future alluvia would wash on to this narrow band of terrain belonging to the State, and would also become State property.

It goes without saying that this had not been the intention of the legislator, who had consciously returned to the old regime of the local law. But this consideration played no part whatsoever in the civil proceedings that were to follow – at least it is not to be found in the motivation of the courts that had to decide on these matters. Maybe this is not surprising at a time when just after the new codification, a strict adherence to the law (Legism) was the common approach. But one notices that the efforts of the Department of the Public Domain met with

28 The story of this affair has been magnificently described by Vos, 'De kwelderkwestie'.

very little sympathy, to put it mildly, and the courts showed great inventiveness in finding ways to throw out the Department's demands. One thing that was never in any doubt, however, and apparently never challenged by anyone, was the applicability of French law in the period 1811–1838.

In the first trial, which the Department started against the city of Groningen, the owner of a large plot of land on the coast in the northern part of the province, the court in Winschoten decided that the land in question was new land situated on the Dollard; that the Dollard must be considered to be a continuation of the river Ems; and that consequently it was a case of alluvion from a river, which according to French law was the property of the owner of the bank. This verdict of 1841 was confirmed by the Court of Appeal of the province.[29]

In another trial which started in 1855, the Court of Appeal considered that the sea to the north of the province of Groningen, the Waddenzee, is really old, submerged land, which cannot be considered as *lais et relais de la mer* in the sense of Article 538 of the *Code Civil.* This decision was confirmed by the Supreme Court (*Hoge Raad*) in 1860.[30] A similar decision by the court at Appingedam of 1866 was confirmed by the Court of Appeal of the province in 1870.[31]

The solution of 1870

No doubt the landowners were winning the trials, but that did not solve the problem. Around the year 1850, the alluvia had already reached such proportions that it would be profitable to dyke them. But there was this problem of legal proceedings, which made the landowners very hesitant to build a new dyke at their expense. Traditionally they paid for the construction of the dyke, but because of the threat of legal proceedings by the Department of the Public Domain, which were calling their rights into question, they did not feel like risking their money. It goes without saying that as far as proper exploitation of the land in question was concerned, this was an undesirable situation.

The problem was finally solved on the initiative of the Groningen provincial government, which in 1869 sent a petition to the King, asking him to promote the speedy and unobstructed dyking of the new terrains. This petition had the desired result. The provincial government received a letter of 4 July 1870 from the Ministry of Finance – of which the Department for the Public Domain is a part – in which it said that its intention was to no longer initiate legal proceedings to claim alluvia in Groningen. Reassured by this letter, the owners of coastal properties decided to have the terrains dyked. On the dyke of the Eemspolder

29 Vos, 'De kwelderkwestie' 160: Rechtbank Winschoten 30 June 1841, *Het Regt in Nederland* III, 132; Provinciaal Gerechtshof Groningen 7 May 1844, (1844) *Regtsgeleerd Bijblad*, 602.

30 Vos, 'De kwelderkwestie' 160: Provinciaal Gerechtshof Groningen 14 September 1858, *Weekblad van het Regt* (*WvhR*) nr 2007; HR 13 January 1860, *WvhR* nr 2171.

31 Vos, 'De kwelderkwestie' 162: Rb Appingedam 28 June 1866, *Regtsgeleerd Bijblad* 1867, 103; Provinciaal Gerechtshof Groningen 29 March 1870, *WvhR* nr 3242.

which was then constructed, there still is a memorial plaque with an inscription, on which a poem records the legal battle of 24 years between the landowners and the Department of the Public Domain.[32]

This, by the way, is only the first half of the story of the alluvion in Groningen. There is a second part which started in the twentieth century and ended roughly in 1954.[33] But French law played no part in this other half, so there is less material there for the comparatist. Suffice it to say that once again, the Department for the Public Domain was the villain – but in the end, there was a solution that satisfied everybody.

Conclusion

By way of conclusion, I would like to remark that this was a very singular case on the borderline between French and Dutch law. In retrospect, one is tempted to criticise the 1838 legislators, who could have avoided the problem by making a transitional provision but failed to do so. Saying that, one must not forget that in the Kingdom of the Netherlands between 1815 and 1830, codification of the law was a very delicate matter. In 1815, the northern and southern Netherlands had been amalgamated, and in the south people were very much attached to the French *Code Civil*. We can imagine that there was no great eagerness to accentuate the differences between the *Code Civil* and the projected new Civil Code. Or one was simply convinced that the textual changes made in 1823 were sufficient to protect the rights of the landowners.

In 1832 the situation was different: no longer was there any need to take into account the preferences of the Belgians. This resulted in Article 577 of the BW-1838, which laid down a clearer regime concerning the alluvion from the sea. Nevertheless, one did not foresee the tactics of the Department of the Public Domain, which were only halted by the creativity of the courts and the involvement of the King. It goes to show that alluvion is a difficult phenomenon for a legislator: since it is a process that stretches over time and progresses almost imperceptibly, it tends to escape the attention.

Looking at it from another point of view, it might be said that around 1830 one was thinking too statically, concentrating on the rights of the landowners, and forgetting about the dynamic phenomenon of alluvion. And one was almost entirely oblivious of the position of who stood to lose by the return to the old

32 It can be found on a culvert near the windmill 'Goliath', a few km. from the Eemshaven. See http://www.bdpoppen.nl/goliath.html, accessed 2 April 2018, where even the text of the poem is given (as in the article by Vos, 'De kwelderkwestie'). Translation: 'The case is now decided. After twenty-four years one finally acquired the rights to this land from the waves. The goal that was set to us long ago has been achieved, and soon the waving wheat will shine on this new field.'

33 This part of the story is also described by Vos, 'De kwelderkwesti who as an advocate represented the owners of the coastal properties in this second legal battle against the Department for the Public Domain.

law: the Department for the Public Domain. Someone, in fact, during the discussions in 1832, raised the point that the public domain had an interest in the matter, but apparently it was thought that this would never lead to any legal proceedings – a lack of foresight that was to have serious consequences.

If we are looking for an illustrative parallel, it is not one of Esin's favourite cooking parallels that comes to mind. This is rather like a case of a medical transplant of a body part that was eventually rejected and amputated again. All seemed well initially – but then it turned out that the transplant had left a nasty infection and the patient fell seriously ill until the King came to the rescue, turning the story almost into a fairy tale. All is well that ends well – but the moral of this story is that legal transplants are to be considered very carefully before making them. You just might get more effects than you were hoping for.

Selected bibliography

M. Chardon, *Traité du droit d'alluvion* (Comynet 1830).

G. Diephuis, *Het Nederlandsch Burgerlijk Regt: Zesde deel* (Wolters 1886).

Christian Dugas de la Boissonny (ed.), *Terre, forêt et droit: Journées internationales d'histoire du droit, Nancy 12–15 Juni 2002* (2006).

A.M.J.J. Dupin (ed.), *Oeuvres de R-J Pothier contenant les Traités du droit français* (vol 5, Tarlier 1831).

P.A. Fenet, *Recueil complet des travaux préparatoires du Code civil* (Videcoq 1827).

C.J. Fortuijn (ed.), *Verzameling van wetten en besluiten en andere regtsbronnen van Franschen oorsprong, in zooverre deze ook sedert de invoering der nieuwe wetgeving in Nederland van toepassing zijn: Derde deel, 1808–1813* (Bij Johannes Müller 1840).

H.G. Kronenberg, *Rechtsgeschiedenis van den Aanwas* (Vilders 1911).

N.K.F. Land, *Verklaring van het Burgerlijk Wetboek: Tweede deel* (Bohn 1901).

PhA. Merlin, *Répertoire universel et raisonné de jurisprudence* (vol 6, 1813).

JTh. de Smidt (ed.), *Joannes van der Linden, Ontwerp Burgerlijk Wetboek, 1807–1808* (Graphic 1967).

J.C. Voorduin, *Geschiedenis en beginselen der Nederlandsche wetboeken, volgens de beraadslagingen deswege gehouden bij de Tweede Kamer der Staten-Generaal (...): III. Deel. Burgerlijk Wetboek* (Robert Natan, akademie-boekhandelaar 1838).

R.A. Vos, 'De kwelderkwestie', in *Pro Excolendo Iure Patrio*: 1761–1961 (JB Wolters 1961).

Alan Watson, *The Digest of Justinian* (revised edn, Penn Press 1998).

10 The rule of law in Turkey

Two steps forward, one step back

Mustafa Koçak[1]

Introduction

The rule of law is the sine qua non of a liberal, pluralist, modern democracy. It requires state authority to be bound, limited, and balanced by law. In this regard, the rule of law rises at the nexus of freedom and law. With a foreseeable and just public policy, it ensures that the law is applied in a fair and reliable manner. In the essence of the concept lies the idea of preventing an arbitrary form of rule that disregards the law. In accordance with the rule of law, the state must establish the boundaries and direction of its actions; determine and protect the free ambits of its citizens and it must not rely on moral discourses that directly or ipso facto lie outside its legal boundaries.[2] From this point of view, a well-performing democracy requires institutions. However, under the rule of law, institutions are not there to protect the state, but the individuals who are vulnerable before it.

As Tom Bingham said,

> [t]he concept of the rule of law is not fixed for all time. Some countries do not subscribe to it fully, and some subscribe only in name, if that. Even those who do subscribe to it find it difficult to apply all its precepts quite all the time.[3]

1 I would like to thank Assistant Professor Nurdan Okur and Assistant Professor Tolga Şirin for their contribution in preparation of this article and Research Assistant Kutlu Tarıman, Armağan Öcal Başer and N. Umut Orcan for the English translation.

2 In his book *Philosophy of Law* dated 1837, G F Stahl has also stated that the state 'should be a state of law (Rechtsstaat), this is the watchword and, in truth, also the tendency of recent times. It should exactly and irrevocably determine and secure the directions and the limits of its activity and the free sphere of the citizen and not enforce on its own behalf or directly any moral ideas beyond the sphere of law. This is the conception of the 'Rechtsstaat' and not that the state should confine itself to administering the law and pursue no administrative purpose or only protect the rights of the individual. It says nothing about the content or aim of the state but defines only the manner and method of achieving them'. Friedrich A. von Hayek, 'The Political Ideal of the Rule of Law (Siyasi Bir İdeal Olarak Hukuk Devleti)', in Ali Rıza Çoban, Bilal Canatan and Adnan Küçük (eds) *Hukuk Devleti Hukuki Bir İlke Siyasal Bir İdeal* (The Rule of Law as Legal Principle and a Political Ideal) (Adres Yayınları 2008) 70.

3 Tom Bingham, *The Rule of Law* (Penguin Group 2010) 174.

Turkey has moved both forwards and backwards with regard to the establishment of the rule of law. In both the 1961 and 1982 Constitutions, the rule of law is embodied under the characteristics of the Republic. Even though the concept found its place in the constitutional texts, putting the principle into practice, in other words, establishing the rule of law culture, has been problematic.

The Development of the rule of law in Turkey

The first attempts to establish respect for the rule of law as it is in the West can be traced back to the Ottoman Empire. Ottoman-Turkish constitutional progress commenced in 1839 with the issuing of *Gülhane Hatt-ı Hümayunu* (the Ottoman Rescript of the Rose Bower).[4] The Rescript also marked the start of the *Tanzimat* (Reformation) era,[5] during which by committing to legal principles over arbitrary governance, providing legal security, and cherishing human rights, a movement towards the limitation of political authority took place.[6]

With the very first constitution of the Turkish Republic, the 1921 Constitution, the nature of sovereignty was fundamentally changed. It was stated in the constitution that 'sovereignty is vested fully and unconditionally in the Turkish Nation' and, together with the 1924 Constitution, the formation of the nation-state began. The priority of both constitutions was not to realise the ideal of the rule of law, but to provide a transition from Monarchy to Republic and to form, albeit belatedly, a nation-state similar to its Western counterparts.

Despite this, the rule of law, as it was said by Jacques Chevalier, did not move out of the 'prosaic area of legal dogma'[7] at that time. It only became a political discourse after the 1980s. Before the 1980s, the concept of the rule of law solely stayed in the confined space of law and did not find its place in the constitutions with such a rich and universal scope as it has today.

4 Concerning the development of the Rule of Law in Turkey see Ibrahim Ö Kaboğlu, 'Türkiye'de Hukuk Devletinin Gelişimi (The Development of the Rule of Law in Turkey)' in Hayrettin Ökçesiz (ed.) *Hukuk Devleti* (Hukuk Felsefesi ve Sosyoloji Arkivi Yayınları: 4, AFA Yayıncılık 1998) 89–116.

5 The term 'Tanzimat' is not always indicative regarding which incidents were included in this period. Tanzimat is sometimes understood as a phase of the relations between the dominant Muslim populations and the Christian societies living in the Ottoman Empire. It is also accepted as the entrance within the occidental civilization Tanzimat includes entirely both ideas and in fact these two main ideas are closely connected. İnalcık, Tanzimat Nedir (What is Tanzimat), in *Tanzimat Değişim Sürecinde Osmanlı Imparatorluğu* The Ottoman Empire during the Tanzimat Changes) (4. Basım, Türkiye İş Bankası Kültür Yayınları 2014) 31.

6 For a broad evaluation of the Tanzimat see Bülent Tanör, *Osmanlı-Türk Anayasal Gelişmeleri* ('The Ottoman-Turk Constitutional Evolution') (Yapı Kredi Yayınları 1998) 117–120; (Tanzimat) 'Dealing with such matters as the security of life, honour and property of the subject, fiscal reform, and the like, the edict goes on to say "these imperial concessions are extended to all our subjects, of whatever religion or sect they may be..."', Bernard Lewis, *What Went Wrong* (Perenial 2003) 91.

7 Ertuğrul Cenk Gürcan, *Hukuk Devleti*, trans. Jacques Chevalier (İmaj Yayınevi 2010) 1.

The 1961 Constitution and the rule of law

In the constitutions of the Republic of Turkey, the 1961 Constitution (promulgated following a *coup d'état*) included the concept of the rule of law for the first time. The preamble of the Constitution stated, 'Guided by desire to establish a democratic rule of law based on juridical and social foundations, which will ensure and guarantee human rights and liberties, national solidarity, social justice, and the welfare and prosperity of the individual and society'.[8] Pursuant to Article 2 of the Constitution, 'The Turkish Republic is a nationalistic, democratic, secular and social state governed by the rule of law, based on human rights, and the fundamental tenets set forth in the preamble'.[9] The 1961 Constitution not only included the principle of the rule of law but also established the rules and institutions that would embed the principle. The 1961 Constitution adopted the principle of the 'separation of powers' and made the supremacy and binding force of the constitution effective by means of Article 8. It stated, 'Laws shall not be in conflict with the Constitution. The provisions of the constitution shall be the fundamental legal principles binding the legislative, executive and judicial organs, administrative authorities and individuals'. Likewise, with Article 145, a Constitutional Court was established for the first time, and important progress was made in the name of the rule of law.

As a matter of fact, in a decision rendered in 1963, the Constitutional Court applied the principle of the rule of law recognised by the 1961 Constitution. According to the Constitutional Court, if a state recognises the rule of law, all the activities of the state should not only be in accordance with the hierarchy of norms, but the content of its legal rules also need to have certain characteristics. Legal rules ought to be impartial, protective of human or natural rights, and conform with peremptory norms.[10]

As is well-known, the rule of law limits the authority of the state over society. It is fundamental not to interfere while the public freely acts. In other words, freedom is the rule and limitation is the exception in a state recognising the rule of law. Thereby, a state recognising the rule of law is a minimal state in which the state respects the autonomy of the citizens by not encroaching on its legitimate authority.[11]

In this regard, in addition to its various reforms on other matters, the 1961 Constitution also contributed to the establishment of the rule of law in three

8 Sadık Balkan, Ahmet E. Uysal and Kemal H. Karpat (trans), 'Constitution of the Turkish Republic', translated for the Committee of National Unity, (Ankara 1961), http://www.anayasa.gen.tr/1961constitution-text.pdf, accessed 1 October 2015.

9 Ibid.

10 Turkish Constitutional Court case dated 11 October 1963, and numbered E 1963/124, K 1963/243, Official Gazette dated 4 November1963 and numbered 11572.

11 Gürcan, *Hukuk Devleti*, 56–57.

main ways.[12] First, the supremacy and binding force of the constitution and the establishment of institutions that made those principles effective were adopted. Second, the separation of powers or distribution of sovereignty was adopted. Before 1961, the centralisation of power and authority was the prevailing approach in Turkey. In addition, the 1961 Constitution set out 'checks and balances' between these distributed powers. Third, this Constitution introduced an adequately protective system to safeguard the fundamental rights and freedoms. The 1961 Constitution not only guaranteed the first-generation rights and freedoms like the preceding Constitution but also expanded the rights list by embodying social rights as fundamental rights and freedoms. Moreover, it adopted 'legality' and 'conformity with the letter and the spirit of the constitution' as general conditions to restrict fundamental rights and freedoms. It also prohibited the law from infringing upon the essence of any right.

However, the system established by the 1961 Constitution did not last long; with the 12 March 1971 Memorandum of Turkish Armed Forces, a legitimate civilian government was forced to resign, and during the interim government formed with the assistance of the military, two substantial amendments to the constitution were made.[13] These changes in 1971 and 1973 weakened the effect of the rule of law and, in the area of fundamental rights and authority of judiciary, significant limitations were imposed.[14]

The 1982 Constitution and the rule of law

The 1982 Constitution, which was also adopted after a *coup d'état*, was a setback compared to the 1961 Constitution in terms of the rule of law. Terminologically, the rule of law expression in the preamble was changed to 'the legal system' and 'based on human rights' to 'respecting human rights'. In provisions regarding rights and freedoms, concepts of the 'duties and responsibilities', 'law', and 'authorised body' were emphasised, and authority of the administration was increased.

12 Bülent Tanör, *İki Anayasa 1961–1982* ('Two Constitutions 1961–1982') (Beta yayınevi 1991) 19–28.

13 For an evaluation of these changes see Tanör, *İki Anayasa 1961–1982*, 39–46.

14 Concerning the Constitutional changes see the Law dated 20 September1971 and numbered 1488, Official Gazette dated 22 September 1971 and numbered 13964 and the Law dated 15 March 1973 and numbered 1699 Official Gazette dated 20 March1973. These negatives changes concerning the Human Rights and The State recognising the Rule of Law can be summarised under five headings:With the military domain's acquisition of some autonomy over the civil government, it started to emerge at least partially, out of political power's influence;The limitation of the judicial control over the political decision-making bodies;The strengthening of the executive while the legislative body was relatively weakened;The strengthening of the of the executive body itself by the diminution of the autonomy of self-regulation organizations included in the executive body;Concerning the fundamental rights and freedoms: the strengthening of the State authority over the individual's and society's rights and freedom.See Tanör, *Osmanlı-Türk Anayasal Gelişmeleri*, 412–418.

While the emphasis on the individual was dominant in the 1961 Constitution, the emphasis in the 1982 Constitution was on authority. In order to decrease this emphasis, numerous amendments have been made since that time.[15] At the beginning of the 2000s, significant steps were taken towards democratisation primarily as a result of Turkey's application for European Union (EU) membership, external dynamics, and struggles in the name of democracy in Turkey. The EU's influence has a particularly important place in these amendments. It was stated in the 2004 progress report that the decision for Turkey to become a candidate in 1999 in Helsinki was a stimulating factor for the extensive constitutional and legal reforms.

After the Helsinki Summit, in this report, these statements were made regarding the Turkish reforms:

> Following decades of sporadic progress and partly because of political consolidation after the 2002 elections, there has been a substantial institutional convergence in Turkey towards European standards. Political reforms have introduced changes ranging from improved civil liberties and human rights to enhanced civilian control of the military. Civil society has grown stronger. The reform process has clearly addressed major issues and importantly, highlighted a growing consensus in favour of liberal democracy.[16]

Besides, in the 2004 progress report, it is indicated that Turkey fulfilled the Copenhagen political criteria, and for this reason accession negotiations had started between Turkey and the EU.[17] After that, reforms were continued in order to align Turkish legislation with the EU acquis.[18] The 2010 Constitutional amendments were examples of progress in this respect.[19]

15 The 1982 Constitution has been amended 17 times in 1987, 1993, 1995, 1999, 2001, 2002, 2004, 2005, 2007, 2008, and 2010.

16 2004 Regular Report on Turkey's Progress towards Accession, SEC(2004) 1201, 14, http://ec.europa.eu/enlargement/archives/pdf/key_documents/2004/rr_tr_2004_en.pdf, accessed 1 October 2015.

17 During the Brussels Summit on 17 December 2004, it was decided that Turkey could start the accession negotiation in 2005. The official negotiations for Turkey started during the intergovernmental Conference taken place in Luxembourg on 3 October 2005.

18 For further information see Ergun Özbudun and Serap Yazıcı, *Democratization Reforms in Turkey, 1993–2004* (TESEV Publications 2004).

19 Concerning the constitutional amendment law dated 7 May 2010 see the Official Gazette dated 13 May 2010 and numbered 27580.

Two steps forward

The 2010 constitutional amendments and rule of law

The constitutional amendment package which was adopted by the 2010 referendum[20] covered changes and additions to the total of 23 articles of the Constitution. These amendments may be summarised as reforms to the civil and military judiciary system, establishment of an Ombudsman system, collective bargaining for civil servants, positive discrimination for women, children and elderly, and removal of judicial immunity under the Provisional Article 15 of the Constitution for the persons who staged the 1980 coup. The 2010 Constitutional amendments should be examined closely.

The Constitutional Court

With the 2010 Constitutional reform, especially in the area of the judiciary, important progress was made. Foremost among these was the reform of the structure and functions of the Constitutional Court. Before the reform, the Constitutional Court was composed of 11 regular and four substitute members. Some of these members were directly, and the rest were indirectly, selected by the President of the Republic. With the amendments, the number of the High Court members was increased to 17, substitute membership was annulled and, by empowering the parliament to select three members, democratic legitimacy, albeit somewhat limited, was conferred. With regard to the structure of the Constitutional Court, a system consisting of two chambers and one general assembly is adopted.

Individual application

Another reform, which was not in the previous Constitution, was the competence of evaluating individual applications. In accordance with the amended Article 148 of the Constitution:

> Everyone may apply to the Constitutional Court on the grounds that one of the fundamental rights and freedoms within the scope of the European Convention on Human Rights which are guaranteed by the Constitution has been violated by public authorities. In order to make an application, ordinary legal remedies must be exhausted.
>
> In the individual application, judicial review shall not be made on matters required to be taken into account during the process of legal remedies.

20 The aforementioned Constitutional amendment law was adopted as a result of a referendum and the related decision of the Supreme Electoral Council of Turkey dated 22 September 2010 and numbered 846 was published in the Official Gazette dated 23 September 2010 and numbered 27708.

The High Council of Judges and Prosecutors (HSYK)

An important amendment with regard to the rule of law was the structure, formation, and functions of the High Council of Judges and Prosecutors.[21] In the original text of the 1982 Constitution, the head of the Council was the Minister of Justice. The Undersecretary to the Ministry of Justice was an ex-officio member of the Council. According to Article 159 of the Constitution, Members of the Council shall be appointed by the President of the Republic from among members of the teaching staff in the field of law, and lawyers; three regular and three substitute members shall be appointed by the General Assembly of the High Court of Appeals from among members of the High Court of Appeals; two regular and two substitute members shall be appointed by the General Assembly of the Council of State from among the members of the Council of State.

In the 2010 Constitutional reform, essential amendments were made regarding the number, composition, and selection of the members of the High Council of Judges and Prosecutors. Composition of the High Council of Judges and Prosecutors were as follows:

> For a term of four years, four regular members of the Council, the qualities of whom are defined by law, shall be appointed by the President of the Republic from among members of the teaching staff in the field of law, and lawyers ... one regular and one substitute member shall be appointed by the General Assembly of the Justice Academy of Turkey from among its members; seven regular and four substitute members shall be elected by civil judges and public prosecutors from among those who are first category judges and who have not lost the qualifications required for being a first category judge; three regular and two substitute members shall be elected by administrative judges and public prosecutors from among those who are first category judges and who have not lost the qualifications required for being a first category judge. (Article 159 of the 1982 Constitution)

Another important amendment regarding the High Council of Judges and Prosecutors was the possibility to partially have judicial recourse against the Council's decisions. According to Article 159/10, 'The decisions of the Council, other than dismissal from the profession, shall not be subject to judicial review'. With these amendments, judicial recourse was made available at least for the dismissal decisions.

Details with regard to the establishment and functioning of the High Council of Judges and Prosecutors are regulated by the High Council of Judges and

21 Concerning this topic see Ergun Özbudun, *Anayasa Hukuku* ('Constitutional Law') (15th edn, Yetkin Yayınları 2014) 389–397; Mustafa Koçak, 'Hukuk Devleti, Yargı Bağımsızlığı ve Yeni Hakimler ve Savcılar Yüksek Kurulu' ('State Recognizing the Rule of Law, İndependence of Judiciary and the new High Council of Judges and Prosecutors') *Demokrasi Platformu*, year 8, number 29, (Ankara 2012) 149–160.

Prosecutors Act No. 6087 dated 11 December 2010.[22] With this Act, the Council's independence from the Executive power had increased, and the influence of the Minister of Justice and the Undersecretary to the Ministry of Justice over the Council's decisions had weakened. Inspection and investigation were to be carried out with the approval of the President (Minister of Justice) only if there was a proposal of the Third Chamber (Article 6 of Act No. 6087). The Undersecretary could not be elected as the Head of Chamber and could not attend the Second and Third Chamber meetings in relation to promotion, allocation of judges as first-class and their disciplinary proceedings but could only attend the Plenary and the First Chamber meetings (Article 8 and 9 of Act No. 6087).

The European Commission for Democracy through Law (Venice Commission) also regarded these changes as generally positive. In the Commission's report dated 29 March 2011, it stated as follows:

> In general, the amendments are to be welcomed. An important element in the amendments consists of provisions transferring powers of supervision from the Ministry of Justice to the HSYK. These changes are to be welcomed as representing a step in the right direction, albeit a relatively modest one. Another welcome amendment concerns the strengthening of the rights of judges and prosecutors to answer disciplinary charges and complaints.[23]

Thereby, these reforms changed the structure and the composition of the Constitutional Court and the High Council of Judges and Prosecutors, which were previously designed by the military government as military tutelage institutions, so as to resemble their counterparts in the democratic world.

The Ombudsman

The Ombudsman system, which it is claimed originated from the Ottoman Empire, provides an independent, impartial, and inexpensive forum or a platform for the people as a dispute resolution mechanism. Due to this mechanism, the complaints of the citizens are settled, human rights are protected, their honour is restored, and their confidence in democratic procedure is increased.[24]

With the 2010 Constitutional reforms, this institution was included in the Constitution under the name of '*Kamu Denetçiliği Kurumu*'. According to the paragraph added on 12 September 2010 with Act No. 5982 to Article 74 of the

22 Official Gazette dated 18 December 2010 and numbered 27789.

23 European commission For Democracy Through Law (Venice Commission), 'Opinion on the Draft Law on Judges and Prosecutors of Turkey', 29 March 2011, CDL-AD (2011) 004, para 101–102.

24 See Howard Gadlin, 'The Ombudsman: What's in a Name?', *Negotiation Journal* (Plenum Publishing Corporation 2000) 45–46.

Constitution, 'Everyone has the right to obtain information and appeal to the Ombudsman. The Institution of the Ombudsman established under the Grand National Assembly of Turkey examines complaints on the functioning of the administration'.

In the 2011 EU–Turkey progress report, it was stated that the draft also provides that transactions by the army of a military nature do not fall under the powers of the Ombudsman. The practice in most EU Member States is that an Ombudsman oversees the military in one way or another. Other provisions of the draft would empower the Ombudsman to respond to individual complaints and recommend improvements in the way the public administration works. There are no provisions allowing the Ombudsman to conduct inquiries on his or her own initiative. Finally, the draft grants Turkish citizens up to 90 days to submit complaints to the Ombudsman. This is short compared with practice at the EU level.[25] However, it was also indicated that the powers of the Ombudsman were limited compared to European counterparts.

Other important reforms

Pursuant to Article 125/2 of the Constitution, 'recourse to judicial review shall be available against all decisions taken by the Supreme Military Council regarding expulsion from the armed forces except acts regarding promotion and retirement due to lack of tenure'. Notice and condemnation, which had been outside the scope of judicial review in the original text of the Constitution, were brought within the scope of the judicial review by means of Article 129 of the Constitution.

In accordance with Article 148/8, 'Application for judicial review may be made against the decisions of the Supreme Court [*Yüce Divan*]. Decisions taken by the General Assembly regarding the application shall be final'. Thus, inconsistency between the previous Constitution and the European Convention on Human Rights that regulated the right to a fair trial was resolved.

In December 2010 and March 2011, with the entry into force of the Acts regarding the Constitutional Court[26] and the High Council of Judges and Prosecutors,[27] the reforms had been accelerated for the restructuring of the judiciary. Therefore, a substantial part of the valid criticisms made in the Accession Partnership Document had been met with these reforms. These changes should be welcomed as substantial progress towards a pluralist democracy.[28] 'In general,

25 Commission Staff Working Paper Turkey 2011 Progress Report, Brussel 2011 http://www.mfa.gov.tr/data/AB/ilerlemeraporu-2011.pdf, accessed 6 October 2015.

26 For the law dated 30 March 2011 and numbered 6216 see the Official Gazette dated 3 April 2011 and numbered 27894

27 For the law dated 11 December 2010 and numbered 6087 see the Official Gazette dated 18 December 2010 and numbered 27789

28 Concerning this topic see Serap Yazıcı, 'Turkey's Last Ten Years: From European Democracy to Autocracy', *Heinrich Böll Stiftung Perspectives*, number 10, October 2014, 24–27. Mustafa Koçak, 'Hukuk Devleti, Yargı Bağımsızlığı ve Yeni Hakimler ve Savcılar Yüksek

these changes were welcomed not only by AKP (Justice and Development Party) supporters, but also a majority of independent liberal democrats and major European institutions such as the EU, the Council of Europe and the Venice Commission'.[29]

One step back

The progress of Turkish democracy towards pluralism was initially put on hold and later suffered a step backwards towards majoritarian democracy with the policies of the government which followed the protests started at the Gezi Park (which started as a protest against cutting trees in the Park) in 2013 and spread nation-wide. In these incidents, 11 people were killed, thousands were injured, and a large number of people were put into custody and arrested. Complaints of the protesters during the incidents centred around the excessive use of force by the police force and these complaints were investigated by the Ombudsman.

The Ombudsman prepared a report regarding the incidents and confirmed the infringements by the law enforcement officers during the incidents. According to the Ombudsman's report on the Gezi Park Protests, there were infringements of the following articles against torture and bad treatment in the Universal Declaration of Human Rights, Torture under the European Convention for the Protection of Human Rights and Fundamental Freedoms, Torture and persecution under the International Covenant on Civil and Political Rights, Torture prevention measures under the Convention on Torture and Other Cruel Inhuman or Degrading Treatment or Punishment and articles of the Turkish Constitution concerning the Fundamental Rights and Freedoms, the Restriction of Fundamental Rights and Freedoms, the Prohibition of Abuse of Fundamental Rights and Freedoms, the Freedom of Expression and Dissemination of Thought, and the Right to Hold Meetings and Demonstration Marches. Police intervention, particularly in Istanbul Gezi Park and in various other cities, was found to exceed the reasonable limits.[30]

Thereby, progress towards pluralist democracy, human rights, and the rule of law since the early 2000s faced a setback.

Kurulu' ('State Recognizing the Rule of Law, Independence of Judiciary and the New High Council of Judges and Prosecutors') 149–160.

29 Ergun Özbudun, 'Turkey's Judiciary and the Drift Toward Competitive Authoritarianism' 50 (2) *The International Spectator: Italian Journal of International Affairs* 42–55 http://dx.doi.org/10.1080/03932729.2015.1020651, accessed 1 October 2015.

30 Ombudsman recommendation number 2013/90, the Ombudsman Institution Annual Report 2013, http://www.ombudsman.gov.tr/contents/files/Raporlar/2013%20kdk_y%C3%84%C2%B1ll%C3%84%C2%B1k_raporu.pdf, accessed 1 October 2015.

Another blow to the rule of law

The rule of law took a second blow on 17 and 25 December 2015 with the 'Corruption operations of December 17, 25'. These operations took place due to the allegations that four ministers of the government, children of the ministers, and a businessman of Iranian origin acquired an illegal personal benefit by corruption. In a state recognising the rule of law, in the presence of such allegations the accused ought to be tried, allegations ought to be assessed by the judiciary, and, as a result, the accused will either be exonerated or sentenced.

However, in Turkey, that was not the case: in order to control the judiciary, a series of legislative regulations took place. These can be summarised as follows: Act No. 2802 on the High Council of Judges and Public Prosecutors, Act No. 2992 on the Governance and Duties of the Ministry of Justice, Act No. 4954 on Turkish Justice Academy, Act No. 6087 on the High Council of Judges and Prosecutors, and Act No. 6216 on the Establishment and Proceedings of the Constitutional Court.[31]

With the mentioned legal changes, achievements regarding the legal guarantee of judges and independence of judiciary which had been made through the 2010 Constitutional amendments and following legal reforms were mostly lost. Among these, the important ones are as follows: First, with the Act on the High Council of Judges and Prosecutors, the Minister of Justice was authorised to decide which member would serve in which chamber. The appointment of administrative staff, which was previously within the capacity of the Deputy President and Secretariat General of the High Council of Judges and Prosecutors, was conferred upon the Minister of Justice. Moreover, all staff, except the members of the High Council of Judges and Prosecutors working at the Academy of Justice, were dismissed and the authority to designate new staff for about 600 vacant positions of the High Council of Judges and Prosecutors and Academy of Justice, pursuant to the new Act, was given to the Ministry of Justice in addition to the authority to designate five Assistant General Secretaries and appoint the President and Vice Presidents of the Academy. The Inspection Board, acting on behalf of the High Council of Judges and Prosecutors, was affiliated to the Ministry of Justice; authorisation to designate the Council President and Vice Presidents was thus taken out of the scope of the High Council of Judges and Prosecutors' competence and put within the scope of the Minister of Justice

Another power granted to the Minister of Justice was regarding the assignment of judges abroad. Here too, decision making power was taken out of the scope of competence of the High Council of Judges and Prosecutors' competence and given to the Minister of Justice Accordingly, the judiciary lost its independence and entered directly into the executive power's influence.

31 For further explanations see Yazıcı, 'Turkey's Last Ten Years' 26–27.

However, the Constitutional Court found most of the articles of Act No. 6524 unconstitutional.[32] Accordingly, the article, which included the 'authorization to designate the President and the Vice Presidents of the Inspection Board of the High Council of Judges and Prosecutors' within the scope of powers and obligations of the Minister of Justice who was at the same time the President of the Council of High Judges and Prosecutors, was found to be unconstitutional. The Constitutional Court also found that the President of the Inspection Board being accountable to the Ministry of Justice was unconstitutional.

Another article, which was rendered unconstitutional, was regarding the Minister of Justice's authority to decide on which members of the High Council of Judges and Prosecutors were to serve as regular or substitute members in which chamber. Pursuant to Article 153/5, the annulment decisions of the Constitutional Court are non-retroactive. Besides, the Constitutional Court also held that this decision would enter into force three months following the issuance of the decision in the Official Gazette. It is important to note that three months was enough time for the government to make fundamental changes at the High Council of Judges and Prosecutors by relying on these quashed provisions, despite the fact that the articles were declared unconstitutional.

Criminal judges of peace and the principle of natural judge

As a follow-up of the 17/25 December operation, with Act No. 6545 dated 18 June 2014, the rule of law was again wounded.[33] The mentioned Act annulled the Criminal Courts of Peace and dismissed the judges of these courts who had served until then. The functions of these courts were transferred to the Criminal Courts of First Instance, with the exception of the issuing of search and arrest warrants. To carry on this exempted issuings, the Criminal Judges of Peace established as a first instance judiciary and only a handful of judges appointed to this duty.

Under this new system, search and arrest warrants issued previously by the Criminal Courts of Peace were now issued by this aforementioned handful of Criminal Judges of Peace.[34] The jurisdiction to challenge these decisions was taken out of the competence of Criminal Courts of First Instance and put within the scope of the other Criminal Judges of Peace.[35] Therefore, with these changes,

32 Turkish Constitutional Court case numbered E.2014/57, K.2014/81, Official Gazette dated 14 May 2014 and numbered 29000.

33 For the full version of the law, see the Official Gazette dated 28 June 2014 and numbered 29044.

34 With the Act No 6545, 38 courts of peace were abrogated and instead of them only six criminal magistrates of peace were re-established, and six criminal judges of peace were assigned to them. http:www.hsyk.gov.tr/duyurular/2014/temmuz/1-bölge-devir.pdf accessed 5 October 2015.

35 Before the aforementioned law entered into force, a person who was sent to the court of Istanbul for arrest could came up before one of the 38 criminal courts of peace judges but

the principle of the natural judge and legal security provided by the rule of law was heavily wounded.[36] Accordingly, Turkey, after the 'Gezi Park Protests', proceeded towards the state of law rather than the rule of law and these developments were highlighted in the report of Venice Commission.

In the report of the Venice Commission dated 20 June 2015,[37] under the heading of the Declaration on Interference with Judicial Independence in Turkey, this serious interference was identified as follows,

> These cases point to a pattern of interference with the independence of the judiciary in clear violation of European and universal standards:
>
> - Judicial decision and requests from prosecutors were not executed in violation of the law;
> - Prosecutors were suddenly removed from cases prepared by them over a long period;
> - Judges and prosecutors allegedly were arbitrarily transferred to other courts;
> - Judges were dismissed for decisions taken by them;
> - Alarmingly judges and prosecutors were even arrested for decisions taken by them.

It is possible to say there is uncertainty for the future. The seat allocation in the parliament following the 7 June 2015 parliamentary elections in Turkey does not allow a single political party to form a government by itself. This uncertainty may either pave the way for pluralist democracy or move the unfavourable tempo towards majoritarian democracy. Since it was not possible to achieve a solution, the President of the Republic decided that the forthcoming parliamentary elections would take place on 1 November 2015. In short, Turkey needs to cover a lot of ground towards pluralist democracy and the rule of law.

---

now one of the six judges will settle the arrest decision. Likewise, in the previous system, it was possible to appeal against the decision taken by one of the 38 judges before the vacation court among the 55 criminal courts of first jurisdiction. for further information see Kemal Gözler, 'Sulh Ceza Hakimlikleri ve Tabii Hakim İlkesi', 29 October 2014, http://www.anayasa.gen.tr/tabii-hakim.htm, accessed 5 October 2015.

36 Concerning the appointments see: http://www.hsyk.gov.tr/arsiv/duyuru/2014.htm, accessed 5 October 2015After the entry into force of the law, the High Council of Judges and Prosecutors appointed the persons who gave a release decision concerning some key persons of the 17 December corruption investigation, for example Reza Zarrab, Süleyman Ateş who was the former president of Halkbank and the children of some ministers. Concerning the critics about the appointment of the judge who clearly shows its admiration for the Prime Minister via the social medias, see the newspapers dated 18.07.2017.

37 http://venice.coe.int/files/turkish%20declaration%20June%202015.pdf, accessed 5 October 2015.

Actions to be taken

In need of a new Constitution:

The first thing to be done is to establish and bring into force a liberal constitution. Only with a new constitution, is it possible to consolidate the institutions that secure the democracy, the rule of law, human rights, the respect and protection of minorities and solve the other substantial problems that have existed in Turkey for a long time. The 1982 Constitution, instead of solving these problems, created new ones.

The 1982 Constitution sanctified the state pursuant to the first sentence of the 1982 Constitution, 'the eternal existence of the Turkish Motherland and Nation and the indivisible unity of the Sublime Turkish State' are affirmed. The emphasis is on the sublimity.[38] However, as the 'opposite of tyrant state', 'the rule of law' gives prominence to the idea of liberty of its citizens (*liberté du citoyen*) against the idea of the sublimity of the state (*gloire de l'etat*). [39]

Due to this and several other reasons, making a new constitution or fundamental amendments to the existing one has been on the agenda since the day the 1982 Constitution entered into force.[40] Some political parties (the Social Democratic Populist Party and the True Path Party) and NGOs (the Industry & Business Association, the Union of Chambers and Commodity Exchanges of Turkey, and the Union of Turkish Bar Associations), have prepared drafts either proposing radical changes to the existing constitution or making a new one and brought these drafts up for public discussion.

In 1992, a report on making a new constitution was prepared by ten scholars led by Prof Dr Erdoğan Teziç on behalf of TÜSİAD[41] and this report was presented to the TBMM presidency by the TÜSİAD President. The draft began with the analysis that the 1982 Constitution was not prepared within a pluralistic environment and the referendum was held with anti-democratic conditions. It was indicated that it is necessary to make a constitution based on national consensus.

Before the 22 July 2007 parliamentary elections, AKP promised a 'civilian constitution'. In its electoral manifesto, AKP stated the general parameters of the 'new constitution' as follows:

38 The Supremacy of the state was a firmly established idea, and this permits the intervention of the state in all areas of activities. Feroz Ahmad, '*İttihatçılıktan Kemalizme* ('From Unionism to Kemalism') (Kaynak Yayınevi 1985) 25.

39 Carl Scmitt, 'Liberal Hukuk Devleti nin İlkeleri ve Hukuk Devletinde Kanun Kavramı' in Ali Rıza Çoban, Bilal Canatan, Adnan Küçük (eds) *Hukuk Devleti, Hukuki ve Siyasal bir İdeal* (2nd edn, Adres Yayınları 2008) 124. 'Der Rechtsstaatliche Bestandteil der modernen Verfassung' *Verfassugslehre* (8 Auflage, Dunker & Humblot 1993).

40 The need for a new constitution for Turkey is not recent. For the history see Ergun Özbudun and Ömer Faruk Gençkaya, *Türkiye'de Demokratikleşme ve Anayasa Yapımı Politikası* (Doğan Kitap 2010). For the English translation see Ergun Özbudun and Ömer Faruk Gençkaya, *Demokratization and the Politics of Constitution-Making in Turkey* (Central European University Press 2009).

41 Türkiye Sanayi ve İş Adamları Derneği, 'The Turkish Industry and Business Association'.

> The new constitution should protect fundamental rights and liberties in the most effective way in accordance with the standards of the Universal Declaration of Human Rights and European Convention on Human Rights while preserving the unamendable characteristics of our Republic such as the democratic, secular and social state based on human rights and the rule of law. The new constitution should be short, precise and understandable, the relations among the legislative, executive and judicial branches should be regulated in line with the parliamentary model in short, clear and understandable terms, the position and powers of the President should be redefined accordingly, a transition from representative democracy to participatory democracy should be provided. The new constitution should be based on the broadest possible consensus.[42]

As is seen, in 2007, the AKP did not envisage a transition to a presidential system but preferred the parliamentary system and to limit the authority of the former President Ahmet Necdet Sezer. But the AKP invited five academics who were led by Professor Dr Ergun Özbudun to draft a new Constitution; this attempt was not successful.

Later, before the 12 June 2011 parliamentary elections, all political parties running for the elections promised a new constitution. With the result of this parliamentary election, the democratic basis for a new constitution was created.[43]

After the election, on 19 October 2011, a Constitutional Reconciliation Committee was established in the parliament. The Committee consisted of three members from each of the four political parties qualified for seat allocation, and it was led by the President of the Parliament. The Committee continued its work until 25 December 2013 and then dissolved due to the fact that it was unable to obtain any results. The uncertainty which began after the 7 June 2015 elections is continuing at the time this article was written.[44]

However, it should be noted that the problems cannot be solved only by making a liberal constitution. A new constitution is essential for Turkey, but it is not

42 Ergun Özbudun, Sivil Anayasa Tartışmaları eleştirileri ve cevaplar (The Criticism and the Answer Concerning the Debates on a Non-Military Constitution), (4 December 2007, Zaman).

43 AKP 49.83% (327 seats), CHP 25.98% (135 seats), MHP 13.01 seats independents 6.57% (35 <seats). see http:www.resmigazete.gov.tr/eskiler/2011/06/20110623-4pdf, accessed 5 October 2015.

44 For further information concerning the establishment and the works of the Constitutional Reconciliation Committee see: Serap Yazıcı, 'Turkey in the Last Decades: From Democratization to Authoritarianism', (2015) 21(4) *European Public Law*, 635–636. Concerning the consensus about the articles of the new constitution see Vahap Çoşkun, 'Anayasa Süreci Nerede Tıkandı' II, (Where Was the Constitutional Process Obstructed? http://anayasaizleme.org/anayasa-sureci-nerede-tikandi-ii-vahap-coskun/, accessed 6 October 2015; also see Serap Yazıcı, *Yeni bir Anayasa Hazırlığı ve Türkiye Seçkincilikten Toplum Sözleşmesine* (The Preparation of a New Constitution and Turkey from Elitism to the Social Contract) (1st edn, Istanbul Bilgi Universitesi Yayınları 2009).

enough. There are other problems for Turkish democracy, beyond the making of a liberal constitution. The success of democracy and the rule of law are closely related to the social structure of the country in which they are implemented. Democracy is a matter of culture and it should be passed on to all segments of society. For instance, although the rule of law culture had started to develop before the thirteenth century, this was not the case in Turkey. Magna Carta, Habeas Corpus, and subsequent developments have their roots in the laws of British society for centuries. The founding fathers of the USA were able to inherit this culture and carry it to North America. From this point of view, in Turkey, the limitation of the state is not the prevailing idea but the 'state being almighty' is.[45] With this and similar reasons, the idea of limited state authority, which arose with liberal thought in the West, is not deeply rooted in Turkey. The idea of limiting state authority through law continues to be seen until today as an interference with the national will by political governments

Intervention relying on national will

Another question that needs to be answered here is whether the national will legitimises the intervention. When they make laws which are incompatible with the rule of law in Turkey, political governments rely on the national will in order to justify, or in other words, legitimise the enactment process. In addition, annulment of some articles of these laws by the Constitutional Court is seen as an interference with the national will.

As it is known, the idea of the national will is based on Rousseau's understanding of the general will. Accordingly, democratic society is a form of the general will, and the aim of the democratic institutions is to enable the governance of the general will. When the majority of the citizens set forth an idea generally, it is not possible to resist or limit this will. This will is not limited. According to this understanding, the will of the majority is the same as the will of the citizens.[46]

However, Lord Acton expressed that majoritarian tendencies pose a danger in democracies, with this statement: 'Power tends to corrupt and absolute power corrupts absolutely'.[47] In reality, the point of origin of the constitutionalism is also summarised with this statement.[48] The idea of constitutional democracy and the rule of law is inconsistent with the control of a pluralist party over the institutions of the state in order to politically dominate and by-pass the instruments of democracy.

Rulers in a state recognising the rule of law are not above the law and their authority has legal limits. This situation, on the one hand, contributes to equipping the law with exclusive power and embedding the respect of law in rulers and

45 Ahmad, *İttihatçılıktan Kemalizme*, 25.
46 Münci Kapani, *Kamu Hürriyetleri* (Public Liberties) (7th edn, Yetkin yayınları 1993) 163.
47 Zühtü Arslan, *Anayasa Teorisi* (Constitutional Theory) (2nd edn, Seçkin 2008) 21.
48 Ibid.

society; on the other hand, it transforms the law into an instrument that legitimises the authority of the rulers.[49]

In recent years, rulers in our country, not only saw law as an instrument to realise the national will but also as a way of restating some existing rules. In addition, they did not follow court judgements, felt free to declare Supreme Courts (Anayasa Mahkemesi, Danıştay, and Yargıtay) as 'acting against national interests' due to their decisions, and publicly discredited the judges.[50] However, in a state recognising the rule of law, the fundamental norm is the internalisation of the rule of law by the legislature itself.

In sum, one of the main problems in Turkey is that the strong political power perceives the democratic state and the rule of law as conflicting notions. As Montesquieu said, the one who seizes the power, a fortiori will tend to abuse it.[51] Governments resulting from democratic elections are not willing to limit themselves with the law. Accordingly, even if the most democratic constitution in the world is in force, as long as this tendency continues, it is likely that the problem will persist. Therefore, it should be stated once again that a liberal constitution is essential but not enough.

Good parliament principle

Another vital constituent of the state recognising the rule of law is the 'good parliament principle'.[52] According to this principle, the parliament ought to give importance to the content of the law, make norms that are clear, applicable, easy to understand without any doubts, and in conformity with the legislative technique. The parliament is a political body. However, drafting norms requires technical information and experience.[53] Lately, norms drafted in Turkey are problematic from this point of view. Negligent norms both in meaning and grammatical construction cause problems in practice, discrepancies, and misconstructions.

49 Gürcan, *Hukuk Devleti*, 57–58.

50 For some examples see: http://www.cnnturk.com/haber/turkiye/erdogan-anayasa-mahkemesini-hedef-aldi, accessed 22 June 2015.http://www.radikal.com.tr/yazarlar/sirin_payzin/anayasa_mahkemesi_gayri_milli_olmak_zorundadır-1191432, accessed 22 June 2015.http://cnnturk.com/haber/turkiye/erdoganin-parlamenter-sistem-bekleme-odasinda-sozune-suc-duyurusu, accessed 22 June 2015.

51 '*Tout homme qui a du pouvoir est porté à en abuser*'.(Montesquieu, *De l'Esprit des Lois*, XI, 4).

52 Matthias Knauf, 'Das Verstandnis von Rechtsstaat un Vorrang des Rechts sowie die Hidernisse bei der Verwirklichung' in Murat Yanık, Hüseyin Özcan and Ahmet Akcan (eds) *International Congress on Constitutional Law Book of Paper 2* (T C İstanbul Kültür Üniversitesi Yayınları) 239 (for the Turkish translation: see ibid. 353).

53 In Turkey, The General Directorate of Legislations (kanunlar genel Müdürlüğü) is present within four bodies: the Ministry of Justice, the Prime Ministry (Başbakanlık) the Speakership of Parliament (Meclis Başkanlığı), and the Presidency (Cumhurbaşkanlığı). 'The language integrity of the texts of legislations issued from the parliament differs from each other's: see Cemil Çiçek (Turkish Parliament Speaker) at the opening of the Constitution's Language Symposium; Ankara, 24 April 2012.

However, one of the main principles of the state recognising the rule of law is 'legal certainty'. The Turkish Constitutional Court defines legal certainty as such: 'Legal regulations need to be clear, plain and understandable without any doubts by the citizens and the administration. Principle of legal certainty is also important in order to provide legal security'.[54]

Omnibus law problem (Torba Kanun)

Another obstacle to the principle of a good parliament in Turkey is the omnibus law problem. An omnibus law can be defined as a proposed law that concerns several different Acts. In other words, it is a proposed law that includes diverse and unrelated code amendments under a single Act. With this method, political authority, relying on its majority in the parliament, prefers passing the amendments otherwise impossible to pass separately in a straightforward way, under a single document without compromise.[55]

The laws drafted with this method reflect the will of the political party that has the majority in the parliament and causes the exclusion of the others from the law-making process. Outside the parliament, with the 'omnibus law' method, the opinions of important actors of pluralist democracy such as trade associations and civil society organisations with regard to the proposed law are mostly disregarded. Even though the Constitution provides for a pluralist democracy and the Internal Regulation of the Parliament stipulates norms regarding this, the political party that has the majority in the parliament prefers a majoritarian but not a pluralist and reconciliatory process.[56] As is mentioned above, the underlying rationale for this behaviour is the belief that while the parliamentary majority represents the national will, the opposition and civil society collides with it. In other words, in Turkey, political parties that have the majority opt for majoritarian democracy and practices that are suitable to it.

54 Turkish Constitutional Court case numbered E.2015/17, K.2015/20, Official Gazette dated 19 June 2015 and numbered 29391.

55 Hasip Kaplan, Deputy of Şırnak. The most important characteristic of democracy is the respect of national will. The omnibus law practice offends the national will see. http://yasaizleme.org.tr/idex.php/33-calistay-tutanakları-ozeti, accessed 26 June 2015; Şeref İba, 'in the Turkish legislation system, every political party will be faced to a legislation crisis. Omnibus law is a law-making technique put into the 6th gear thought to be a solution with regard to procedural economy', http://www.yasaizleme.org.tr/index.php/33-calistay-tutanaklari-ozeti, accessed 26 June 2015;

56 The Parliament Speaker Çiçek emphasised that omnibus laws were issued because of the lack of effectiveness and efficiency in law-making, Çiçek who pointed out the fact omnibus laws caused serious justice quality problems said 'we hope that it would be the last (omnibus) law. We worked a lot for this but there are still difficulties concerning the links between the different norms and the structure within which they would take place. The Government should make the law, and the opposition should contribute in which way they see it fit. These possibilities exist, we do not discover anything new.' (newspapers date 29 September 2014).

When the recent events are considered, the following statement with regard to the aim of the omnibus law is justified:

> in order to shape the legal order by the political preferences of the AKP leading staff and dominate the executive order and judiciary bureaucracy according to the tendency of the majority party. It is obvious that such a tendency is not compatible with the concepts of pluralism and the rule of law that forms the basis of the European democracy.[57]

Norm inflation

The essence of law-making is not only making norms that are clear, applicable, and easy to understand beyond any doubt, but also to comply with the legislative technique. This is without a doubt essential but not enough. One of the aims of the rule of law is to ensure legal stability. In other words, legal security not only requires the law to be attainable, but also necessitates qualified law-making and the avoidance of legal instability.[58]

The danger with regard to the rule of law not just in Turkey but in other democratic countries as well as to be drowned under the legislation anarchy. Statutes replicate in number at an unprecedented pace and head towards regulating the communal life extensively. This situation, named 'norm inflation' (inflation normative) in Chevalier's words, diminishes the value of law and causes the non-fulfilment of law's regulatory function as it should be.[59] Not to mention the fact that norm inflation turns the legislation from the protection of freedom, one of the essential characteristics in a state recognising the rule of law, to a weapon of the absolute sovereign. Governments, in this way, have the opportunity to intervene in all fields of communal life. The magnitude of the problem of norm inflation in Turkey is greater than other liberal democracies. Whatever the reason, in recent years, many statutes are drafted including the fundamental statutes such as the Turkish Criminal Code, the Code of Criminal Procedure, the Code of Civil Procedure, the Code of Obligations, and the Turkish Commercial Code. Part of the statutes that entered into force was amended again and again due to the inconveniences caused in practice. For instance, the Turkish Criminal Code No. 5237, dated 26 September 2004, was amended five times in nine years following its entry into force and one of its articles was rendered unconstitutional by the Constitutional Court.[60]

57 Yazıcı, 'Turkey's Last Ten Years' 27.

58 Gürcan, *Hukuk Devleti*, 101.

59 Mustafa Koçak, 'Hukuk Devleti ve Türkiye' ('The State Recognizing the Rule of Law and Turkey') in Murat Yanık, Hüseyin Özcan and Ahmet Akcan (eds) *International Congress on Constitutional Law Book of Paper 2* (T C İstanbul Kültür Üniversitesi Yayınları) 320.

60 The Constitutional Court declared the Article 230/5, 6 which stated conducting religious marriage ceremony before civil marriage as a crime unconstitutional under Article 20 titled

Non-compliance with the principles of democracy, pluralism, and participation in law-making, lack of transparency in parliamentary practice and restraints in active participation of civil society organisations during Commission meetings on top of short-lived regulations that need to be amended continuously, make the country a 'cancelled Statutes dump'. This rapid change, which is extremely challenging even for lawyers to comprehend, causes the law to be unclear and unpredictable for the citizens.

As it is known, the ECtHR decided that constantly changing laws and contradictory court decisions create an insecure legal setting and weaken the belief in the judiciary. According to the Court, 'the public's confidence in the judicial system, is one of the essential components of a State based on the rule of law'.[61]

Need for eligible judges

The rule of law also requires a proper administration of justice. This in turn mandates a reliable and high-quality court system with well-educated and honest judges, prosecutors and advocates.[62] Independent and impartial judges, equipped with legal knowledge and life experience, who can guide the administrators, prevent the invasions against the legal order, are the sine qua non of state recognition of the rule of law.

As stated by Judge Marshall in *Marbury v Madison*,

> It is emphatically the province and duty of the judicial department to say what the law is. Those who apply the rule to particular cases, must of necessity expound and interpret that rule. If two laws conflict with each other, the courts decide on the operation of each.[63]

A hierarchy of norms can only be effective if it is confirmed by the judiciary. Fundamental rights can only be applied if there are judges protecting them. Due to the fact that the promotion of judges and prosecutors and membership election to the Constitutional Court, the Court of Cassation, and the Council of State (Danıştay) does not depend on an objective merit system, it is possible to say the system does not encourage being a good lawyer.

For the reasons mentioned above, Turkey is not considered a liberal democracy but in the category of illiberal democracies. It is also possible to say Turkey is a partly free country, as Freedom House did.[64]

'Privacy of Private Life' and Article 24 titled 'Freedom of Religion and Conscience of the Constitution'. E:2005/103, K:2005/89 dated 23 November 2005.

61 *Păduraru v Romania* App no. 63252/00 (ECtHR, 1 March 2006), para 98; *Albu and Others v Romania* App no. 34796/09 (ECtHR, 10 August 2012), para 34.

62 Bingham, *The Rule of Law*, 172.

63 Marbury v Madison, 1.Cranch137 (5 U.S137) (1803).

64 Özbudun, 'Turkey's Judiciary and the Drift Toward Competitive Authoritarianism' 42–55.

Conclusion

Turkey's movement towards democracy and the rule of law can be compared to the march of Ottoman Military Band, i.e. 'two steps forward, one step back'. On occasion, important democratic reforms are made and put into practice in succession and other times there have been setbacks. Democratic reforms started in the 2000s were turned back with the 'Gezi Park Incidents' and '17/25 December Corruption Files' and in recent years, Turkey has shown a tendency towards what Özbudun has termed 'competitive authoritarianism'.[65]

As a result of the 7 June 2015 parliamentary elections, four political parties qualified for the seat allocation and the political power lost its majority in the parliament and so was unable to form a government. Coalition negotiations remained inconclusive. Now, Turkey moves towards another election. When this article is published, the forthcoming election will probably have already taken place. It is possible that the results of the election ignite reforms for democracy and the rule of law or vice versa.

From an optimistic point of view, if a government which would give importance to the reforms is formed, it will have to take numerous actions in the name of the rule of law, such as making a new pluralist constitution, amending the abovementioned anti-democratic norms and expediting the EU reforms that were put on hold. The rule of law 'remains an ideal, but an ideal worth striving for, in the interests of good government and peace, at home and in the world at large'. [66]

To emphasise it once again, the success of democracy and the rule of law are closely related to the social structure and the democratic and legal culture of the country in which they are recognised.[67]

Selected bibliography

Feroz Ahmad, *İttihatçılıktan Kemalizme* (Kaynak Yayınevi 1985).
Zühtü Arslan, *Anayasa Teorisi* (2nd edn, Seckin 2008).
Sadık Balkan, Ahmet E. Uysal and Kemal H. Karpat (trans), 'Constitution of the Turkish Republic' (1961), http://www.anayasa.gen.tr/1961constitution-text.pdf, accessed 1 October 2015.
Tom Bingham, *The Rule of Law* (Penguin Group 2011).

65 Ibid.
66 Bingham, *The Rule of Law*, 174.
67 The Turkish general election of November 2015 was held on 1 November 2015. The election resulted in a single-party majority government. Afterwards, a constitutional referendum was held throughout Turkey on 16 April 2017 on whether to approve 18 proposed amendments to the Turkish Constitution that were brought forward by the governing Justice and Development Party (AKP) and the Nationalist Movement Party (MHP). The amendment transformed the country from a parliamentary democracy into so-called *a la Turca* Presidential System (*Cumhurbaşkanlığı sistemi*). This can be the subject matter of another article.

Vahap Çoşkun, 'Anayasa Süreci Nerede Tıkandı' http://anayasaizleme.org/anayasa-sureci-nerede-tikandi-ii-vahap-coskun/, accessed 6 October 2015.

Howard Gadlin, 'The Ombudsman: What's in a Name?' *Negotiation Journal* (2000).

Ertuğrul Cenk Gürcan, *Hukuk Devleti*, trans. Jacques Chevalier (İmaj Yayınevi 2010).

Friedrich A von Hayek, 'Siyasi Bir Ideal Olarak Hukuk Devleti' in Ali Rıza Çoban, Bilal Canatan, Adnan Küçük (eds), *Hukuk Devleti Hukuki Bir İlke Siyasal Bir Ideal* (Adres Yayınları 2008).

Ibrahim Ö Kaboğlu, 'Türkiye'de Hukuk Devletinin Gelişimi' in Hayrettin Ökçesiz (ed.), *Hukuk Devleti* (AFA Yayıncılık 1998).

Münci Kapani, *Kamu Hürriyetleri* (7th edn, Yetkin yayınları 1993).

Matthias Knauf, 'Das Verstandnis von Rechtsstaat un Vorrang des Rechts sowie die Hidernisse bei der Verwirklichung' in Murat Yanık, Hüseyin Özcan and Ahmet Akcan (eds), *International Congress on Constitutional Law: Book of Paper 2* (T C İstanbul Kültür Üniversitesi Yayınları 2011).

Mustafa Koçak, 'Hukuk Devleti, Yargı Bağımsızlığı ve Yeni Hakimler ve Savcılar Yüksek Kurulu' (2012) 8(29) *Demokrasi Platformu* 149.

Bernard Lewis, *What Went Wrong* (Perenial 2003).

Ergun Özbudun, *Anayasa Hukuku* (15th edn, Yetkin Yayınları 2014).

Ergun Özbudun, 'Turkey's Judiciary and the Drift Toward Competitive Authoritarianism' 50(2) *The International Spectator: Italian Journal of International Affairs* 42, http://dx.doi.org/10.1080/03932729.2015.1020651, accessed 1 October 2015.

Ergun Özbudun and Ömer Faruk Gençkaya, *Demokratization and the Politics of Constitution-Making in Turkey* (Central European University Press 2009).

Ergun Özbudun and Serap Yazıcı, *Democratization Reforms in Turkey, 1993–2004* (TESEV Publications 2004).

Carl Scmitt, 'Liberal Hukuk Devleti nin İlkeleri ve Hukuk Devletinde Kanun Kavramı' in Ali Rıza Çoban, Bilal Canatan, Adnan Küçük (eds), *Hukuk Devleti, Hukuki ve Siyasal bir Ideal* (2nd edn, Adres Yayınları 2008).

Bülent Tanör, *İki Anayasa 1961–1982* (Beta yayınevi 1991).

Bülent Tanör, *Osmanlı-Türk Anayasal Gelişmeleri* (Yapı Kredi Yayınları 1998).

Serap Yazıcı, *Yeni bir Anayasa Hazırlığı ve Türkiye Seçkincilikten Toplum Sözleşmesine* (1st edn, Istanbul Bilgi Universitesi Yayınları 2009).

Serap Yazıcı, 'Turkey's Last Ten Years: From European Democracy to Autocracy' (2014) 10 *Heinrich Böll Stiftung Perspectives* 24.

Serap Yazıcı, 'Turkey in the Last Decades: From Democratization to Authoritarianism' (2015) 21(4) *European Public Law* 635.

11 The method of comparative law reconsidered in the light of legal epistemology and the reception of Roman law[1]

Laurens Winkel

Introduction

Comparative law is, like all parts of legal science, in the last instance based on philosophy.[2] For this short article, I would like to concentrate on epistemology.[3] As far as I can see comparative law is linked with at least five fundamental epistemological questions ranging from general questions to more specific ones:

- How do we know?
- How do we acquire knowledge of what is good?
- How do we know the law?
- How do we know customs and customary laws?
- How do we know and recognise foreign legal rules?

Of course, this is not the moment to go deep into the first two epistemological questions in general. Aristotle dealt with them in his treatises *De Anima*, *Metaphysics*, and *Analytica Priora* and *Posteriora*.[4] Aristotle also dealt with the

1 This chapter is an elaborated version of a paper given in Spring 2015 at the University of Glasgow, in honour of my dear colleague Esin Örücü and on the occasion of her 75th birthday. It was repeated in a different form at the Eötvös Loránd University in Budapest, 14 November 2016. The paper was discussed during a Paul Scholten seminar on legal philosophy at the University of Amsterdam in February 2018. I thank Professor Sean Donlan (University of the South Pacific School of Law), Professor Aukje van Hoek (University of Amsterdam) and the participants of the Paul Scholten seminar for their critical comments and suggestions.

2 Cf. A.E. Örücü, 'Symbiosis Between Comparative Law and Theory of Law – Limitations of Legal Methodology' (Inaugural lecture, Erasmus University Rotterdam, 1982); A.E. Örücü, 'Method and Object of Comparative Law' in H.W. Blom and R.J. de Folter (eds) *Methode en object in de rechtswetenschappen* (Tjeenk Willink 1986) 57–69.

3 Mitchel de S-O-l'E Lasser, 'The Question of Understanding' in P. Legrand and R. Munday (eds) *Comparative Legal Studies: Traditions and Transitions* (CUP 2003) 197ff goes into practical, not theoretical epistemological questions.

4 I. During, *Aristoteles* (Carl Winter Universitätsverlag 1966) 105: see especially Anal. Post. Book II; W.K.C. Guthrie, *A History of Greek Philosophy, VI: Aristotle* (CUP 1981) 130–134, 170–202.

third question, about knowledge of the law in his *Nicomachean Ethics*.[5] The last two questions are normally a bit neglected in legal literature, although they are quite important and it is therefore good to attempt to clarify them.

How do we know the law?

In Antiquity, the standard for legal knowledge was the man with an average amount of diligence (*anèr spoudaios*[6]), in Roman law the Latin expression *diligens pater familias* applied.[7] The perspective changed in the early modern period with the gradual rise of individualism, starting in the seventeenth and eighteenth centuries. From the eighteenth century on, the emphasis was put more on the – albeit theoretical – possibility of knowing the law; hence, we find all the provisions on promulgation especially after the French Revolution, e.g. in the *Code Civil* in Article 1 and in the Austrian ABGB in § 2, in a prominent place. In this respect, the nineteenth century was a century of the legal positivism of the legislator and of political liberalism.[8]

A further striking observation is that epistemological problems with the perception of facts are extensively discussed from Plato in his *Theory of Ideas*[9] to modern philosophers like Bertrand Russell, who starts his well-known introductory book on the problems of philosophy with epistemology in a way not very different from Plato.[10] On the other hand, the literature on the epistemological problems of *normative* phenomena is scarce in later theoretical scholarship. After Aristotle, who is in this respect fundamental, Roman jurists like Marcus Antistius

5 Book III and to a lesser degree Book V, see L. Winkel, *Error iuris nocet, I Rechtsirrtum in der griechischen Philosophie und im römischen Recht bis Justinian* (Terra 1985) 22–35, where Aristotle's doctrine is fully explained.

6 Aristotle embedded this notion in the Theory of the Mean, cf. Aristoteles, Eth. Nic. III, 4, 4–6, 1113 a 25–1113 b 2 and Eth. Nic. V, 6, 6, 1130 a 32–1130 b 5.

7 W. Kunkel, 'Diligentia' 45 *Zeitschrift der Savigny Stiftung für Rechtsgeschichte, romanistische Abteilung* (1925) 266–351.

8 Mistake of law and the maxim *everyone is supposed to know the law* was one of the themes in the congress of the Académie de Droit Comparé in Uppsala in 1966. The general report was written by the Hungarian comparative lawyer Imre Szabó: Le rôle actuel de la maxime 'Nul n'est censé ignorer la loi', *Rapports généraux au VII*[e] *congrès international de droit comparé, Uppsala 1966* (Acta Instituti Upsaliensis jurisprudentia comparativa, Stockholm 1966) 82–93. Previously the theme of mistake of law in criminal law was on the agenda of the congress of the Académie de Droit Comparé in Paris in 1954, whereas during the 1978 congress of the same society in Budapest the topic '*La réglementation pénale de l'erreur' was discussed again, when the 'rapporteur général'* was I. Andrejew (Poland).

9 Main source: Republic (*Politeia*), Book VII, 514A–520A; Guthrie, *A History of Greek Philosophy, IV* (CUP 1977) 512ff.

10 B. Russell, *The Problems of Philosophy* (repr. OUP 1973) 1ff. Russell starts his book with an explanation of the problems of cognition in a vocabulary that reminds of Plato's theory of ideas. He further distinguishes between *knowledge by description* and *knowledge by acquaintance*, ibid. 25ff. He does not deal, however, with the knowledge of norms as a separate epistemological problem.

Labeo who lived at the beginning of the Christian era or Julius Paulus in the first decades of the third century AD[11] addressed the issue. In later history, Thomas Aquinas' opinion is somewhat aprioristic for a modern reader: 'To the first question we must therefore say that the promulgation of natural law stems from what God has inserted in the human mind to enable it to know this [law] in a natural way'.[12]

There is a link here with the medieval maxim '*ens et bonum convertuntur*', that is, existing things coincide with the good, as expounded elsewhere by Aquinas.[13] More important, however, is the nineteenth-century Neo-Aristotelian Franz Brentano (1838–1917),[14] who raised the topic after a long silence.[15] In Neo-Kantianism, too, the knowledge of normative phenomena are sometimes dealt with, but in this branch of philosophy the perception of norms is obscured by the Kantian strict separation between *is* and *ought*.[16] In the existing contemporary literature there is much attention to the perception of facts or fictions, but the basic problems of the knowledge of norms are somewhat neglected.

11 See esp. the (extract) of his *Liber singularis de iuris et facti ignorantia* in D. 22,6,9. Labeo's opinions in D. 22,6,9, 2-3; further biographical references for those Roman jurists in W. Kunkel, *Herkunft und soziale Stellung der römischen Juristen* (Graz/Wien/Köln 1967) 32–34: Marcus Antistius Labeo; 244–245: Julius Paulus.

12 Own translation of Summa Theologiae I, II, Quaestio 90, Art. 1: *Ad primum ergo dicendum quod promulgatio legis naturae est ex hoc ipso quod Deus eam mentibus hominum inseruit naturaliter cognoscendam.*

13 See Thomas Aquinas, *Quaestiones disputatae de veritate*, Quaestio 21 de bono: *Secundo quaeritur utrum ens et bonum convertantur secundum supposita.* More information on these particular scholastic topics in O. Lottin, 'La nature du péché d'ignorance' (1932) 27 *Revue Thomiste*, 634–652, 723–738; L. Oeing-Hanhoff, *Ens et unum convertuntur* (Aschendorf, 1953) 179ff (Das Eine und das Gute).

14 Teacher of the founder of phenomenology Edmund Husserl (1859–1938), see W. Stegmüller, *Hauptströmungen der Gegenwartsphilosophie* (Alfred Kröner 1978) 1ff (Brentano), 49ff (Husserl).

15 Franz Brentano, *Vom Ursprung sittlicher Erkenntnis* (Felix Meiner Verlag 1969); cf L.C. Winkel, 'Das erneuerte Interesse für die erkenntnistheoretischen Aspekte der aristotelischen Ethik in Deutschland und England im 19. und 20. Jahrhundert' in A. Földi, I. Sándor and I. Siklósi (eds) *Ad geographiam historico-iuridicam ope iuris romani colendam – Studia in honorem Gábor Hamza* (ELTE Eötvös K 2015) 405–408: Brentano had a substantial influence on the ideas of G.E. Moore, an important British philosopher on ethics at the beginning of the 20th century. M. Warnock, *Ethics since 1900* (OUP 1978) 1–30, deals extensively with G.E. Moore, but Brentano is as far as we can see not even mentioned.

16 See R. Mallachow, *Rechtserkenntnistheorie und Fiktionslehre* (Rösl & Cie 1922); following to a certain extent Hans Vaihinger, *Die Philosophie des Als-Ob* (Reuther & Reichard 1913); which was recently translated into Dutch: *De filosofie van het alsof* (Samenwerkende Uitgevers Vof 2013). Both philosophers belonged to Neo-Kantianism.

How do we know customs and customary law?

The knowledge of customs and customary law are typically either dealt with in the eternal debate on natural law[17] or, in a different way, in legal anthropology.[18] In society, people tend to develop a set of rules which are not based on morality only, but also or mainly serve practical purposes, e.g. keeping right or keeping left on the road. Hugo Grotius (1583–1645) would have called these kinds of rules '*ius gentium voluntarium*', rules based on the collective volition of peoples. But such regulations were also close to the rules based on morality he called '*ius gentium necessarium*', literally: the necessary common rules of peoples.[19]

According to a common view, natural law is supposed to be implanted in everyone's conscience. That supposition, as we have tried to show elsewhere,[20] is too simplistic. Historically speaking, natural law is not an idea with an unchallenged eternal truth, hence the changing positions over time on the content of natural law. Natural law is, in the Western tradition, mostly based on equality, though sometimes based on inequality, for example in the philosophy of some Greek sophists in Antiquity like Kallikles, in the philosophy of Friedrich Nietzsche and in the National-Socialist legal theory with its notion of '*gesundes Volksempfinden*'.[21]

There is a subsidiary problem on another level concerning customary law: here we are in the middle of the opposition between factual and normative levels. The epistemological problem is dealt with in legal anthropology.[22] Interestingly enough in investigating the problem of 'how we know customary law', there is a link with nineteenth-century colonialism, when colonial powers got acquainted with indigenous legal rules. This was at the time during which European colo-

17 M. Armgardt and T. Repgen (eds), *Naturrecht in Antike und früher Neuzeit* (Mohr Siebeck 2014).

18 Henry Sumner Maine, *Ancient Law* (repr. University of Arizona Press1986) esp. 109ff (Primitive Society and Ancient Law).

19 *De iure belli ac pacis*, 1,2, 4,1-2, following in this respect Francesco de Vitoria (*Relectio de Indis* III,4) who was the first to recognise kind of majority rule in volitional *ius gentium*. cf L. Winkel, 'The Peace Treaties of Westphalia as an Instance of the Reception of Roman Law' in R. Lesaffer (ed.) *Peace Treaties and International Law in European History* (CUP 2004) esp. 227ff.

20 L. Winkel, 'Deux conceptions du droit naturel dans l'Antiquité' (2015) 93 *Revue historique de droit français et étranger* 341–350.

21 Literally: common sense/opinion/experience of the people. The German expression stems from the nineteenth century, but became an instrument in the national-socialist legal doctrine, especially to underpin racist opinions. Further references in Fabian Wittreck, *Nationalsozialistische Rechtslehre und Naturrecht* (Tübingen 2008). For the revival of natural law philosophy in Germany after the Second World War in a humanistic sense based on human equality see: H. Coing, *Die obersten Grundsätze des Rechts, ein Versuch zur Neubegründung des Naturrechts* (Heidelberg 1947); F. Bydlinski, *Fundamentale Rechtsgrundsätze* (Wien/New York 1988) 1ff.

22 Cf. T. Bennett, 'Customary Law in Comparative Studies: The Colonial Encounter' in M. Reimann and R. Zimmermann (eds) *The Oxford Handbook of Comparative Law* (OUP 2006) 642–645.

nies and colonial systems were being developed, infrastructure was built, and ethnographical, and later anthropological research was carried out. This was, for example, the case in the Dutch East Indies from about 1850.[23] The investigation of indigenous culture was further enhanced after the moment when colonial exploitation ceased to be the official aim of the European presence in the colonies, being replaced by education leading to an independent political identity. In the Dutch East Indies, this was the case since 1901.[24]

In this framework, we would like to draw the attention to a methodological principle developed by a famous Dutch legal historian Henk Hoetink (1900–1964) for 'understanding foreign law'.[25] This was in fact the title of his inaugural lecture at the Law School in Batavia (now Jakarta, the capital of Indonesia) in 1929, the predecessor of the present Universitas Indonesia. For Hoetink, it was a problem to understand and to classify Indonesian indigenous law, the *adat*. He submitted that it was only possible to describe and understand such foreign legal phenomena when one refers implicitly or explicitly to one's own legal system. Hoetink's inaugural lecture had already resounded before the Second World War. Hans Winkel,[26] admitted as an unsalaried lecturer in comparative legal history at the University of Utrecht in 1936, adhered to the opinions of Hoetink and showed their great relevance to the method of comparative law and comparative legal history.[27] In a later publication, Hoetink generalised this epistemological problem of *adat* law and extended it to legal history as a whole: we only can understand historical legal rules when we make a kind of restatement of them in modern legal terminology. According to Hoetink, there is a necessarily inherent form of anachronism in every description of history. Otherwise understanding the (legal) past is impossible.[28] Emilio Betti (1890–1968), an important Italian legal historian, came later to similar, even somewhat more radical, conclusions.[29]

23 The *Bijdragen tot de taal-, land- en volkenkunde van Nederlandsch-Indië* were published since 1853, the Koninklijk Instituut voor Taal-, Land- en Volkenkunde, the predecessor of the still existing Royal Netherlands Institute of Southeast Asian and Caribbean Studies was founded in 1851, see M. Kuitenbrouwer, *Dutch Scholarship in the Age of Empire and Beyond* (Leyden 2014).

24 The introduction of the so-called ethical politics in 1901 in the Dutch Indies, cf. A.D.A. de Kat Angelino, *Le problème colonial, II: Les Indes-Néerlandaises* (The Hague 1932) 442ff.; J.A. Somers, *Nederlandsch Indië, Staatkundige ontwikkelingen binnen een koloniale relatie* (Zutphen, 2005) 121ff.

25 H.R. Hoetink, 'On understanding foreign law' in H.R. Hoetink, *Opera Selecta* (Zutphen 1986) 23–52.

26 Father of the author of these lines.

27 H. Winkel, 'De methode der rechtsvergelijking' (Inaugural public lecture as unsalaried university lecturer, Utrecht, 1936) 11ff.

28 H.R. Hoetink, 'Les notions anachroniques dans l'historiographie du droit' (1955) 23 *Tijdschrift voor Rechtsgeschiedenis/The Legal History Review* 1–20; Hoetink, *Opera Selecta*, 216–237.

29 E. Betti, *Allgemeine Auslegungslehre als Methodik der Geisteswissenschaften* (Tübingen 1967) 98ff.

How do we know and recognise *foreign* legal rules?

There is a striking recent example of the defective knowledge of foreign law: the widespread astonishment in the press outside the UK, but also among some jurists, about the Brexit case heard in the British Supreme Court in January 2017 and its outcome. In this case, the Court applied on Brexit, purely and simply, the old rule and unbroken tradition of sovereignty of Parliament.[30] The bottom line of the astonishment was the question of whether a well-established rule of English constitutional law as described by A.V. Dicey[31] could be put aside by only a *consultative* referendum. Clearly the answer was: no. However, the situation in the UK, with an 'unwritten constitution' is more complicated than in countries with a written constitution. In the latter countries, but not only there, Hans Kelsen's theory of the Basic Norm can be helpful[32] for exploring foreign legal rules and their embedding within the constitutional order. For a codified legal order with a constitution, the constitution can be considered the *Grundnorm*. A characteristic quotation from Kelsen runs as follows:

> But since the cognition of law, like any cognition, seeks to understand its subject as a meaningful whole and to describe it in noncontradictory statements, it starts from the assumption that the conflicts of norms within the normative order, which is the object of this cognition, can and must be solved by interpretation.[33]

This implies high confidence in the structure of the (foreign) legal order, but this approach through the *Grundnorm* also helps us to get to know and understand the structure and content of foreign legal rule. Contextualisation can be a tool in understanding foreign legal rules; for example, the constitutional and systematic place in the legal order. In modern Anglophone legal philosophy, we might hear an echo of Basic Norm theory in the philosophy of the English positivist legal philosopher H.L.A. Hart in what he calls the '*rules of recognition*'.[34]

Knowledge of foreign law is also implied when a judge applies the *public order exception* in Private International Law cases. There, the judge refuses to apply foreign legal norms that are not in accordance with important principles of the domestic legal order. The application of this exception can only follow when a judge has acquired a sufficient amount of knowledge of the foreign legal order and its rules.

30 UK Supreme Court 24 January 2017, full text: uksc-2016-0196-judgment.pdf, consulted 25 April 2017.

31 A.V. Dicey, *Introduction to the Study of the Law of the Constitution* (8th edn, 1915) 3–104 [published on internet by the Liberty Fund, Indianapolis, and directly accessible] where the term 'sovereignty of parliament' is coined and extensively discussed.

32 H. Kelsen, *Reine Rechtslehre* (Wien 1976) 202ff.

33 Ibid., 210.

34 H.L.A. Hart, *The Concept of Law* (OUP 1994) 100ff, 212ff. There is no room here to elaborate on the comparison between Kelsen and Hart.

Remarks on the methodologies of legal history and comparative law

Our still provisional point of view is the following: the epistemological problems related to how to know and how to approach ancient or foreign legal phenomena are basically the same in legal history and in comparative law, respectively. This applies especially to private law on which we will now concentrate. In so far as we share Hoetink's opinions as expounded before. This might not be surprising for a legal historian of his school. Moreover, it is consistent, for example, with the opinions of most British legal historians such as the late Peter Stein (1926–2016) and Alan Watson, experts in both legal history and comparative law. Each extensively studied the relation between Roman law, common law, and comparative law.

However, we would like to add to their observations some elements that are not often dealt with. Besides epistemology, the methods of comparative law and legal history have one more element in common: they both have to deal with the differences in the level of abstraction of the foreign or old legal system,[35] a problem somewhat underestimated in modern scholarship. The far more abstract rules of the German BGB can be compared in a useful manner to the more concrete legal provisions in the French *Code Civil.* This is possible by going back to the common roots, in this case the tradition of European private law as a result of the reception of Roman law and by taking into account the history of the codification. Even a great scholar like Alan Watson could have put even more emphasis on this point where knowledge of a foreign legal system is at stake.[36]

For the legal historian, the history of the reception of Roman law provides much useful information for this comparison. Indeed, Roman law was not taken over in the form of the legal literature of the classical period in Antiquity on the European continent, nor in the form of the legislation of Justinian from the sixth century AD, but in a more or less systematic form that was the result of medieval legal scholarship, starting with the teaching of Roman law at the University of Bologna after 1088.[37] The so-called Glossators (c. 1100–1400) started to restate Roman case law in the form of general rules and exceptions.[38] Justinian's *Corpus Iuris Civilis* was indeed full of contradicting texts. Therefore one text was taken as an example for a more abstract general principle; another text was considered

35 Classical Roman law is basically case law, just as the Common Law. In Civil Law codifications there are considerable difference between e.g. the German codification of private law (BGB) and the French Code civil. The BGB uses far more abstract notions than the Code civil does.

36 A. Watson, *Legal Transplants* (EUP 1974) 16ff; A. Watson, *Roman Law and Comparative Law*, (Athens/London, 1991) 147–181.

37 Traditional and authoritative overview in P. Koschaker, *Europa und das römische Recht* (München, 1966); Peter Stein, *Roman Law in European History* (CUP1999).

38 P. Stein, *Regulae iuris – From Juristic Rules to Legal Maxims* (EUP 1966) 1ff. with interesting remarks on the difference between the rise of Roman law and English law, the former made by jurists in the later Roman Republic, the latter by professional judges in the Middle Ages.

as an exception to that general principle.[39] This was the main contribution of both Glossators and 'Post-Glossators' to legal science and an important step towards the ultimate codification of private law in the eighteenth century and later on in the European continent. In the early modern period since 1500, the 'humanistic jurisprudence' of the sixteenth century tried to impose an order of the second grade: the medieval set of rules and exceptions were put together in a system derived from the *Institutes* of Justinian, a student text that served to provide a systematic structure for private law. The main authors who contributed to the further development of this institutional system[40] were Hugo Donellus,[41] Hugo Grotius,[42] Arnold Vinnius,[43] and Johann Gottlieb Heineccius.[44]

Today, there is additional room for admitting that the English common law was influenced by Roman law. But this form of influence was certainly very different from the reception of the *ius commune* on the European continent. As far as we can see, there is not yet a complete overview of the role of Roman law in common law. Some facts are, however, well researched in the existing literature: from a starting point in the time of Vacarius, a former student in Bologna, who was teaching in England around 1170.[45] Later, in the thirteenth century there is Bracton with his work *De legibus et consuetudinibus Angliae*,[46] and in the eighteenth century we find William Blackstone with his *Commentaries on the Laws of England*.[47] Both authors show the influence of learned Roman law. Reinhard Zimmermann, who emphasises in many publications the original unity

39 Ibid., 131ff.

40 P. Stein, 'The Fate of the Institutional System' in *Studies in Justinian's Institutes in memory of J.A.C. Thomas* 164ff, now in *The Character and Influence of the Roman Civil Law – Historical Essays*, (Ronceverte 1988) 73ff.

41 R. Feenstra, 'Hugues Doneau et les juristes néerlandais du XVIIe siècle: l'influence de son système sur l'évolution du droit privé avant le Pandectisme' in R. Feenstra, *Legal Scholarship and Doctrines of Private Law 13th –18th Century* (Variorum 1996) 231–243.

42 L. Winkel, 'Problems of Legal Systematization from *De iure praedae* to *De iure belli ac pacis: De iure praedae* Chapter II and the *Prolegomena* of *De iure belli ac pacis* compared' (2005–2007) 26–28 Grotiana, New Series 61–78.

43 Arn. Vinnii *in quattuor libros Institutionum imperialium commentarius* (ed quarta, Amstelodami 1665); cf Arnold Vinnius, *Institutionenkommentar Schuldrecht.* Text und Übersetzung. Ins Deutsche übersetzt v. Klaus Wille, mit einer Einführung von Reinhard Zimmermann (Heidelberg 2005). Wille translated the 1726 edition.

44 We consulted the edition J.G. Heineccius, *Elementa iuris civilis secundum ordinem Institutionum* (Amstelodami, 1738, first published 1725). Interestingly enough Heineccius also published a survey of Roman law respecting the *ordo legum* of the Digest: *Elementa iuris civilis secundum ordinem Pandectarum* (Amstelodami, 1731, originally published 1727); see K. Luig, 'Heineccius, Johann Gottlieb' in M. Stolleis (ed.) *Juristen – Ein biographisches Lexikon* (München, 1995) 279–280.

45 Stein, *Roman law in European History*, 56; P. Stein, 'Vacarius and the Civil Law' in *The Character and Influence of the Roman Civil Law*, 167ff.

46 P. Stein, 'Roman Law and English Jurisprudence, Yesterday and Today' in *The Character and Influence of the Roman Civil Law*, 151ff; on Bracton, 153ff.

47 P. Stein, 'Continental Influences on English Legal Thought' in *The Character and Influence of the Roman Civil Law*, 216ff.

of European legal science,[48] elaborated once on the example of the 'implied condition' in continental and common law.[49] His view was that in the development of this notion of implied condition in common law, Roman law undeniably played a role. On the other hand, Pierre Legrand[50] criticises – as far as we can see, not very convincingly – the opinions of Stein, Birks, and Zimmermann in this respect. Interestingly enough, Legrand goes back to epistemology and concludes that there will always be a gap in knowledge, between Italian and English lawyers, of the English law of contract.. He even states that 'there are two cognitive modes of experiencing the world'.[51] Here, Legrand implicitly repeats elements of the romantic view of Friedrich Carl von Savigny's *Volksgeistlehre* expounded as early as 1814 in *Vom Beruf unserer Zeit für Gesetzgebung und Rechtswissenschaft*: it is in the lawyer's mind that we find consciousness of what the law is.[52]

In comparisons between civil law and common law there turn out to be many elements of Roman origin in the common law, but a comparison in the field of private law in a more global way is only possible through a scheme that in the last instance is derived from the *Institutes* of Justinian. The late Peter Birks (1941–2004), at a time Regius Professor at Oxford University, once said of the common law that '[t]he bridge between Contract and Tort is Justinian's *Institutes*'.[53] As mentioned before, this also has an implication for epistemological questions.

The varieties of private law in civil law countries can sometimes be understood by differences in qualifying Roman legal texts as main rules or as exceptions.

48 R. Zimmermann, 'Der europäische Charakter des englischen Rechts: Historische Verbindungen zwischen civil law und common law', 1 *Zeitschrift für Europäisches Privatrecht* (1993) 4–51.

49 R. Zimmermann, 'Heard Melodies Are Sweet, But those Unheard Are Sweeter' (1993) 193 *Archiv für die civilistische Praxis*, 121ff.; cf his magnum opus, R. Zimmermann, *The Law of Obligations – Roman Foundations of the Civilian Tradition* (Cape Town, 1990) and his collection of essays, R. Zimmermann, *Roman Law, Contemporary Law, European Law* (OUP 2001).

50 P. Legrand, 'Legal Traditions in Western Europe, the Limits of Communality' in R. Jagtenberg, E. Örücü and A. de Roo (eds) *Transfrontier Mobility, of Law* (The Hague/London/Boston, 1995) 65ff.

51 Legrand, quoted in the previous footnote, at 71. Cf. S. Donlan and D. Heirbaut, 'A Patchwork of Accommodations: Reflections on European Legal Hybridity and Jurisdictional Complexity' the introduction to Donlan and Heirbaut (eds) *The Law's Many Bodies: Studies in Legal Hybridity and Jurisdictional Complexity, c1600–1900* (Duncker & Humblot 2015) 13ff. Donlan and Heirbaut seem to put much emphasis on the complexity and open character of the legal order in the period before codification and written constitutions which, however, do not exclude the lines of influence of learned law (Roman law, canon and feudal law) as sketched here in the scholarly pan-European legal debate.

52 Cf. F. Wieacker, *Privatrechtsgeschichte der Neuzeit* (Göttingen, 1967) 357ff. On *idem*, 355 remarks on the relation of Savigny's theories with preceding ideas in Montesquieu's *De l'Esprit des Lois* published in 1748.

53 Cf. *108 Zeitschrift der Savigny Stiftung, romanistische Abteilung* (1991) 708–715, an account of a speech given by Peter Birks. Not without reason the title of the Essays in Memory of Peter Birks, Oxford 2006 (edited by Andrew Burrows and Lord Rodger of Earlsferry) is *Mapping the Law*.

Differences in modern private law systems can be explained in other cases again by the critical restatements of Roman law after legal humanism. Maybe one of the best-known examples is the contract of sale and the transfer of ownership: according to classical and Justinian Roman law, a *causa* is required for the informal transfer of ownership after a valid contract, the *traditio*. All this was criticised in the 'Natural Law School' of the eighteenth century when the model of natural law was central, and emphasis was put on the individual in private law relations. The question was: when two people with a reasonable mind, the seller and the buyer, have a common aim – i.e. that the sold object was no longer in the ownership of the vendor but should pass to that of the buyer – why is there a law saying that there are additional requirements for this transfer than this mutual consent? Hence the doctrine that ownership passes in principle from the seller to the buyer at the very moment of the conclusion of the contract. The origin of this opinion can be found in Grotius, *De iure belli ac pacis*,[54] where Grotius quoted Seneca to underpin his statement. This approach was not, however, adopted by Jean Domat or Robert Pothier,[55] who both adhered to the traditional view of the *ius commune*. This separation between the contract and transfer of ownership also found an echo in the works of other jurists of the eighteenth century like Samuel Pufendorf.[56]

Handing over the sold object has, in Grotius's doctrine described above, only a factual significance and is only important for – factual – possession and for the effect of the transition of ownership for third parties. Curiously here, this principle not only applies in French private law, but is also the principle of the Sale of Goods Act in England where movables or personal property are concerned. In French law, under the influence of Grotius and other scholars, and in common law, in respect of movables the contract of sale implies transition of ownership.[57]

In German private law, on the other hand, we know the *Abstraktionsprinzip*; according to which the transfer of ownership is part of a separate legal transaction (*Rechtsgeschäft*) whose validity is independent from the previous contract.[58] Here we have to take into account the results of Pandectism in Germany. A whole set of abstract legal terms like *Rechtsgeschäft* in modern private law have their origin in the works of Bernhard Windscheid and his colleagues. They are so common that we are hardly aware of their origin anymore. Examples are 'legal act', 'minority',

54 II, 12,15,1.

55 See Jean Domat, *Les loix civiles dans leur ordre naturel*, Livre I, Titre II, Sect, II : Des engagements du vendeur envers l'acheteur (Paris, 1756) 34ff.; J. Pothier, *Traité des obligations*, Partie 1, Chap. I, Sect. 1, Art. 1 (Paris/Orléans, 1768) 16; cf D. Deroussin, *Histoire du droit des obligations* (Economica 2007) 233–247.

56 *De iure naturae et gentium*, 5,5,2, Londini etc. 1672, 645.

57 W.J. Zwalve and A.J.B. Sirks, *Grundzüge der europäischen Privatrechtsgeschichte, Einführung und Sachenrecht* (Wien-Köln-Weimar 2008) 308ff.; W.J. Zwalve, *C.Æ. Uniken Venema's Common Law & Civil Law*, (Deventer 2000) 201–205.

58 See § 929–931 BGB; V. Beuthen and W. Hadding (eds) *Studienkommentar zum BGB* (Frankfurt, 1979) 600ff.

'*potestas alienandi*', 'nullity', 'annullability,' and many more. Even in the description of English common law, we cannot avoid these categories.

One of the main aims of comparative law is the harmonisation of laws, and maybe in the long run even unification of them. This very example shows us that unification even of technical structures in private law is far from simple. The *Draft Common Frame of Reference* maintains on the whole the Roman system of a separate 'delivery' in IV A –2:102, possibly going back to Ernst Rabel who wrote on the law of sale, not only as a legal historian but also as a comparatist.[59]

Of course, the measure of abstraction has some relation with the moment of codification of private law in the different European countries. Whereas the *Code Civil* was introduced in France as early as 1804, the codification of German private law took nearly a century longer, and the *Bürgerliches Gesetzbuch* (BGB) was only introduced in 1900. This also reflects the different approaches to comparative law in the nineteenth century, the period in which comparative law was born as an academic discipline. It certainly also has had an impact on the *method* of comparative law. The emphasis in nineteenth-century French comparative law was based on comparing legislation; in Germany it was on legal science, or '*législation comparée*' in France, and '*vergleichende Rechtswissenschaft*'. In Germany, this was due not only to the late codification of private law but also to the long period during which legal science (legal doctrine) was a direct source of law in most of the German-speaking countries. This occurred under the spell of von Savigny, who in 1814 succeeded in convincing German jurists to postpone codification on a national scale and concentrate on systematising the surviving Roman law in a far more radical way.[60] So the *form* and *extension* of the reception of Roman law on the continent was not similar everywhere either.

Conclusions

The debate between those who study legal history and comparative law is not only between those who study diachronic and synchronic comparative law:[61] fundamental epistemological questions are also involved. Legal history and

59 Timo Utermark, *Rechtsgeschichte und Rechtsvergleichung bei Ernst Rabel* (Peter Lang AG 2005). On the biography of Ernst Rabel: G. Kegel and Ernst Rabel, 'Vorkämpfer des Weltkaufrechts' in H. Heinrichs e.a (Hrsg) (ed.) *Deutsche Juristen jüdischer Herkunft* (München, 1993) 571–594. On the uniform law of sale: E. Rabel, *Das Recht des Warenkaufs* vol. 1 (Berlin/Leipzig, 1936) 194–213.

60 Marc Ancel, *Unité et méthode du droit comparé* (Neuchâtel, 1971) 14–17; cf J.A. Jolowicz, 'Comparative Law in Twentieth-century England' in J. Beatson and R. Zimmermann (eds) *Jurists Uprooted – German-speaking Emigrant Lawyers in Twentieth-century Britain* (OUP 2004) 347. See also L. Winkel, 'Review of Elmar Wadle, Einhundert Jahre Rechtsvergleichende Gesellschaft in Deutschland, Baden-Baden 1994', 63 *Tijdschrift voor Rechtsgeschiedenis/ The Legal History Review* (1995) 414.

61 We do agree here with our predecessor in Rotterdam, C.M.G. ten Raa, 'Beschouwingen over rechtshistorie' in H.W. Blom and R. de Folter (eds) *Methode en object in de rechtswetenschappen* (Zwolle 1986) 73–91, but we leave aside some of his niceties in Dutch terminology:

comparative law are, so we would like to defend, similar on the level of method and approach, but they also share common features on the level of epistemology. For diachronic and synchronic comparison, Roman law in whatever form is the *tertium comparationis*, not only in concrete cases, like sale, hire, or representation, but also where legal systems as a whole are considered. The use of this *tertium comparationis*[62] is often unconscious. It would be far better if this was a matter of conscious deliberation. For more general comparative remarks – at least in the field of private law – the institutional system is nearly always present, where it concerns contemporary law or when the history of private law is involved. The measure of abstraction of legal norms can be a further parameter in this comparative process. We are, however, by far not the first to come to these kinds of conclusions,[63] but we hope nevertheless they will please Esin Örücü, the author of many thought-provoking books and articles on comparative law.[64]

Selected bibliography

Marc Ancel, *Unité et méthode du droit comparé* (Neuchâtel, 1971).

S. Donlan and D. Heirbaut, 'A Patchwork of Accommodations: Reflections on European Legal Hybridity and Jurisdictional Complexity' in S. Donlan and D. Heirbaut (eds) *The Law's Many Bodies: Studies in Legal Hybridity and Jurisdictional Complexity*, c1600–1900 (Duncker & Humblot 2015).

H.R. Hoetink, 'Les notions anachroniques dans l'historiographie du droit' (1955) 23 *Tijdschrift voor Rechtsgeschiedenis/ The Legal History Review* 1–20.

H.R. Hoetink, *Opera Selecta* (Zutphen 1986) 216–237.

J.A. Jolowicz, 'Comparative Law in Twentieth-century England' in J. Beatson and R. Zimmermann (eds) Jurists Uprooted – German-*Speaking Emigrant Lawyers in Twentieth-Century Britain* (OUP 2004).

P. Legrand, 'Legal Traditions in Western Europe, the Limits of Communality' in Annie J. de Roo, Esin Örücü, and Robert W. Jagtenberg (eds) *Transfrontier Mobility of Law* (Kluwer 1995) 5.

R. Mallachow, *Rechtserkenntnistheorie und Fiktionslehre* (Rosi & Cie 1922).

Marieke Oderkerk, 'The Need for a Methodological Framework for Comparative Legal Research' (2015) 79 *Rabels Zeitschrift für ausländisches und internationales Privatrecht*, 589–623.

Esin Örücü, *The Enigma of Comparative Law* (Martinus Nijhoff Publishers 2004).

Peter Stein, *Roman Law in European History* (CUP 1999).

Timo Utermark, *Rechtsgeschichte und Rechtsvergleichung bei Ernst Rabel* (Peter Lang AG) 2005.

Ten Raa distinguishes – as far as we can see unnecessarily – between *rechtsgeschiedenis* and *rechtshistorie*.

62 Important remarks on the concept of *tertium comparatonis* in Marieke Oderkerk, 'The Need for a Methodological Framework for Comparative Legal Research' (2015) 79 *Rabels Zeitschrift für ausländisches und internationales Privatrecht* 589–623, esp 610ff.

63 Cf. W.J. Zwalve, 'Het Janushoofd der rechtsvergelijking' (inaugural lecture, Groningen, 1988) 10.

64 cf Esin Örücü, *The Enigma of Comparative Law* (Martinus Nijhoff Publishers 2004) *passim*.

Alan Watson, *Legal Transplants* (EUP 1974).
Alan Watson, *Roman Law and Comparative Law* (University of Georgia Press 1991).
L.C. Winkel, 'Das erneuerte Interesse für die erkenntnistheoretischen Aspekte der aristotelischen Ethik in Deutschland und England im 19. und 20. Jahrhundert', in A. Földi, I. Sándor, I. Siklósi (eds), *Ad geographiam historico-iuridicam ope iuris romani colendam – Studia in honorem Gábor Hamza* (Teoria e Storia del Diritto Privato 2015) 405–408.

12 Hybrid law and culinary metaphor – empty coquetting or something else?

Jaakko Husa

By far the greatest thing is the use of metaphor.

Aristotle, *Poetics*[1]

Introduction

Scholars in different academic fields follow different modes of writing across disciplines and fields of study. In short, what makes perfectly decent scholarly writing in chemistry might be regarded as grossly out of place in political philosophy. Yet, it would be an exaggeration to argue that there could not be significant similarities when it comes to the academic texts produced by scholars. For instance, there are clear structural similarities in academic research texts; it is commonplace to start with an introduction and to end with a conclusion. However, it would be a mistake to assume that even within a certain field or discipline, all of the authors would write in a similar style. Perhaps a leopard cannot change its spots, but not all leopards are similar.

Accordingly, in law as an academic discipline, there are different styles of writing depending on the subfield and purpose of the text. Legal historians, legal philosophers, doctrinalists, or comparatists tend to compose their texts by using different styles. Also, the purpose of a text is a meaningful factor because a vivid and heavily theory-laden style may work wonderfully in, for example, a legal theoretical or law and literature type of analysis, whereas using a similar style in an introductory doctrinal textbook would quite likely end in an epic failure. For this reason, a metaphor-loving doctrinalist might soon end up having a rather limited readership indeed.

In the same fashion, comparative law as an academic discipline seems to have its own conventions when it comes to composing different scholarly texts. Consequently, some of the authors have followed the conventions of doctrinal

1 '*πολὺ μέγιστον τὸ μεταφορικὸν εἶναι*', *Ἀριστοτέλης, Περὶ ποιητικῆς*, 1459a, 'Aristotelis De arte poetica liber', in Rudolf Kassel (ed.) *Oxford Classical Texts* (E Typographeo Clarendoniano (Clarendon Press) 1965) (source: Perseus Digital Library, http://perseus.tufts.edu). For Aristotle, being a master of metaphor was something that cannot be learnt from others and, moreover, it is also a sign of literary genius.

legal writing, whereas others have been influenced by other disciplines like historiography, philosophy, or economics.[2] One curious feature in comparative law language, used by some but certainly not by all scholars, has been the use of metaphors to express ideas, findings, and conclusions. But what actually is a metaphor, and how well does it fit into academic comparative law? According to the OED, a metaphor is 'a figure of speech in which a name or descriptive word or phrase is transferred to an object or action different from, but analogous to, that to which it is literally applicable'.[3]

In my view, there is a reason why comparatists in particular use metaphors in their writing. This reason is found, it will be argued in this chapter, in the comparative nature of the research. In essence, metaphor is a comparison between two things; so, it is based on resemblance or similarity of certain qualities without using 'like' or 'as'. In other words, metaphor is not merely a rhetorical device belonging to certain comparatists' personal writing style, but it is an intrinsic part of the attempt to think comparatively. In essence, as defined by Kenneth Burke, metaphor is a 'device for seeing something in terms of something else'.[4] And, importantly, comparatists always see something else, i.e. foreign laws and legal cultures that are different than their own.[5]

This chapter discusses the use of metaphor in comparative law by looking at an example from macro-comparative law by Esin Örücü, who has used culinary terms as metaphors while discussing mixed legal systems. The purpose of the following analysis is to illustrate the particular epistemic benefits of using metaphors in comparative legal literature. Accordingly, it will be argued that metaphors have a special place, especially in comparative law literature.

This paper is structured as follows: after this short introduction, the context of macro-comparative law is explained. This is followed by a concrete example of metaphorical conceptualisation concerning mixed legal systems. The final part contains a theoretical conclusion on the use of metaphors in macro-comparative law.

2 For example, texts from Gunter Frankenberg or Pierre Legrand are also stylistically very different from the texts of Rodolfo Sacco or Reinhard Zimmermann.

3 Oxford University Press, 'Metaphor' (*OED Online* March 2016), www.oed.com/view/Entry/117328?redirectedFrom=metaphor, accessed 22 April 2016. Of course, this definition basically relies on Aristotle's definition from *Poetics* (1457b): 'metaphor is the application of a strange term' *('μεταφορὰ δέ ἐστιν ὀνόματος ἀλλοτρίου ἐπιφορὰ').*

4 Kenneth Burke, *A Grammar of Motives* (University of California Press 1969) 503.

5 Finn Makela speaks of domain mapping, which refers to the fact that metaphors should be seen as speech acts that propose a hypothesis of similarity between two separate domains, see Finn Makela, 'Metaphors and Models in Legal Theory' (2011) 52 *Les Cahiers de droit* 397.

About macro-comparative law

In the theory of comparative law, *law groups*, *legal families*, *legal cultures*, and *legal traditions* are frequently discussed.[6] Such classifications mainly refer to whole systems, and they represent what is called macro-comparison. Other comparative typologies with a lower abstraction level are built around different substantive sectors of law, like, for example, in a comparative constitutional study where as a result of comparison different typologies of models for controlling the constitutionality of laws can be presented. Now, when constructing *legal families*, the comparatist tries to illustrate the general nature of legal cultural phenomena and the reasons for their manifestations. This is how we classify legal systems into Roman-Germanic (civil law) or common law systems, or how we regard Nordic law as a separate legal family that is legal-culturally closer to the legal cultural sphere of civil law rather than common law.[7] So, in essence, *legal families* or other macro-constructs are conceptual and theoretical tools for outlining the core content of a foreign legal system in a very broad and generalising manner.[8]

In macro-comparison, contrasting takes place between legal systems or even between *legal families*. Accordingly, the levels of abstraction and generalisation are both very high. Macro-comparison does not concentrate on individual legal rules, cases, institutions, or concrete problems and the ways to solve them. Comparison may, for example, be aimed at issues that concern legislative methods, the style of writing provisions, the systematisation and division of the different fields of law, and the doctrine of legal sources, or even the style of entire legal systems, i.e. legal cultural features characteristic of them.[9] Today, the two most important and virtually overarching *legal families* are civil law and common law.[10] However, not all systems can be classified as civil law or common law, and this poses an epistemic challenge for macro-comparatists. This challenge is caused by *hybridity*, which in this case refers to a mixture of different elements resulting in a mixed composition of rules, principles and institutions whose elements are derived from different *legal families*.[11]

To clarify the above, mixed legal systems (or hybrid legal systems) refer to systems that simultaneously contain key characteristics of other *legal families*.

6 About the distinction between micro-comparison and micro-comparison, see e.g. Konrad Zweigert and Hein Kötz, *An Introduction to Comparative Law* (2nd edn, Oxford University Press 1998) 4–5.

7 Jaakko Husa, *A New Introduction to Comparative Law* (Hart Publishing 2015) 25.

8 Ibid., 225–229.

9 Ibid., 102.

10 See e.g. Thomas Lundmark, *Charting the Divide between Common and Civil Law* (Oxford University Press 2012).

11 See Seán Patrick Donlan, 'Comparative Law and Hybrid Legal Traditions – An Introduction' in Eleanor Cashin-Ritaine, Seán Patrick Donlan, and Martin Sychold (eds) *Comparative Law and Hybrid Legal Traditions* (Lausanne, Swiss Institute of Comparative Law, 2010) 9–18 (arguing that hybridity challenges legal nationalism, positivism, centralism, and monism which are all part of the legal families approach).

Reasons for hybridity are always related to legal history, yet, each legal system has had different routes to hybridity. For example, together with British imperialism, common law also spread to areas where other types of law (indigenous, traditional, and religious) had earlier been used. If the law that had preceded common law was legal-culturally strong, little by little systems were formed where there were features of both local law and common law. In some well-known cases, like Louisiana and Quebec, mixed systems are mixes between civil law and common law. Unlike in the past, mixed legal systems are nowadays seen by some as an independent *legal family*, which are by no means dying out and which are legal-culturally equal to common law and civil law.[12] The best example of this novel epistemic move can be seen in the book edited by Vernon V. Palmer called *Mixed Jurisdictions Worldwide.*[13] According to Palmer, the third legal family is 'conceived for purposes of convenience, utility, and explanatory power' and it can be used 'only if it provides better insights than comparative analysis has provided in the past'.[14] In any case, for macro-comparative law, legal cultural hybridity remains a problem of classification even though the phenomenon itself is hardly any novelty.[15]

The oldest of the classical mixed systems is probably that of Scotland because it was independent for a long time before it formed a union named Great Britain (1707) with England and Wales. Scotland had connections with Continental law and, thus, assumed many Roman law/*ius commune* influences. Also, in the law of the province of Quebec in Canada there are similar features of mixed legal systems where common law has mixed with the civil law elements implanted earlier: branches like property law and civil law are of a French civil law type, but public law and criminal law are of a common law type. Besides, in Africa, common law has mixed with the customary law of the tribes and in Asia with a legal tradition that could, due to its main cultural features, be characterised as Confucian.[16] Thus, there are many kinds of legal cultural hybridities and resulting legal pluralism.

In the same way, there are systems that belong to the family of Continental European law, for example, in Latin America, Africa, and Asia, where civil law has intermingled with common law. Crucially, European systems are these days so close to each other due to the European Union (EU) that some comparatists

12 Husa, *A New Introduction to Comparative Law*, 215.

13 Vernon Valentine Palmer (ed.), *Mixed Jurisdictions Worldwide: The Third Legal Family* (2nd edn, Cambridge University Press 2012).

14 Palmer, 'Introduction to the Mixed Jurisdictions' 16.

15 See also Lundmark, *Charting the Divide between Common and Civil Law*, 33–38 (discusses legal families and takes into account mixed legal systems). For an interesting discussion about legal history and hybridity, see Seán Patrick Donlan, 'Remembering: Legal Hybridity and Legal History' (2011) 2 *Comparative Law Review* 1 (pointing out that there are no pure types).

16 See e.g. Patrick H. Glenn, *Legal Traditions of the World: Sustainable Diversity in Law* (5th edn, Oxford University Press 2014) ch 9.

classify the EU law as a kind of mixed law containing elements from national systems (common law and civil law) mixed with public international law and *sui generis* EU elements.[17] In a comparative law view, the EU legal system is not a unitary entity but consists of different legal cultural elements, and in this sense it is a hybrid and needs to be studied as such.[18]

Some of the former socialist countries, too, are as a matter of fact in a state of mixed law, although in Europe they mainly belong to the sphere of civil law.[19] For example, Czech law is legal-culturally a complicated entity where remnants of socialist law (itself a Marxist variant of civil law) are still to be found in civil law, labour law, and family law. On the other hand, in the Czech system, commercial law is clearly Romano-Germanic. The earlier Czech picture has been further mixed by later legal loans from Western law, and, due to this, the system is systematically fragmented and contains certain inconsistencies. Today, it is part of the EU, which has a huge impact on the law and legal culture of the Czech Republic.[20] Because of all these reasons, it is difficult for the macro-comparatist to generalise and conceptualise systems that are mixed or undergoing a process of transformation from one legal family to another.[21]

To continue the above discussion, further examples of hybrids or mixed systems are South Africa where common law and Roman-Dutch law are combined and Malta that combines common law and Italian Continental law. Similar examples are the Philippines and Puerto Rico, both of which combine the law of Spanish origin with common law. In addition, in practice all Islamic systems are also hybrids mixing Western, local, and Muslim ingredients.[22] Now, the purpose of this section is not to exhaustively list mixed legal systems but, rather, to provide an illustrative overview of various types of mixed legal systems so that the difficulties of macro-comparison become visible. As shown above, there are various mixtures and hybridities when it comes to the legal systems of the world. Nevertheless, it may be useful to note that the condition of being 'mixed law' or 'hybrid law' is not necessarily immutable, but there are differences between systems: some systems seem able to retain their constituent *mixité*, whereas others have a more endangered status as hybrid systems. These potential future

17 See e.g. Peter de Cruz, *Comparative Law in a Changing World* (2nd edn, Cavendish 1999) ch 5.

18 cf Paul James Cardwell and Tamara Hervey, 'Bringing in the Technical into the Socio-Legal' in David Cowan and Daniel Wincott (eds) *Exploring the 'Legal' in Socio-Legal Studies* (Palgrave 2016) 157–182, 166.

19 Husa, *A New Introduction to Comparative Law*, 216.

20 See Bohumil Havel, 'The Czech Republic' in Jan Smits (ed.) *Elgar Encyclopedia of Comparative Law* (Edward Elgar Publications 2012) 279–285.

21 Simply, in many cases the macro-comparatist uses crude determining factors when systematising the legal systems of the world. A key factor has traditionally been the 'fact that common law systems accept judge-made law as a source of law' (Lundmark, *Charting the Divide between Common and Civil Law*, 49).

22 See e.g. Farid S. Shuaib, 'The Islamic Legal System in Malaysia' (2012) 21 *Pacific Rim Law & Policy Journal* 85.

developments are well presented and discussed in the recent book titled *A Study of Mixed Systems*.[23] Correspondingly, the world of law is plural, and this unorthodox plurality poses an epistemic problem for those who try to generalise and describe legal systems from the perspective of macro-comparison.

On the whole, different ingredients are mixed into different legal pluralistic entities depending on local applications and historical paths, like for instance colonialism. What results is normally a mix between various cultural ingredients combining Western and Non-Western, modern and traditional, and religious and secular. Thus, for macro-comparative law, these systems are epistemologically problematic because they are hard to conceptualise using vocabulary that is originally based on the distinction between civil law and common law. Hence, this is where metaphorical conceptualisation may become a useful tool as we will see in the following section.

Mixed legal systems and culinary metaphor

It is important to realise that whatever one thinks of the classification of the world's legal systems, and especially of mixed legal systems, it is an undeniable fact that some systems are hybrids by their legal cultural nature. There is hybridity that cannot be explained away; some systems just are hybrid by their nature. Typically, these systems are more complex mixes than is the case with the European mixes. For example, Morocco's system follows structurally and institutionally French models, yet its family law has modified but clear Islamic features.[24] Or, to take another example, Mauritius' legal system has structurally and institutionally heavy British influences, whereas its civil law follows French models (the *Code Napoleon*, i.e. *Code Civil*) and there are also customary law elements included.[25] And, this specific quality of hybridity makes them difficult to conceptualise in a standard comparative law language in a compelling and handy manner. Simply, we seem to have rather poorly fitting words (statutory law, case law, religious law, customary law etc.) for the task. The reasons for this terminological inadequacy are not difficult to grasp.

Normally, a mixed legal system is the result of the transmigration of law and the outcome of a mismatch between the recipient and the original model. In the resultant, i.e. hybrid legal system, diverse legal elements co-exist simultaneously.[26] And, therein lies the problem for macro-level description. Mixed ingredients are hard to generalise about and, furthermore, they are in a constant state of flux

23 Sue Farran, Esin Örücü and Seán Patrick Donlan (eds), *A Study of Mixed Systems: Endangered, Entrenched or Blended* (Ashgate Publishing 2014).

24 See e.g. Katie Zoglin, 'Morocco's Family Code: Improving Equality for Women' (2009) 31 *Human Rights Quarterly* 964.

25 See e.g. A.H. Angelo, 'Mauritius: The Basis of the Legal System' (1970) 3 *Comparative and International Law Journal of Southern Africa* 228.

26 Esin Örücü, 'Law as Transposition' (2002) 51 *International and Comparative Law Quarterly* 205, 212.

between differing legal cultural enticements. All this does not make it easy for a macro-comparatist to conceptualise mixed systems in a general and understandable manner. In brief, the question is this: how can we descriptively explain mixed systems in a concise and understandable manner? One possible answer is to rely on metaphorical conceptualisation; the usage of metaphor may open up new ways of understanding and studying various legal mixtures.[27]

Basically, the problem of macro-comparative law's mainstream approach is that its presentations of mixed legal systems are not very imaginative, and they lack certain intellectual appeal and gravity. Anyone who reads comparative law literature soon finds out that mixed legal systems are kind of a remainder of an attempt to classify and characterise the world's legal systems from a macro-comparative viewpoint. For these reasons, Örücü's discussion of mixed legal systems through the use of culinary metaphors is particularly interesting because they simplify an otherwise tremendously complicated subject matter. Regardless of complexity, these metaphors give an instant feeling of being spot on because they convey an intuitively proper general mental image. In other words, they tell a story of a legal system with a minimal amount of words. Hence, metaphor is a narrative compressed into a linguistically minimal space. Moreover, it would seem, the use of culinary metaphor makes this kind of macro-comparative law analysis more personal and memorable. And, no doubt, also intellectually more appealing to many readers who are jaded with boring and dull descriptive macro-comparative law texts focusing on positive laws and the so-called Great *legal families*.[28] It is almost needless to say that comparative law literature is filled with common-law-this and civil-law-that discussions and descriptions. Metaphor may be a way out.

Basically, Örücü has distinguished between four different kinds of mixed legal systems which are: (1) *mixing bowl* systems where distinct elements are integrated within similar legal institutions, (2) *salad bowl* systems where both legal elements and institutions are distinct, (3) *salad plate* systems where there is legal dualism or pluralism, and (4) *purée* systems where *legal traditions* that form the basis for legal elements and institutions have become genuinely blended.[29] This metaphorical structure uses the level of integration as the foundation: at one end there is a mixing bowl where legal elements are interacting but not totally blended, at the other end there is a *purée* where legal elements are truly fused together making it difficult to distinguish between them. In practice, however, most mixed systems are situated somewhere in between these extreme ends.

27 This point is also made by Cardwell and Hervey, 'Bringing in the Technical into the Socio-Legal' 164 in the context of EU law.

28 For a recent discussion of legal families see Mariana Pargendler, 'The Rise and Decline of Legal Families' (2012) 60 *American Journal of Comparative Law* 1043 and Jaakko Husa, 'The Future of Legal Families' (*Oxford Handbooks Online* May 2016) DOI: 10.1093/oxfordhb/9780199935352.013.26.

29 Örücü, 'Law as Transposition' 213. For more detailed earlier discussion, see Esin Örücü, 'Mixed and Mixing: A Conceptual Approach' in Esin Örücü and Elspeth Attwooll and Sean Coyle (eds) *Studies in Legal Systems: Mixed and Mixing* (Kluwer 1996) 335–351.

On one occasion, Örücü visualises mixed systems along a spectrum and continues by conceptualising her culinary mixed legal system metaphor in the following manner:

> When elements from socio-culturally similar and legal-culturally different legal systems come together forming mixed systems of the already mentioned 'simple' kind – the 'mixing bowls' – the ingredients are still in the process of blending but in need of further processing if a 'purée' is to be produced. Next to 'simple' mixes come the 'complex' mixed systems, where the elements are both socio-culturally and legal-culturally different. I have called this type elsewhere the 'Italian salad bowl' where, although the salad dressing covers the salad, it is easy to detect the individual ingredients clearly through the side of the glass bowl. A good example of this is Algeria. Then, there is what I called the 'English salad plate', the ingredients sitting separately far apart on a flat plate with a blob of mayonnaise at the side into which the different ingredients can be dipped before consumption. Examples of this are the Sudan and Zimbabwe – legal pluralisms –, which lie towards the far end of the spectrum. The examples become more extreme along the path, ending in 'curdling', with a dysfunctional legal system, as already mentioned.[30]

To be sure, this is not a boring way to write about macro-comparative law. Undoubtedly, it is also a personal and memorable way to conceptualise legal hybridity. Albeit, the question is: does this kind of metaphorical composition really work? And, if it works, what makes it work?

As one can see from the above lengthy quote, the culinary metaphor is really about explaining how socio-culturally and legal-culturally different legal elements form mixed outcomes of various kinds. Essentially, culinary metaphors are not important as such, but, rather, they are a means to an end. Accordingly, the macro-comparative compressed narrative told with the help of a metaphor transfers words describing legal elements (institutions, sources, processes, actors etc.) into culinary ones so that 'salad bowl' and other words enable the reader to conceive the described world of law in terms of dishes. But what really takes place here? What happens is that this metaphor actually stimulates the reader to visualise a mixed legal system because these non-conventional words (in a conventional legal context) awaken the reader's perception into a form of imagery – mixed legal system X transforms into mental representation of a salad bowl of law or into a salad plate of legal institutions. In this process of metaphorising, the abstract macro-comparative terms and concepts become legal theoretical grand-scale images enabling the reader to instantly picture what they are reading and also to remember and, at best,

30 The quote is taken from Esin Örücü, 'What Is a Mixed Legal System: Exclusion or Expansion?' (2008) 12 *Electronic Journal of Comparative Law*, www.ejcl.org/121/art121-15.pdf, accessed 24 May 2016.

instantly conceive what they are reading.[31] By the same token, a culinary metaphor is also an allusion because it draws on sources relating to a kitchen or cookery, which are outside the world of law and the sphere of legal systems.

For example, mentally visualising Scots law as a mixing bowl, where there are distinct civil law and common law elements integrated with similar legal institutions, is an intellectually clever manner of expressing the overall state and nature of Scots law as a mixed legal system. In short, the whole point in this kind of use of metaphor is to create a mental image that enables quick understanding of a complicated thing.[32] For an attempt to grasp and generalise hybrid systems comparatively this kind of understanding may be particularly beneficial. Under these circumstances, metaphor is a comparative generalisation that makes complicated mixed systems cognitively less complex, i.e. metaphorising is *an act of epistemic simplification* – something which is always crucial for macro-comparative law.[33]

Moreover, the fact that metaphor fits so well in theoretically oriented comparative law writing should not be a surprise for anyone. Along similar lines, I agree with Finn Makela when he claims that legal scholars who venture beyond the doctrinal study of law 'tend to think of themselves as engaging in some form of social science or philosophy. As such, we tend to view metaphors with some suspicion'. But as he continues, metaphor may be a powerful methodological tool for generating new understanding.[34] Moreover, we can argue that legal language in general is strongly metaphorical because law is 'an abstract and intellectually-indeterminate idea', and as such we need 'to describe it in figurative words and phrases that evoke concrete and readily-comprehensible sensory phenomena'.[35]

Now, the culinary macro-comparative metaphor used by Örücü implies that metaphor functions as a methodological tool generating new understanding (i.e. as an act of perceiving) by creating mental images of different kinds of mixed legal systems.[36] This kind of metaphor is profoundly innovative as to its nature or what

31 This kind of understanding of a text is metaphorical as it relies on the use of non-literal meaning which is connected to the context of the text. So, 'the word is always the bearer of the "emergent meaning" which specific contexts confer upon it', Paul Ricoeur, *Hermeneutics & the Human Sciences*, ed. John B. Thompson (Cambridge University Press 1995) 166. Clearly, the specific context in this case is macro-comparative law in general and discourse on mixed legal systems in particular.

32 I have argued elsewhere that this kind of function is an elemental part of the concept of 'legal family', which is also a metaphorical device used to conceptualise complicated things. See Jaakko Husa, 'Family Affair – Comparative Law's Never Ending Story?' *Annuario di diritto comparato e di studi legislativi* (Napoli, Edizioni Scientifiche Italiani 2014) 21–48.

33 One could also argue that, in fact, reality is metaphorical so that metaphor forms a kind of a bridge which traverses the cognitive gap between the scholar and reality. See Gary Watt, 'The Matter of Metaphor in Language and Law' (2012) 6 *Pólemos* 49.

34 Makela, 'Metaphors and Models in Legal Theory' 415.

35 Bernard J. Hibbits, 'The Metaphor is the Message' (1995) 22 *International Journal for the Semiotics of Law* 53.

36 However, metaphorical language can also be used in a doctrinal sense so that it frames 'the world in ways which are presented as unquestionable' as has been the case with EU law,

Paul Ricoeur calls 'a momentary creation of language … which does not have a status in the language as something already established'.[37] Importantly, metaphors are built of creative compositions that invite the reader along a journey of understanding (foreign law) with the author.[38] In the end, metaphorical writing contributes to an imaginative comparative law that finds its own ways of doing things, and it does this without relying too much on the conceptual help from other disciplines that may be alien to the hermeneutical character of the comparative study of law.[39]

Conclusion

As shown above, it can be concluded that metaphorical writing has merits in non-doctrinal comparative law writing. In an essential sense, macro-comparative culinary metaphors are legal theoretical images and, as noted by Maks Del Mar, these kinds of images allow theoretical constructions to be built, so in this sense metaphors are 'constructive; like islands of belief dotting the oceans of doubt'.[40] And, often comparatists are indeed sailing in an ocean of doubt caused by the epistemic challenges posed by hybrid legal systems. Ultimately, metaphors are helpful precisely because they provide islands of belief but also, crucially, they provide points of understanding – making cognitive sense of foreign legal systems and legal hybridities.[41] This core task of making sense of the foreign lies at the heart of comparative law as an academic discipline.

Altogether, the use of metaphor in comparative law has many benefits of which some are even quintessential as to their nature.[42] One of the most crucial dimensions relates to the nature of comparative law research. Basically, comparative knowledge produced by the comparatist is typically relative as to its nature. This is to say that there is no certain knowledge but that the research results are well-founded interpretations

Cardwell and Hervey, 'Bringing in the Technical into the Socio-Legal' 174. Yet, Örücü's metaphors seem more open-ended and clearly far less unquestionable as to their nature.

37 Ricoeur, *Hermeneutics and the Human Sciences* (n 30) 174.

38 In a more general view, we might argue that the literary model (which metaphorical expression follows) has a contribution to make to comparative law as one tool in the comparatist's toolbox. See Eric Heinze, 'The Literary Model in Comparative Law' (2014) 9 *Journal of Comparative Law* 17, 27.

39 However, it would be a mistake to think that any metaphor would work. It is clear that foreign legal texts cannot be freely interpreted or metaphorised because they present 'a limited field of possible constructions' as reminded by Paul Ricouer, *Interpretation Theory: Discourse and the Surplus of Meaning* (Texas Christian University Press 1976) 79.

40 Maksymilian Del Mar, 'Thinking in Images in Legal Theory', in Maksymilian Del Mar and Claudio Michelon (eds) *The Anxiety of the Jurist* (Routledge 2013) 43–57, 64.

41 It is likely that metaphorical use of legal language is also 'a potent constitutive mechanism for creating and sustaining communities, including legal communities' as noted by Cardwell and Hervey, 'Bringing in the Technical into the Socio-Legal' 157.

42 Watt goes further and argues that 'law as cultural ordering may be considered to be a reflection of the internal ordering of the mind', 'The Matter of Metaphor in Language and Law' 62.

rather than fully objective scientific results.[43] So, while using metaphors, comparatists have in fact revised the absolute knowledge claim of metaphors in the comparative study of law. Of course, recognition of the use of metaphorical language is also about accepting the interpretative character of comparative law research in general.[44] If we accept this view, then, metaphors are strictly speaking non-scientific (as in an exact science) but at the same time are rather intrinsic to constitutive forms in constructing our hermeneutic knowledge of foreign legal systems.[45] But to claim that metaphor is not scientific is not to undermine its value, on the contrary, because 'law is a major area in which reality is metaphorical' as Gary Watt notes.[46]

Along these lines, the function of metaphors is not really to explain the differences and similarities found in scholarship. Instead, it is to offer holistic projections that help comparatists to understand their subject matter and to make it easier for readers to grasp the essential message (in the form of mental images) which the comparatist seeks to convey. In other words, metaphor constructs a resemblance of two different objects relying on some common characteristics; i.e. metaphor is comparison inside comparison. On balance, there is one significant problem when it comes to using these kinds of macro-comparative metaphors. It seems to me that most or at least a large number of readers will epistemically benefit from macro-comparative metaphors by creating instant legal theoretical images when reading, but this is not necessarily so for all readers. In short, there may be readers who do not form such mental images naturally. And, of course, for such readers, heavy reliance on metaphors may become dramatically counterproductive. Simply, not everyone visualises in the form of mental imagery and understands in the form of picture-like representations. Moreover, metaphors may also confuse readers because they are necessarily imperfect as to their nature, i.e. they are able to cover certain aspects but certainly not all.[47] Of course, this limitation also concerns Örücü's metaphors. And, it goes without saying that failed metaphors end up obscuring things and prevent understanding as cognitive obstacles. Accordingly, *Cicero*'s ancient warning about the use of metaphor is good to bear in mind:

> A metaphor is a short form of simile, contracted into one word; this word is put in a position not belonging to it as if it were its own place, and if it is recognizable it gives pleasure, but if it contains no similarity it is rejected.[48]

43 See for more detailed discussion, Mark Van Hoecke, 'Methodology of Comparative Legal Research' (2015) 5 *Law and Method*, www.bjutijdschriften.nl/tijdschrift/lawandmethod/2015/12/RENM-D-14-00001.

44 See also John Bell, 'Legal Research and the Distinctiveness of Comparative Law', in Mark Van Hoecke (ed.) *Methodologies of Legal Research* (Hart Publishing 2011) 155–176.

45 See also Husa, *A New Introduction to Comparative Law*, 61 (discussing the scholarly nature of comparative law research).

46 Watt, 'The Matter of Metaphor in Language and Law' 63.

47 As such this is perfectly normal and a part of the macro-comparative endeavour, see Husa, 'Family Affair – Comparative Law's Never Ending Story?'.

48 Cicero, *De Oratore* III 157, in A.S. Wilkins (ed.) Libri de oratore tres (E Typographeo Clarendoniano (Clarendon Press) 1902) (source: Perseus Digital Library, http://perseus.tufts.edu.

It remains the responsibility of a comparatist to make sure that metaphor contains a sufficient degree of similarity or it will be rejected.

One final thought. For most readers, macro-comparative metaphors probably work well, but relying too extensively or too imaginatively on metaphors may be over the top, thus turning this otherwise useful comparative device into scholarly coquetting which nobody really benefits from. As the ancient carving in *Apollo*'s temple in Delphi says 'nothing in excess' – and that works well with the use of metaphors in comparative law too.[49]

Selected bibliography

David Cowan and Daniel Wincott (eds), *Exploring the 'Legal' in Socio-Legal Studies* (Palgrave 2016).

Seán Patrick Donlan, 'Remembering: Legal Hybridity and Legal History' (2011) 2 *Comparative Law Review* 1.

Susan Farran, Esin Örücü, Seán Patrick Donlan (eds), *A Study of Mixed Systems: Endangered, Entrenched or Blended* (Ashgate 2014).

Patrick H. Glenn, *Legal Traditions of the World: Sustainable Diversity in Law* (5 edn, OUP 2014).

Eric Heinze, 'The Literary Model in Comparative Law' (2014) 9 *Journal of Comparative Law* 17.

Jaakko Husa, *A New Introduction to Comparative Law* (Hart 2015).

Thomas Lundmark, *Charting the Divide between Common and Civil Law* (OUP 2012).

Esin Örücü, 'Mixed and Mixing: A Conceptual Approach' in Esin Örücü, Elspeth Attwooll, Sean Coyle (eds) *Studies in Legal Systems: Mixed and Mixing* (Kluwer 1996).

Esin Örücü, 'Law as Transposition' (2002) 51 *International and Comparative Law Quarterly* 205.

Finn Makela, 'Metaphors and Models in Legal Theory' (2011) 52 *Les Cahiers de droit* 397.

Vernon Valentine Palmer (ed.), *Mixed Jurisdictions Worldwide: The Third Legal Family* (2nd edn, CUP 2012).

Gary Watt, 'The Matter of Metaphor in Language and Law' (2012) 6 *Pólemos* 4.

'Similitudinis est ad verbum unum contracts brevitas, quod verbum in alieno loco tanquam in suo positum si agnoscitur, delectat, si simile nihil habet, repudiatur'. Cicero spoke of a chain of metaphorical words used to describe something as 'a valuable stylistic ornament' (De Oratore III 167; 'magnum ornamentum orationis'). Yet, Cicero also cautioned the users of this ornament and warned them to avoid obscurity.

49 In classical Greek upper-case letters 'ΜΗΔΕΝ ΑΓΑΝ' (in lower case μηδὲν ἄγαν). For a short explanation, see Casper J. Kraemer, Jr., 'ΜΗΔΕΝ ΑΓΑΝ: An Additional Note' (1927) 22 *Classical Philology* 223.

Index

For Product Safety Concerns and Information please contact our EU representative GPSR@taylorandfrancis.com
Taylor & Francis Verlag GmbH, Kaufingerstraße 24, 80331 München, Germany

www.ingramcontent.com/pod-product-compliance
Ingram Content Group UK Ltd.
Pitfield, Milton Keynes, MK11 3LW, UK
UKHW011013180926
475701UK00004B/728

* 9 7 8 1 0 3 2 0 8 3 2 2 3 *